Advance Praise

'Mariana Velasco-Rivera analyzes, through *The Politics of Constitutional Rigidity*, an apparently technical and abstract issue: constitutional rigidity and the formal requirements established for constitutional reform. However, what we find in this book is a masterful study on a topic that touches the very heart of constitutional theory: the conflictive relationship between democracy and constitutionalism. Better still, Velasco-Rivera examines the topic in a way that helps us to think better and more critically about current processes of constitutional change, such as the (tragic) judicial reform adopted in Mexico in 2024.'

Roberto Gargarella, Professor of Constitutional Theory and Political Philosophy, Universidad de Buenos Aires and Universidad Torcuato Di Tella

'The 1917 Mexican Constitution is one of the most amended constitutions in the world. Yet there is little scholarship exploring how and why this is the case. Enter Mariana Velasco-Rivera's brilliant new book, *The Politics of Constitutional Rigidity*—providing a highly original account of the role of constitutional culture, political parties and individual actors in turning a formally rigid constitution into a functionally dynamic one, or even one characterized by a pattern of 'hyper-amendment'. The book should be compulsory reading for anyone interested in constitutionalism in Mexico or constitutional amendment dynamics around the world. It is a deeply important work by a rising star in the field of comparative constitutional studies.

Rosalind Dixon, Professor of Law, University of New South Wales

'At the same time an absorbing account of the law and politics of constitutional change in Mexico, and an important contribution to scholarship on the strategic foundations of constitutional transformation and stalemate more generally, *The Politics of Constitutional Rigidity* is an essential read for anyone interested in the real, non-idealized interplay between constitutionalism and democracy. Highly recommended.'

Ran Hirschl, University Professor and the David R Cameron Distinguished Professor in Law and Politics, University of Toronto

OXFORD COMPARATIVE CONSTITUTIONALISM

Series Editors

The Politics of Constitutional Rigidity

OXFORD COMPARATIVE CONSTITUTIONALISM

Series Editors

Richard Albert, William Stamps Farish Professor of Law,
The University of Texas at Austin Law School

Robert Schütze, Professor of European and Global Law,
Durham University and College of Europe

Comparative constitutional law has a long and distinguished history in intellectual thought and in the construction of public law. As political actors and the people who create or modify their constitutional orders, they often wish to learn from the experience and learning of others. This cross- fertilization and mutual interaction has only accelerated with the onset of globalization, which has transformed the world into an interconnected web that facilitates dialogue and linkages across international and regional structures. Oxford Comparative Constitutionalism seeks to publish scholarship of the highest quality in constitutional law that deepens our knowledge of local, national, regional, and global phenomena through the lens of comparative public law.

ALSO PUBLISHED IN THIS SERIES

Courts and LGBTQ+ Rights in an Age of Judicial Retrenchment
Rehan Abeyratne

Ex-Ministers as Constitutional Judges
Mathias Möschel

Redefining Comparative Constitutional Law
Essays for Mark Tushnet
Edited by Madhav Khosla and Vicki C. Jackson

Foreign Relations Federalism
The EU in Comparative Perspective
Thomas Verellen

Responsive Judicial Review
Democracy and Dysfunction in the Modern Age
Rosalind Dixon

Outsourcing Rulemaking Powers
Constitutional limits and national safeguards
Cedric Jenart

Abusive Constitutional Borrowing
Legal globalization and the subversion of liberal democracy
Rosalind Dixon and David Landau

A Theory of African Constitutionalism
Berihun Adugna Gebeye

Eternity Clauses In Democratic Constitutionalism
Silvia Suteu

Deliberative Peace Referendums
Ron Levy, Ian O'Flynn, and Hoi L. Kong

Scales of Memory Constitutional Justice and Historical Evil
Justin Collings

The Global South and Comparative Constitutional Law
Edited by Philipp Dann, Michael Riegner, and Maxim Bönnemann

The Politics of Constitutional Rigidity

Unveiling Pathways to Change in Mexico

MARIANA VELASCO-RIVERA

OXFORD
UNIVERSITY PRESS

OXFORD
UNIVERSITY PRESS

Great Clarendon Street, Oxford, OX2 6DP,
United Kingdom

Oxford University Press is a department of the University of Oxford.
It furthers the University's objective of excellence in research, scholarship,
and education by publishing worldwide. Oxford is a registered trade mark of
Oxford University Press in the UK and in certain other countries.

Published in the United States of America by Oxford University Press
198 Madison Avenue, New York, NY 10016, United States of America.

British Library Cataloguing in Publication Data

Data available

Library of Congress Control Number: 2025932450

ISBN 9780192887320

DOI: 10.1093/9780191981876.001.0001

Printed and bound by
CPI Group (UK) Ltd., Croydon, CR0 4YY

The manufacturer's authorised representative in the EU for product safety is Oxford University Press España S.A. of El Parque Empresarial San Fernando de Henares, Avenida de Castilla, 2 – 28830 Madrid (www.oup.es/en or product.safety@oup.com). OUP España S.A. also acts as importer into Spain of products made by the manufacturer.

FSC
www.fsc.org
MIX
Paper | Supporting
responsible forestry
FSC® C013604

No one really knows how the parties get to 'Yes'
The pieces that are sacrificed in every game of chess
We just assume that it happens
But no one else is in the room where it happens

Leslie Odom Jr and Lin-Manuel Miranda,
'The Room Where It Happens'

Acknowledgements

This book started as an attempt, during my doctoral studies, to understand why Mexico's constitution had been modified so frequently despite being a rigid constitution on paper. I intuitively knew that Mexico's formal constitutional change dynamics posed a long-term risk for the survival of constitutional democracy, but I was mainly intrigued by what I thought to be a rather theoretical question. At that point in time, I had spent two years abroad experiencing two legal cultures that were quite different to that of Mexico. In 2009, I spent one year in Bogotá, Colombia at Universidad de los Andes as part of an academic exchange during my undergraduate studies. In August 2015, when I was starting my doctoral studies, I had just finished my LLM at Yale Law School in the United States. During my time in both places I was most struck by the prominent role the Constitutional Court and the Supreme Court had in the legal cultures of Colombia and the United States, respectively. Both countries aligned to what I had learned in the classroom: in democratic contexts, when apex courts are empowered with judicial review powers, they will inevitably become prominent and consequential political actors.

Even though Mexico, like Colombia, had joined the wave of 'new' constitutionalism in the wake of its transition to democracy in the 90's with the judicial reform of 1994 that empowered the Supreme Court with new judicial review powers, my lived experience of the legal culture surrounding the court was quite different from what I had experienced abroad. After being kept at the sidelines for most of the twentieth century, in the decades that followed the judicial reform of 1994, the Mexican Supreme Court, no question, acquired much relevance through its competence allocation and abstract review powers, as well as through individual constitutional complaints. Still, when it came to high profile cases, for different reasons (eg design features of the judicial review mechanisms), the Supreme Court seemed to often fall short in its role of upholding the constitution. In a context where the master text constitution had been amended several hundred times since its enactment in 1917, the constitutional review of constitutional amendments, I thought, had to be the litmus test to assess not only how powerful the Supreme Court was but also the assumptions of the model of 'new' constitutionalism and the theories of the judicialization of politics. Yet, unlike the Colombian Constitutional Court, the

Mexican Supreme Court had (and still has) consistently refused to review the constitutionality of constitutional amendments.

Against this backdrop, and the context of democratic backsliding around the world, my research topic eventually revealed itself as more than a theoretical question. In particular because—as we know—amending the constitution to do away with democratic checks is a prominent tool in the toolkit of would-be autocratic governments. In this context, the academic discussion in the field of comparative constitutional studies, which was already court-centric, became interested in figuring out whether and to what extent apex courts have the ability to prevent or slow down democratic erosion. In Mexico, the amendment rate seemed to suggest that nothing was off the table and given the absence of an unconstitutional constitutional amendment doctrine, the threat to the survival of constitutional democracy was, thus, ever present. However, turning to the Supreme Court to understand the scope and limits of the amendment power was a non-starter. To find answers to this question, the Mexican context forced me to step away from the traditional path of inquiry and to look beyond it. What started as a theoretical inquiry about the rate of constitutional amendments in Mexico became an endeavour attempting to explain the interaction between relevant political actors and the constitution, in particular, the amendment rule. It is precisely in that interaction where the limits of the amendment power reside. Understanding such interaction resulted in a useful tool to understand, not only why the Mexican constitution changes the way it does but also the process of democratic erosion in Mexico.

I have been very lucky to find different people at different stages of this project who have supported me and, most importantly, believed in me. I am grateful to my doctoral supervisor at Yale, Jack Balkin, who believed in this project from the very beginning and who pushed me way beyond what I thought I was capable of. The time I spent as a postdoctoral fellow (October 2019–August 2021) at the Alexander von Humboldt Chair of Comparative Constitutionalism held by Ran Hirschl at the University of Göttingen in Germany was consequential in turning my doctoral thesis into this book. I am grateful to Ran for his mentorship and generosity and to him and Ayelet Shachar for their always incisive feedback and for the incredible academic experience they managed to create in Göttingen during the extremely challenging times that the COVID pandemic brought for all of us. The isolation that came along with the pandemic was perhaps a blessing in disguise in that it gave me time to rethink things I had included in my doctoral thesis that I would have probably left untouched if the book proposal review had not been delayed because of the pandemic. The delay not only gave me time to rethink some things but to share them with and get feedback from my colleagues in Göttingen: Berihun Gebeye, Alex Hudson, Lisa Harms, Sam Schmid, among others.

Old and new colleagues have been, at different stages, very generous in many respects such as with their time to read and give feedback on drafts of different chapters and/or engage in conversation about the project. To all of them I am very grateful for their support: Richard Albert, Carlos Bernal Pulido, José Antonio Caballero, José Ramón Cossío Díaz, Morelos Canseco, Manuel Cepeda Espinosa, Gráinne de Búrca, Rosalind Dixon, Oran Doyle, Roberto Gargarella, Juan Jesús Garza Onofre, Marie Gren, Carlos A. Gudiño Cicero, José Omar Hernández Salgado, Aileen Kavanagh, David Kenny, Mattias Kumm, Javier Martín Reyes, Gabriel Negretto, Jaclyn Neo, Francisca Pou Gimenez, Andrea Pozas-Loyo, Dominik Rennert, Laura Rojas Zamudio, José Roldán Xopa, Suryapatrim Roy, Zim Nwokora, Jaime Olaiz, Wojciech Sadurski, Scott Stephenson, Adrienne Stone, Alec Stone Sweet, Silvia Suteu, Sergio Verdugo, Joseph Weiler. Thanks are also due to three anonymous reviewers for their useful comments and feedback.

Special thanks are due to Joel Colón-Ríos, Raúl Mejía Garza, Carlos Velasco Rivera and Ángela Zorro Medina—who either read countless drafts of different chapters, engaged with me in endless conversations and/or were generous with their time giving me a helping hand to deal with different issues related to my data. For your time, friendship and support, I will be forever grateful.

Thanks are also due to my academic home, Maynooth University's School of Law and Criminology where I found the much-needed support to bring this project over the finish line. In particular, I am grateful to Michael Doherty and Fergus Ryan. I am also grateful to other institutions that have hosted me in different capacities and at different stages of this project: El Colegio Nacional in Mexico; the Center for Global Constitutionalism at the WZB Berlin Social Science Center; the Trinity Centre for Constitutional Law (TriCON) at Trinity College Dublin; the Gilbert + Tobin Centre of Public Law at the University of New South Wales in Australia; Academia Sinica in Taiwan; the University of Göttingen; the Max Planck Institute for the Study of Religious and Ethnic Diversity in Göttingen; the Jean Monnet Center for International and Regional Economic Law & Justice at New York University School of Law; the IACL Junior Scholars Forum; the Yale Fox International Fellowship; and, Yale Law School.

Finally, I would like to thank my family and friends who were an important source of emotional support in different moments during the long process that started with my doctoral studies and that culminates in this book.

Thank you: mom, dad, Carlos, Anna, Ángela, Gaby, Julio, Joel, Violeta, Regina, Raúl, Julian, and Ximena. And to my partner, Kieran: thank you for always reminding me about the things that truly matter and for brightening up my days.

Dublin, February 2025

Contents

Table of Cases

INTERNATIONAL JUDGMENTS

FOREIGN JUDGMENTS

Table of Legislation

Table of Constitutional Amendments

1
The Mexican Challenge

I. Introduction

Between September and November 2024, the Mexican Constitution was modified beyond recognition. Several amendments were introduced to, among other things, overhaul the judicial branch at the federal and state level, deepen the militarization of public life, and dissolve several independent agencies such as the Instituto Nacional de Transparencia (INAI), the body in charge of guaranteeing the right of access to public information and data protection.[1] In particular, the judicial overhaul undid the judicial reform of 1994 through which Mexico joined the judicialization of politics wave whereby unprecedented power was transferred to apex courts around the world.[2] Among other things, the 1994 reform sought to consolidate the Supreme Court as a constitutional tribunal and created the Judicial Council, the body in charge of overseeing federal judges to guarantee judicial independence. The changes introduced in 2024 replaced the judicial appointment systems at the federal and state levels with the popular election of *all* judges: only at the federal level about 1,600 judges, from district judges to Supreme Court Justices, were to be unseated after the elections took place. The Judicial Council was abolished and replaced with a judicial administration body and a Judicial Discipline Tribunal. The latter was granted broad powers to oversee and sanction judges (including removal from office) for unspecified behaviours such as acting against the principles of 'objectivity', 'impartiality', 'professionalism', 'independence', and

[1] Constitution of 1917, articles 17, 20, 76, 89, 94, 95, 97, 97, 98, 99, 100, 101, 105, 107, 110, 111, 113, 116, 122, and 123, as amended, Diario Oficial de la Federación (15 September 2024); Constitution of 1917, articles 13, 16, 21, 32, 55, 73, 76, 78, 82, 89, 123, and 129, as amended, Diario Oficial de la Federación (30 September 2024); Elia Castillo Jiménez, 'El Senado extermina siete órganos y entes autónomos, incluido el INAI' *El País México* (29 November 2024) <https://elpais.com/mexico/2024-11-29/el-senado-extermina-siete-organos-y-entes-autonomos-incluido-el-inai.html> accessed 29 November 2024.

[2] Ran Hirschl, *Towards Juristocracy: The Origins and Consequences of the New Constitutionalism* (Harvard UP 2004); Tom Ginsburg, *Judicial Review in New Democracies: Constitutional Courts in Asian Cases* (CUP 2003).

The Politics of Constitutional Rigidity. Mariana Velasco-Rivera, Oxford University Press.
 DOI: 10.1093/9780191981876.003.0001

'excellence'.[3] The decisions of the Tribunal are not subject to appeal. The same model is replicated at the state level.[4]

The process through which the judicial overhaul was adopted happened at a vertiginous speed: it was approved by the Chamber of Deputies and the Senate in two separate overnight sessions, and ratified by the required seventeen state legislatures in less than twenty-four hours.[5] The fastest ratification, by the legislature of the State of Oaxaca, came four hours after it had been approved by Congress. The session in which the amendment was 'deliberated' and approved in that state legislature took six minutes.[6] Unsurprisingly, given the magnitude and gravity of the judicial overhaul, it was challenged on multiple fronts: in addition to country-wide student-led protests in the months and weeks leading to its adoption, affected sitting judges and human rights organizations, as well as parties in the opposition and dissident state legislatures, brought cases to the judiciary through *amparos* (ie individual constitutional complaints) and *acciones de inconstitucionalidad* (ie abstract review). When the intervention of the Supreme Court in original jurisdiction (ie through abstract review) became imminent, the government moved to adopt yet another reform to shield the judicial overhaul from scrutiny by introducing a blanket ban on judicial review of constitutional amendments.[7] Just like the judicial overhaul, this amendment was rammed through Congress and state legislatures. It took nine days for it to wend through all the relevant steps of the constitutional amendment process, from initiative to publication. The floors of the Senate and the Chamber of Deputies 'deliberated' it in one session, respectively, and it was ratified by twenty-three out of thirty-two state legislatures in less than twenty-four hours.[8]

[3] Constitution of 1917, article 100, as amended, Diario Oficial de la Federación (15 September 2024).

[4] The amendment also introduced changes that are problematic from a due process perspective such as faceless judges in organized crime cases.

[5] 'Reforma al Poder Judicial Será Ley: Es Aprobada Por 17 Congresos, ¿qué Estados la Aprobaron?' *El Financiero* (12 September 2024) <www.elfinanciero.com.mx/nacional/2024/09/11/reforma-judicial-aprobacion-en-congresos-de-los-estados-cuales-votaron-a-favor-en-vivo> accessed 23 October 2024.

[6] 'Morena y Aliados Aprueban la Reforma Judicial en 24 Congresos Estatales; Querétaro y Jalisco la Rechazan' (15 September 2024) <https://animalpolitico.com/politica/congreso-oaxaca-avala-reforma-judicial> accessed 23 October 2024.

[7] Constitution of 1917, articles 105 and 107, as amended, Diario Oficial de la Federación (31 October 2024).

[8] See 'Senado aprueba en fast track "supremacía constitucional"; hará intocables reformas de Morena frente a la Corte' *El Universal* (25 October 2024) <www.eluniversal.com.mx/nacion/senado-aprueba-en-fast-track-supremacia-constitucional-hara-intocables-reformas-de-morena-frente-a-la-corte> accessed 28 October 2024; Melín Angélica, 'Supremacía Constitucional Sale en fast track en San Lázaro' (*MVS Noticias*, 30 October 2024) <https://mvsnoticias.com/nacional/2024/10/30/supremacia-constitucional-avanza-paso-acelerado-en-san-lazaro-663436.html> accessed 21 November 2024; 'En tiempo récord, estados avalan reforma de Supremacía Constitucional; ya van 20 entidades' *El Universal* (31 October 2024) <www.eluniversal.com.mx/nacion/supremacia-pasa-por-congreso-de-los-estados> accessed 21 November 2024; 'Presidencia publica en DOF decreto sobre supremacía constitucional' *La*

The rash approval of changes of such magnitude would be surprising in any context. But it is perhaps most surprising because, on paper, Mexico's Constitution is rigid. Article 135, the amendment rule, establishes a stringent amendment procedure: it requires a two-thirds majority of each chamber of the bicameral Congress and ratification of half of the state legislatures. Additionally, since 1988, the year in which the Partido de la Revolución Instituticional (PRI) lost the ability to amend the Constitution on its own, no single political party has had the power to do so without collaborating with other parties. The judicial overhaul was passed by a coalition between Movimiento de Regeneración Nacional (MORENA, the party in government), Partido del Trabajo (PT), and Partido Verde Ecologista de México (PVEM).

The reader might wonder: is this judicial overhaul an extraordinary, unusual, or exceptional happening? Does it mean that the wave of democratic backsliding has arrived in Mexico? Is Mexico, perhaps, living in an era of abusive constitutionalism[9] or autocratic legalism?[10] While the reader would not be incorrect in thinking all of those things, framing it simply as an unusual constitutional development risks overlooking the fact that far from exceptional, rash approvals are part and parcel of constitutional reform processes in Mexico. The judicial overhaul was in many ways the result of deeply engrained unwritten rules of political behaviour, beliefs, and understandings around the function of constitutional amendments that was built over the span of three decades, in particular by the three main political parties of the time, the PRI, Partido Acción Nacional (PAN), and Partido de la Revolución Democrática (PRD), as well as by the Supreme Court. It is those unwritten rules, beliefs, and understandings that shape the flexibility of Mexico's theoretically rigid Constitution.

II. Constitutional Rigidity: Theory versus Reality

The question of how constitutions change is a loaded one: it goes straight to the heart of the relationship between constitutionalism and democracy. Often, it comes with important normative assumptions about what constitutions are, how they should change, and the nature of the acts and politics surrounding them. One of the main assumptions associated with constitutions is that they

Jornada (31 October 2024) <www.jornada.com.mx/noticia/2024/10/31/politica/presidencia-publica-en-dof-decreto-sobre-supremacia-constitucional-2537> accessed 21 November 2024.

[9] David Landau, 'Abusive Constitutionalism' (2013) 47 UC Davis Law Review 189.
[10] Kim Lane Scheppele, 'Autocratic Legalism' (2018) 85 The University of Chicago Law Review 545.

have a direct link to the popular will. Constitutions in this sense are understood as the product of an exercise of popular sovereignty that involves foundational political acts substantively different from other acts or decisions that take place in the realm of ordinary politics.[11] The adoption of constitutional changes is thought to involve extraordinary happenings different in nature from those that result in the enactment of ordinary laws. Even though both types of acts are frequently carried out by the same or similar actors (ie the members of legislative bodies), the former are attributed to the people and the latter to their representatives, mainly because the processes to produce one and the other involve different requirements.[12]

In this context, amendment mechanisms and the question of constitutional rigidity are of paramount importance. Stringent constitutional amendment procedures are supposed to guarantee the status of constitutions as higher laws while protecting a self-governing people's most fundamental decisions. These decisions, the theory goes, should be difficult to change but not to the point where they end up trapping present generations in choices made in the far past (which creates the risk of revolutionary constitutional replacement).[13] Accordingly, given that the democratic legitimacy and endurance of constitutional orders depend, at least in some ways, on the capacity of constitutions to respond to present popular values, striking a balance between constitutional

[11] See eg Bruce A Ackerman, *We the People, Volume 1: Foundations* (Harvard UP 1993); Bruce Ackerman, 'Higher Lawmaking' in Sanford Levinson (ed), *Responding to Imperfection: The Theory and Practice of Constitutional Amendment* (Princeton UP 1995) 63–88; Thomaz Pereira, 'Constituting the Amendment Power' in Richard Albert, Xenophon Contiades, and Alkmene Fotiadou (eds), *The Foundations and Traditions of Constitutional Amendment* (Hart Publishing 2017) 105; Dieter Grimm, *Constitutionalism: Past, Present, and Future* (OUP 2016) 200 (arguing 'constitutional and ordinary law have different sources. Since constitutional law brings forth legitimate political power it cannot emanate from that same power. It is made by or attributed to the people').

[12] See eg Grimm (n 11) 200 (arguing 'the making of constitutional law differs from the making of ordinary law. It is usually a special body that formulates constitutional law and its adoption is subject to a special procedure in which either the people takes the decision or, if a representative body is called upon to decide, a super-majority is required'); Ackerman, *We the People, Volume 1* (n 11); Ackerman, 'Higher Lawmaking' (n 11).

[13] This concern, commonly known as the 'dead-hand problem', was present in Thomas Jefferson's constitutional thought and it is also present in contemporary constitutional theory. See Thomas Jefferson, '*Thomas Jefferson to James Madison*': *The Papers of Thomas Jefferson*, vol 15 (Julian P Boyd ed, Princeton UP 1958) ('it may be proved that no society can make a perpetual constitution, or even a perpetual law. The earth belongs always to the living generation. They may manage it then, and what proceeds from it, as they please, during their usufruct. They are masters too of their own persons, and consequently may govern them as they please. [. . .] Every constitution then, and every law, naturally expires at the end of 19 years. If it be enforced longer, it is an act of force, and not of right'); Ackerman, 'Higher Lawmaking' (n 11); Bruce Ackerman, *We the People, Volume 2: Transformations* (Harvard UP 2000); Akhil Reed Amar, 'The Consent of the Governed: Constitutional Amendment Outside Article V' (1994) 94 Columbia Law Review 457.

rigidity and flexibility has been an ever-present problem for constitutional theorists and designers alike.[14]

Perhaps the best-known case of 'extreme' constitutional rigidity is that of the Constitution of the United States (US)—which has been classified as one of the most difficult to amend in the world.[15] In the US, the idea that constitutional rigidity is institutionally determined is largely taken for granted. The formal hurdles imposed by Article V,[16] which has been described as an 'iron cage', are assumed to make constitutional amendments close to impossible.[17] This idea (that formal hurdles such as supermajority requirements determine how difficult it is to change the text of a constitution) is in fact a well-established proposition in constitutional theory that may be traced back to the founding of the US.[18] In 'The Federalist No. 43', James Madison argued that Article V would guard 'equally against that extreme facility, which would render the Constitution too mutable; and that extreme difficulty, which might perpetuate its discovered faults'.[19] Yet, if an observer looks at the amendment reality in

[14] See eg Grimm (n 11) 141–42 (arguing 'constitutional amendments are appropriate only when the constitution conflicts with practical constraints and this makes violation of its own provisions likely, or when the constitution prevents desirable developments and thereby undermines its inherent legitimacy. Constitutional amendment is thus constitutional improvement'); Donald Lutz, 'Toward a Theory of Constitutional Amendment' in Sanford Levinson (ed), *Responding to Imperfection: The Theory and Practice of Constitutional Amendment* (Princeton UP 1995) 245; Zachary Elkins, Tom Ginsburg, and James Melton, *The Endurance of National Constitutions* (CUP 2009).

[15] Lutz (n 14); Arend Lijphart, *Patterns of Democracy* (Yale UP 2012) 206–11; Elkins, Ginsburg, and Melton (n 14) 101.

[16] Article V of the US Constitution provides: 'The Congress, whenever two thirds of both Houses shall deem it necessary, shall propose Amendments to this Constitution, or, on the Application of the Legislatures of two thirds of the several States, shall call a Convention for proposing Amendments, which, in either Case, shall be valid to all Intents and Purposes, as Part of this Constitution, when ratified by the Legislatures of three fourths of the several States, or by Conventions in three fourths thereof, as the one or the other Mode of Ratification may be proposed by the Congress; Provided that no Amendment which may be made prior to the Year One thousand eight hundred and eight shall in any Manner affect the first and fourth Clauses in the Ninth Section of the first Article; and that no State, without its Consent, shall be deprived of its equal Suffrage in the Senate.'

[17] Sanford Levinson, *Our Undemocratic Constitution: Where the Constitution Goes Wrong (and How We the People Can Correct It)* (OUP 2006).

[18] Perhaps the most prominent example of this view is the influential work of Sanford Levinson. See ibid. This assumption, however, is widely shared in the scholarly literature both in law and political science. See eg Lutz (n 14); Arend Lijphart, *Patterns of Democracy: Government Forms and Performance in Thirty-Six Countries* (Yale UP 1999) 206–11; Joel I Colon-Rios, *Weak Constitutionalism: Democratic Legitimacy and the Question of Constituent Power* (Routledge 2012) 66; Stephen M Griffin, 'The Nominee Is . . . Article V' in Sanford Levinson, William N Eskridge, and Murphy Institute of Political Economy (eds), *Constitutional Stupidities, Constitutional Tragedies* (New York UP 1998) 51–53; Heather K Gerken, 'The Hydraulics of Constitutional Reform: A Skeptical Response to Our Undemocratic Constitution' (2006) 55 Drake Law Review 925; Dieter Grimm, 'Types of Constitutions' in Michel Rosenfeld and András Sajó (eds), *The Oxford Handbook of Comparative Constitutional Law* (OUP 2012) 111; Aziz Z Huq, 'The Function of Article V' (2013) 162 University of Pennsylvania Law Review 1165.

[19] James Madison, 'Federalist No 43' (The Avalon Project) <https://avalon.law.yale.edu/18th_century/fed43.asp> accessed 23 January 2020.

the US and Mexico side by side, they will realize that Madison may have been wrong on both counts. Formal hurdles, like the ones imposed by Article V, neither guard against extreme facility in constitutional amendment nor necessarily make constitutional change extremely difficult.

Like the US, Mexico is a federal and presidential system with a rigid and old Constitution (enacted in 1917). Similar to the US, the amendment rule of the Mexican Constitution requires a two-thirds majority of each chamber of the bicameral Congress and ratification of half of the state legislatures for constitutional amendments to be passed. Methodologically speaking, from a most-similar-case approach, Mexico is an ideal case to test the validity of the claim that amendment difficulty stems from the formal hurdles imposed by amendment rules.[20] Interestingly, in Mexico, the amendment mechanism has been successfully used 257 times, resulting in over 772 discrete amendments to the constitutional text since 1917.[21] By contrast, Article V has been successfully used fewer than twenty times (as the first ten—the Bill of Rights—were proposed and ratified at once). Mexico's formal constitutional change reality seriously questions the validity of the traditional claim about constitutional rigidity. The dynamics of constitutional change in that country show that the design of the amendment mechanism often does very little to prevent a constitution from being amended with 'extreme facility' and therefore from becoming 'too mutable'.

Madison's view rested on a reasonable assumption about the relationship between design and rigidity that became part of the US Constitution (Article V) without much scrutiny.[22] This assumption is still present in contemporary constitutional thought. Constitutional scholars still regard Article V as one important, if not the main, obstacle to fix structural governmental flaws embedded in the Constitution and, thus, as a threat to American democracy.[23]

[20] Ran Hirschl, *Comparative Matters: The Renaissance of Comparative Constitutional Law* (OUP 2014) 245–46.

[21] These figures account for the constitutional amendments adopted until 31 July 2024. Importantly, the number of discrete changes refers to the number of constitutional articles modified in each presidential administration, which is different from the number of amendment decrees. Amendment decrees normally include the modification of more than one article and clauses within articles. Therefore, the number of decrees will always be lower than the number of discrete modifications to articles and clauses of the constitutional text. See Cámara de Diputados, Reformas Constitucionales por Artículo <www.diputados.gob.mx/LeyesBiblio/ref/cpeum_art.htm> accessed 20 October 2024; and Cámara de Diputados, Reformas Constitucionales por Decreto en Orden Cronológico <www.diputados.gob.mx/LeyesBiblio/ref/cpeum_crono.htm> accessed 20 October 2024.

[22] Melissa Schwartzberg, 'The Arbitrariness of Supermajority Rules' (2010) 49 Social Science Information 61, 72.

[23] This idea may be found in the constitutional thought of one of the founders of modern political science, John W Burgess. See John W Burgess, *Political Science and Comparative Constitutional Law*, vol 1 (1893) 151 (arguing, 'When I reflect that, while our natural conditions and relations have been requiring a gradual strengthening and extension of the powers of the central government, not a single step

Of course, as Aziz Huq rightly points out, Madison did not possess the empirical resources to establish with certainty whether Article V would indeed strike a balance between 'extreme facility' and 'extreme difficulty'.[24] Looking at the amendment realities of Mexico and the US side by side should give contemporary scholars pause to reconsider the prevailing assumptions about constitutional change and rigidity.

III. Outline of the Book

The book is organized as follows. Chapter 2 argues that the literature that grapples with the question of constitutional rigidity can be divided in two camps: *formalists*—those who believe that amendment difficulty is institutionally determined;[25] and *anti-formalists*—those who, by contrast, maintain that it is determined by non-institutional factors.[26] This body of literature, on the one hand, does not offer a conclusive answer as to what are the institutional and non-institutional determinants of constitutional rigidity and, on the

has been taken in this direction through the process of amendment prescribed in that article, except as the result of civil war, I am bound to conclude that the organization of the sovereign power within the constitution has failed to accomplish the purpose for which it was constructed. . . . when a state must have recourse to war to solve the internal questions of its own politics, this is indisputable evidence that the law of its organization within the constitution is imperfect; and when a state cannot so modify and amend its constitution from time to time as to express itself truthfully therein, but must writhe under the bonds of its constitution until it perishes or breaks them asunder, this is again indisputable evidence that the law of its organization within the constitution is imperfect and false. To my mind the error lies in the artificially excessive majorities required in the production of constitutional changes'). More recently, a vocal advocate of this idea has been Sanford Levinson; see Levinson (n 17).

[24] Huq (n 18) 1176.

[25] Cristina Bucur and Bjørn Erik Rasch, 'Institutions for Amending Constitutions' in Roger D Congleton, Bernard Grofman, and Stefan Voigt (eds), *The Oxford Handbook of Public Choice, Volume 2* (OUP 2019) 156–76. See eg Lutz (n 14); Astrid Lorenz, 'How to Measure Constitutional Rigidity: Four Concepts and Two Alternatives' (2005) 17 Journal of Theoretical Politics 339; Levinson (n 17); Lijphart (n 18); Kathleen M Sullivan, 'Constitutional Constancy: Why Congress Should Cure Itself of Amendment Fever Address' (1995) 17 Cardozo Law Review 691; Bjørn Erik Rasch and Roger D Congleton, 'Amendment Procedures and Constitutional Stability' in Roger D Congleton and Birgitta Swedenborg (eds), *Democratic Constitutional Design and Public Policy: Analysis and Evidence* (MIT Press 2006) 319-342.

[26] See eg Tom Ginsburg and James Melton, 'Does the Constitutional Amendment Rule Matter at All? Amendment Cultures and the Challenges of Measuring Amendment Difficulty' (2015) 13 International Journal of Constitutional Law 686; Vicki C Jackson, 'The (Myth of Un)Amendability of the US Constitution and the Democratic Component of Constitutionalism' (2015) 13 International Journal of Constitutional Law 575; Rosalind Dixon and Richard Holden, 'Constitutional Amendment Rules: The Denominator Problem' in Tom Ginsburg (ed), *Comparative Constitutional Design* (CUP 2012); Gabriel Negretto, 'Replacing and Amending Constitutions: The Logic of Constitutional Change in Latin America' (2012) 46 Law and Society Review 749; Richard Albert, *Constitutional Amendments: Making, Breaking, and Changing Constitutions* (OUP 2019); George Tsebelis, 'Constitutional Rigidity Matters: A Veto Players Approach' [2020] British Journal of Political Science 48.

other, tends to rely on normative assumptions that obscure the direct drivers of constitutional change—in particular, the role of political parties.[27] In fact, since they heavily rely on the normative dimension of constitutionalism and constitutional design, these works are unable to systematically capture the non-institutional and political factors that affect constitutional rigidity. The chapter contends that the formalist and anti-formalists tend to either conflate the normative and empirical aspects of constitutional change and/or oversimplify constitutional experiences, therefore obscuring the direct drivers of constitutional change. Importantly, these critiques and shortcomings apply to both legal and social science approaches. In particular, I provide examples of the ways in which aggregated quantitative studies dealing with questions about amendment difficulty present explanatory limitations that call for in-depth single case studies that capture the rich context in which formal constitutional change takes place. Mexico's constitutional change dynamics strongly suggest that the determinants of amendment difficulty are not to be found in the design of the amendment rule alone. It is therefore an ideal case to deepen our knowledge of the determinants of constitutional rigidity and flexibility.

This book contends that if we are to understand how and why constitutions change the way they do, a new approach is necessary. That approach ought to be less normative and more descriptive so that it is able to account for the direct drivers of constitutional change. Given that in contemporary democracies constitutional change is largely a mediated phenomenon—meaning that specific actors have the legal power to activate the mechanisms that can be used to modify the constitutional text—offering an account that sheds light on the direct drivers of constitutional change means shifting our attention towards those actors. In contemporary democracies, these actors are, as a general rule, political parties. But political parties are not monoliths and do not act in a vacuum. They are constituted by rational, self-interested individuals whose actions, preferences, and choices are shaped by the constitutional culture in which they operate—which includes but is not limited to the unwritten political norms and practices driving their behaviour.

This book is an attempt to move in that direction. Building on an in-depth study of the dynamics of constitutional change in Mexico, with particular

[27] For an in-depth analysis of the absence of political parties and party systems in constitutional theory and comparative constitutional law, see Tarunabh Khaitan, 'Political Parties in Constitutional Theory' (2020) 73(1) Current Legal Problems 89. Negretto and Hudson have done crucial work on shifting the attention to political parties when grappling with questions of constitutional change. See Negretto (n 26); Gabriel Negretto, *Making Constitutions: Presidents, Parties, and Institutional Choice in Latin America* (CUP 2013); Alexander Hudson, *The Veil of Participation: Citizens and Political Parties in Constitution-Making Processes* (CUP 2021).

attention to the period between 1988 and 2024, Chapter 3 offers an analytical framework that incorporates the political dimension of constitutional change, one that can explain why a high amendment rate is possible in the context of a formally rigid constitution. In so doing, it takes a strategic-realist approach[28] to develop an analytical framework that seeks to disrupt the conflation of the normative and empirical aspects of constitutional change and capture the descriptive dimension of constitutional change.[29] The analytical framework systematically identifies different non-institutional and political factors that influence constitutional rigidity—namely, political parties and party systems, constitutional culture, and the choices made by key political actors, all of which take place in what I will call an economy of constitutional change.

The economy of constitutional change operates based on three important assumptions: it views politics from a rational choice perspective—that is, as a 'process of exchange through which individuals seek to advance their interests';[30] it views constitutional amendments as politics by other means; and, therefore, when choosing to amend the Constitution, 'rather than acting in a self-defeating way, said identifiable actors act motivated by self-interest'.[31] Moreover, the economy of constitutional change is determined by three key elements: (i) political parties and party systems; (ii) a country's constitutional culture (understood as the beliefs, understandings, assumptions, and attitudes of the relevant actors regarding constitutional change); and (iii) the choices of key political actors among the *available* means of entrenchment in a given constitutional order. The availability of the mechanisms of entrenchment will be determined by the interplay of (i), (ii), and (iii) in an economy of change whereby constitutional change (formal and informal) is a function of political entrenchment.

Chapter 4 seeks to shed light on the first key element of the analytical framework offered in Chapter 3: the role of political parties and the party system in determining the availability of constitutional amendment in Mexico's economy of constitutional change. Based on an original data set covering all constitutional amendments in the period between 1997 and 2024, Chapter 4 measures the time a proposal spends in each of the stages (from initiative to

[28] Ran Hirschl, 'The Strategic Foundations of Constitutions' in DJ Galligan and Mila Versteeg (eds), *Social and Political Foundations of Constitutions* (CUP 2013) 157–81.

[29] ibid 165.

[30] Tom Ginsburg, 'Public Choice and Constitutional Design' in Daniel A Farber and Anne Joseph O'Connell (eds), *Research Handbook in Public Choice and Public Law* (Edward Elgar 2010) 261. See also Jack M Balkin and Sanford Levinson, 'Understanding the Constitutional Revolution' (2001) 87 Virginia Law Review 1045.

[31] Hirschl (n 28) 157, 166.

publication) of the process. Contrary to the normative assumptions about amendment rules identified in Chapter 2 (eg that they ensure deliberation and heighten transparency), this chapter identifies a fast-track trend in the adoption of amendments and a general lack of opposition by state legislatures. Perhaps most importantly, the stages that are supposed to be characterized by deliberative practices—that is, when proposals are considered on the floor of the chambers of Congress—are the shortest: the vast majority of proposals are approved on the same day they are submitted to the floor. This, in turn, suggests three main features about Mexico's party system: the ability to cooperate across party lines; strong party discipline; and a high centralization of constitutional decision-making. Building on those findings, the chapter turns to shed light on the cross-party cooperation dynamics and politics surrounding the coalitions that have allowed constitutional amendment to remain available in Mexico's economy of constitutional change.

Chapter 5 analyses the second key element of the analytical framework offered in Chapter 3: constitutional culture as a non-institutional factor influencing the availability of constitutional amendment in Mexico's economy of constitutional change. The chapter explores in what ways constitutional culture (here understood as the beliefs, understandings, assumptions, and attitudes of the actors who have the legal power to activate the amendment mechanism) around constitutional change may contribute to explaining the formal constitutional change trends identified in Chapter 4. In so doing, it focuses on the governing elite subculture; in particular, on the unwritten rules that allowed presidents to exercise unchecked power which, at the same time, eased access to the amendment mechanism since the late nineteenth century and throughout most of the twentieth. Since, for over a century, the governing elite subculture enjoyed disproportionate power to access the amendment mechanism, its study is central to understanding the constitutional amendment dynamics in Mexico. The chapter shows that both presidents who enjoyed wide levels of popular support (eg Benito Juárez and Lázaro Cárdenas) and presidents with less democratic credentials such as Porfirio Díaz or José López Portillo were interested in and able to access the amendment mechanisms to fulfil a wide array of political needs—for example, lifting presidential term limits, gaining control over judicial appointments, capturing the judiciary, dealing with a rising political opposition, and resetting the national narrative to cope with serious legitimacy crises. Such disproportionate power to access the amendment mechanism, the chapter argues, shaped the country's constitutional culture that understands the amendment rule as a political entrenchment mechanism. The expectation was that with democratization, the unwritten rules that formed throughout a century would disappear and the constitutional system of separation of powers and checks and balances would begin to effectively constrain power, and therefore constitutional amendment would cease to be easily accessible. Instead, the chapter argues, as the PRI hegemonic regime unravelled, new unwritten rules, inevitably influenced by old ones, gave way to the emergence of a regime where cross-party entrenchment enables continued access to the constitutional amendment mechanism: the cross-party entrenchment regime (CPER). As a result, in the CPER, the Constitution continues to play a central role in public discourse as well as in protecting the interests of the ruling elite.

Chapter 6 sheds light on the third element of the economy of constitutional change: the choices made by key political actors. In so doing, it seeks to show how the choices made during the the nineties had a lasting impact on the trajectory of constitutional change in Mexico and the consolidation of the CPER. Particular attention is drawn to a key choice: the deployment of what I call the *consensus rationale*—the championing of the idea of consensus as a necessary condition for the realization of democracy. Through embracing the consensus rationale, the PRI set the ground for perpetuating the centralization of constitutional decision-making, and in so doing secured the continued availability of constitutional amendment in the country's economy of constitutional change. In particular, it enabled the government's ability to cut deals with the political opposition and facilitated the centralization of decision-making. The deployment of the *consensus rationale* resulted in the formation of a new unwritten rule: the rule of cooperation—which has been the main driver of the CPER. The rule of cooperation operates through party discipline and its effect is the centralization of decision-making—which allows the continued use of the amendment mechanism for political entrenchment despite political fragmentation. The chapter traces the formation of the rule of cooperation by shedding light on the choices and decisions made by key political actors (including but not limited to Presidents Carlos Salinas and Ernesto Zedillo, the last two PRI presidents before the transition to democracy) to deal with the political reality they faced as the hegemonic party unravelled.

Chapter 7 explores the role the Supreme Court has played in Mexico's economy of constitutional change. The centralization of decision-making that characterizes the CPER has negative implications in terms of the values and principles that, in a liberal constitutional democracy, the state is supposed to guarantee and protect—such as the separation of powers, the system of checks and balances, transparency, non-arbitrary state action, and accountability. In theory, under a 'new constitutionalism' and juristocracy logic, the Court is a constitutional actor in a position to enforce those principles. Far from it: through its constitutional doctrines on the question of the reviewability of constitutional amendments, the Court has been consequential in maintaining the amendment mechanism available in Mexico's economy of constitutional change. In particular, the non-justiciability of constitutional amendments doctrine and the constitutional restrictions doctrine, which are largely based on the notion of a 'permanent constituent power', shield the amendment power from scrutiny and accountability, making such power arbitrary. In this way, the chapter argues, the Court's doctrines have done two things: they have disempowered citizens, leaving them without legal mechanisms to defend themselves from abuses of power; and they have informed the understandings, attitudes, and beliefs politicians have about the scope and limits of the amendment power. Chapter 8 concludes.

2

The Formalist and Anti-Formalist Approaches to Constitutional Rigidity

I. Introduction

A growing body of literature has engaged with the question of constitutional rigidity in different ways and for different purposes. For instance, Zachary Elkins, Tom Ginsburg, and James Melton are interested in understanding the relationship between constitutional rigidity and survival (in their view, flexible constitutions have better chances to survive political crises).[1] Arend Lijphart, on the other hand, focuses on measuring constitutional rigidity as a variable to test his model of patterns of democracy.[2] Donald Lutz is interested in the institutional features that would ensure an optimal level of constitutional amendments.[3] More generally, others have sought to identify the features of amendment rules that explain constitutional amendment rates,[4] while some have focused on extra-constitutional or non-institutional factors.[5] The overarching question, for these scholars, is whether one can predict the stability

[1] Zachary Elkins, Tom Ginsburg, and James Melton, *The Endurance of National Constitutions* (CUP 2009) 100.

[2] Arend Lijphart, *Patterns of Democracy* (Yale UP 2012).

[3] Donald S Lutz, 'Toward a Theory of Constitutional Amendment' (1994) 88 The American Political Science Review 355.

[4] John Ferejohn, 'The Politics of Imperfection: The Amendment of Constitutions' (1997) 22 Law and Social Inquiry 501, 523 (arguing that 'special majorities or separate majorities in different legislative sessions or bicamerality [are] the key variable to explaining amendment rates'); Astrid Lorenz, 'How to Measure Constitutional Rigidity: Four Concepts and Two Alternatives' (2005) 17 Journal of Theoretical Politics 339; Bjørn Erik Rasch and Roger D Congleton, 'Amendment Procedures and Constitutional Stability' in Roger D Congleton and Birgitta Swedenborg (eds), *Democratic Constitutional Design and Public Policy: Analysis and Evidence* (MIT Press 2006); Rosalind Dixon and Richard Holden, 'Constitutional Amendment Rules: The Denominator Problem' in Tom Ginsburg (ed), *Comparative Constitutional Design* (CUP 2012) (finding that the size of legislative bodies has a negative relationship to the rate of constitutional amendments in different states in the United States).

[5] See eg Tom Ginsburg and James Melton, 'Does the Constitutional Amendment Rule Matter at All? Amendment Cultures and the Challenges of Measuring Amendment Difficulty' (2015) 13 International Journal of Constitutional Law 686; Vicki C Jackson, 'The (Myth of Un)Amendability of the US Constitution and the Democratic Component of Constitutionalism' (2015) 13 International Journal of Constitutional Law 575; Richard Albert, *Constitutional Amendments: Making, Breaking, and Changing Constitutions* (OUP 2019) 95–138.

The Politics of Constitutional Rigidity. Mariana Velasco-Rivera, Oxford University Press.
 DOI: 10.1093/9780191981876.003.0002

of the constitutional text by looking only (or even mainly) at the amendment rule. In other words, can one expect a negative relationship between the stringency of the amendment rule and the frequency of amendments?

This body of literature can be classified in two main streams: the formalists and the anti-formalists. The *formalists* are those who consider that constitutional rigidity is institutionally determined.[6] That is to say, the difficulty of amendment can be analysed, assessed, measured, and predicted from an institutional design point of view (which in some cases may include substantive limits to constitutional change[7]). The *anti-formalists*, on the other hand, are sceptical about the weight and impact the design of amendment rules has on amendment rates. While they do not necessarily think that amendment rules are irrelevant to understanding constitutional rigidity, they believe that other extra-constitutional or non-institutional factors have much more weight in determining the ease or difficulty with which a constitution can be amended.[8] To be sure, there is no such a thing as an absolute formalist or anti-formalist. Some authors seem to place a lot of weight on institutional design and others either implicitly or explicitly are more or less open to the idea that non-institutional factors affect constitutional rigidity. Moreover, the question of what exactly are the determinants of constitutional rigidity is far from being settled.[9] Thus, it is most helpful to think about these two extreme positions as existing on a spectrum. Section II of this chapter discusses the formalist stream of the literature and Section III the anti-formalist. Section IV identifies the pitfalls of the formalist and anti-formalist approaches to questions of constitutional rigidity. Finally, drawing on some of the explanatory limitations of current social science approaches, in Section V a case is made for in-depth single case studies.

[6] See eg Lutz (n 3); Donald Lutz, 'Toward a Theory of Constitutional Amendment' in Sanford Levinson (ed), *Responding to Imperfection: The Theory and Practice of Constitutional Amendment* (Princeton UP 1995); Arend Lijphart, *Patterns of Democracy: Government Forms and Performance in Thirty-Six Countries* (Yale UP 1999); Sanford Levinson, *Our Undemocratic Constitution: Where the Constitution Goes Wrong (and How We the People Can Correct It)* (OUP 2006); Lorenz (n 4).

[7] For an in-depth study on the different functions eternity clauses have in constitutional democracies, see Silvia Suteu, *Eternity Clauses in Democratic Constitutionalism* (OUP 2021).

[8] See eg Gabriel Negretto, 'Replacing and Amending Constitutions: The Logic of Constitutional Change in Latin America' (2012) 46 Law and Society Review 749; Ginsburg and Melton (n 5); Jackson (n 5); Mila Versteeg and Emily Zackin, 'Constitutions Unentrenched: Toward an Alternative Theory of Constitutional Design' (2016) 110 American Political Science Review 657; Albert (n 5); George Tsebelis, 'Constitutional Rigidity Matters: A Veto Players Approach' [2020] British Journal of Political Science 48.

[9] For a helpful review of the literature on this question, see Cristina Bucur and Bjørn Erik Rasch, 'Institutions for Amending Constitutions' in Roger D Congleton, Bernard N Grofman, and Stefan Voigt (eds), *The Oxford Handbook of Public Choice, Volume 2* (OUP 2019) 156–76.

II. The Formalists

At one extreme of the constitutional rigidity determinants spectrum, one finds works according to which the institutional design of the amendment mechanism is the key factor explaining constitutional rigidity. Perhaps the most prominent example of this position is Sanford Levinson's writings on Article V of the US Constitution. Levinson regards Article V as an 'iron cage' that prevents 'changing some of the most important aspects of our political system'.[10] Inasmuch as Article V is the main factor preventing formal constitutional change, Levinson maintains that it threatens the democratic legitimacy of the Constitution. Accordingly, one must take the threat posed by Article V very seriously. Similarly, Kathleen Sullivan also regards Article V as the key factor making formal constitutional change difficult in the US. However, in contrast to Levinson, Sullivan believes Article V serves important functions in the US constitutional system. For example, it secures the stability of the constitutional order and sets the boundaries between law and politics and between higher and ordinary law.[11]

There are also quantitative empirical works that reflect the formalist approach. This is exemplified in the efforts of some political scientists to develop ways of measuring how difficult it is to amend a constitution. In simple terms, this approach consists of developing difficulty indexes by classifying diverse (and ideally all) possible forms of constitutional amendment rules and assigning them an estimated score of difficulty based on the relevant requirements. Lutz and Lijphart's influential works are prominent examples of this approach.

In his pioneering work on constitutional rigidity, Lutz found a strong negative relationship between the stringency of amendment rules and the amendment rate—meaning that the more difficult the formal amendment process (ie the more hurdles that must be surpassed before an amendment can be adopted), the lower the amendment rate, and vice versa.[12] Based on this finding, Lutz turns to argue that it is possible to predict the amendment rate based on the design of the amendment rule—'one can with some confidence

[10] Levinson (n 6) 159–66. See also Rosalind Dixon, 'Updating Constitutional Rules' [2009] The Supreme Court Review 319, 319; Richard H Fallon Jr, 'Constitution Day Lecture: American Constitutionalism, Almost (but Not Quite) Version 2.0' (2012) 65 Maine Law Review 77, 92 (arguing, 'Even under the best of circumstances, the requirement that three-fourths of the states must ratify constitutional amendments makes it nearly impossible to achieve significant change in our written Constitution through the Article V process').

[11] Kathleen Sullivan, 'Constitutional Amendmentitis' [2001] *The American Prospect* <http://prospect.org/article/constitutional-amendmentitis> accessed 15 August 2024.

[12] Lutz (n 3) 362.

achieve a moderate rate of amendment by selecting an appropriate range of amendment difficulty'—and continues to suggest that 'certain amendment strategies are better in this regard than others'.[13] In his view, different designs of amendment rules reflect different commitments and assumptions about constitutionalism (ie popular sovereignty, deliberation, the distinction between ordinary and constitutional matters) and have definite and predictable consequences for the political process.[14] Lutz concludes that institutions matter and operate to a great extent independently of the cultural, historical, geographic, or political context.[15]

Similarly, Lijphart develops an index of constitutional rigidity which takes into account the strength of judicial review as a central explanatory variable to test his model of patterns of democracy (consensual and majoritarian).[16] Similarly to Lutz's, Lijphart's index of rigidity operates under the premise that institutional design determines constitutional rigidity. His index identifies four rigidity levels based on the size of the majority required by the amendment mechanism (ie ordinary majorities, supermajorities but less than two-thirds, two-thirds, and supermajorities greater than two-thirds).[17] Notably, Lijphart takes into account how the majorities required by the amendment rules are elected as a variable to his rigidity classification—assuming that supermajorities in plurality systems are less constraining than in proportional ones.[18] Even though Lijphart uses this variable to adjust levels of rigidity, he relies on the design of the electoral system at hand.[19]

[13] ibid 363.

[14] See ibid 363–64 (arguing, 'it was determined earlier that the amendment rate is highly correlated with the degree of difficulty. It is now apparent that different amendment strategies, which reflect different combinations of assumptions about constitutionalism, have certain levels of difficulty associated with them. That is, institutions have definite [and in this case predictable] consequences for the political process').

[15] See ibid 364–65 (arguing, 'Among more general conclusions, the first is that institutions have consequences and that the effects of institutional definitions in constitutions can be studied empirically. Second, the similarity in amendment patterns between the American state constitutions and the national constitutions raises the possibility that for other aspects of constitutional design, one set of documents may be useful in developing propositions for studying the other set and therefore that there are basic principles of constitutional design operating independently of cultural, historical, geographic, and short-term political considerations. Third, the first two general conclusions together suggest the possibility of discovering a set of principles that can be used to design constitutions with predictable results'); Lorenz (n 4) 340 (arguing, 'Lutz concludes that, first, institutions matter and, second, that they operate more or less independently of cultural, economic or other structures or actors').

[16] Lijphart (n 2) 204–26. As discussed by Lorenz, Lijphart measures constitutional rigidity as 'one of a complex set of variables which he uses to test the character and performance of different patterns of democracy (consensus and majoritarian model). Combined with the strength of judicial review, rigidity is seen as a central explanatory constitutional variable'. See Lorenz (n 4) 340.

[17] Bucur and Rasch (n 9) 164.

[18] Lijphart (n 2) 209.

[19] ibid 206–11. But see Lorenz (n 4) 343 (reporting that the correlation between the voting system and actual majorities is overestimated).

As for measuring the strength of judicial review of legislation, Lijphart's classification is based, first, 'on the distinction between the presence and absence of judicial review, and, second, on three degrees of activism in the assertion of this power by the courts'.[20] Based on this classification, Lijphart shows a correlation between constitutional rigidity and judicial review, whereby the more rigid a constitution, the stronger judicial review will tend to be (it is not clear, however, what are the criteria to determine the degree of activism).[21] One problem with this approach is that it is static and thus unable to capture transformations of the party system across time (eg the level of institutionalization, coalition-making ability, or party discipline). Similarly, Lijphart's determination of the degrees of activism is determined solely by the presence of judicial review in the jurisdiction at hand and does not make any distinctions based on institutional design variation. For example, according to his index, Mexico's would be classified among the most rigid constitutions of the world (together with, eg, the US, Argentina, Australia, Canada, and Japan) because its amendment rule requires a two-thirds majority plus approval by state legislatures, majorities are elected by a system of proportional representation, and there is a system of judicial review that Lijphart would probably regard as strong (even though it is not entirely clear what criteria he uses to determine the degree of activism). However, as will be seen in Chapter 4, in practice, the Mexican Constitution is not rigid and, as shown in Chapter 7, contrary to what Lijphart would expect, there are good reasons to argue that the exercise of judicial review by the Supreme Court is rather weak in practice.

Other formalist authors have tried to measure constitutional rigidity and refined the indexes described above.[22] However, as reported by Bucur and Rasch, it has proven nearly impossible to reach a consensus on the measurement of both dependent and independent variables in the relationship of amendment difficulty and amendment rate—in general, measures show poor correlations.[23] In other words, the formalist approach in quantitative studies has important explanatory limitations. Bucur and Rasch suggest that these poor correlations might be explained by 'the different definitions used by various authors, as well as [by] the different country samples and periods of analysis' which may reflect different beliefs about what makes constitutional amendment difficult.[24] This observation is crucial in that it highlights a concern that

[20] Lijphart (n 2) 214.
[21] ibid 218–20.
[22] Lorenz (n 4); Rasch and Congleton (n 4).
[23] Bucur and Rasch (n 9) 163 and 165.
[24] ibid 165.

informs my analysis and that, in my view, should inform comparative politics and comparative constitutional law studies that seek to understand what makes a constitution difficult to change. That is, the explanatory limitations of rigidity measures underscore the need for case studies that shed light on the factors and rich context in which constitutional phenomena take place. Based on those case studies, one would be better placed to draw theoretical (and ideally testable) propositions about constitutional rigidity.[25] Aggregated quantitative studies can be immensely valuable in identifying common factors across jurisdictions that influence the different trajectories of constitutional amendment. However, the trade-off is the risk of oversimplifying reality and losing key parts of the story that might be crucial to understand constitutional phenomena.

The formalist approach in comparative constitutional law and theory

Have these studies created a confirmation bias in other fields despite their explanatory limitations? Perhaps. For one, Lutz's work is explicitly referenced in Levinson's.[26] Regardless, the *formalist* view of constitutional rigidity is pervasive in constitutional theory and manifests itself in different ways. Normatively, a lot of faith is placed in stringent constitutional amendment rules. For instance, these kinds of rules are understood as a means to protect constitutional democracy and self-government.[27] Amendment processes are

[25] Kathleen M Eisenhardt and Melissa E Graebner, 'Theory Building from Cases: Opportunities and Challenges' (2007) 50 Academy of Management Journal 25.

[26] See Levinson (n 6) 21 (arguing, 'Donald Lutz has conclusively demonstrated, the U.S. Constitution is the most difficult to amend of any constitution currently existing in the world today').

[27] See eg Stephen Holmes, *Passions and Constraint* (The University of Chicago Press 1995) 155 (arguing, 'The unwieldiness of the amending power, while permitting useful changes, is meant to discourage frivolous attempts to revise the Constitutions every time political deadlock occurs. The unavailability of constitutional amendments as an ordinary political strategy encourages democratic processes of bargaining and mutual learning. Obligatory delays also heighten the quality of successful amendments, because cumbersome procedures give all parties time for thought. Jefferson's scheme was unrealistic, Madison thought, because it ignored the nerve-wracking psychology of interregna and the way periodic opportunities to rescind the entire Constitution would both [mis]shape preferences and squander scarce resources'); Christopher L Eisgruber, *Constitutional Self-Government* (Harvard UP 2001) 11–12 (arguing, 'In particular, I will contend that we should regard inflexible written constitutions, including the American one, as practical, procedural devices for implementing relatively ordinary, albeit non-majoritarian, conceptions of democracy . . . barriers to amendment may actually enhance the capacity of people to govern themselves, and that the Constitution is best understood not as a departure from democracy but as an effort to implement it'); Samuel Issacharoff, 'The Enabling Role of Democratic Constitutionalism: Fixed Rules and Some Implications for Contested Presidential Elections Symposium—Precommitment Theory in Bioethics and Constitutional Law: Constitutional and International Law' (2002) 81 Texas Law Review 1985, 1995 (arguing that 'successful democratic governance requires a credible belief that the rules will remain fixed should the opposition of today muster sufficient support to be the majoritarian preference of tomorrow').

believed to help promote commitments to transparency, deliberation,[28] and the rule of law;[29] and as devices to protect constitutional commitments such as rights and liberties.[30] For instance, the often implicit assumption of theories that view constitutions as precommitment devices is that the institutional design of amendment rules would effectively place certain decisions beyond the reach of ordinary politics and ensure a settled framework to order the political process—providing stability and continuity to make democracy work.[31] In short, stringent constitutional amendments rules are supposed to play a very important role as *the* device that would make it more difficult to dishonour earlier commitments.[32]

More descriptively, the literature on the judicialization of politics assumes the existence of a rigid constitution, a rigidity that seems to be formally determined.[33] This scholarship posits that when judicial review mechanisms are adopted, courts are expected to become powerful political actors due to their ability to produce informal constitutional change through constitutional interpretation. The underlying premise behind these theories is that the power

[28] Jon Elster, 'Don't Burn Your Bridge before You Come to It: Some Ambiguities and Complexities of Precommitment Symposium—Precommitment Theory in Bioethics and Constitutional Law: General Issues' (2003) 81 Texas Law Review 1751.

[29] Rosalind Dixon, 'Constitutional Amendment Rules: A Comparative Perspective' in Tom Ginsburg and Rosalind Dixon (eds), *Comparative Constitutional Law* (Edward Elgar Publishing 2011) 98; Stephen M Griffin, 'The Nominee Is . . . Article V' in Sanford Levinson, William N Eskridge, and Murphy Institute of Political Economy (eds), *Constitutional Stupidities, Constitutional Tragedies* (New York UP 1998) 53 (arguing, 'If we value deliberative change, we should favor making constitutional amendment less difficult'); John Rawls, *Political Liberalism* (expanded edn, Columbia UP 2005).

[30] See eg Dixon (n 29) 102; John Ferejohn and Lawrence Sager, 'Commitment and Constitutionalism Symposium: Precommitment Theory in Bioethics and Constitutional Law—Constitutional and International Law' [2003] Texas Law Review 1929, 1946 (arguing, 'Like all external commitments, external constitutional commitments are independent of the first-order internal commitments they serve; they are valued for that reason, and in principle can be replaced wholly without regret if they are not needed. They are mechanisms designed as means to the end of making it more likely that internal constitutional commitments will be honored'); Lawrence Sager, 'The Birth Logic of a Democratic Constitution' in John Ferejohn, Jack N Rakove, and Jonathan Riley (eds), *Constitutional Culture and Democratic Rule* (CUP 2001) 100–46; Elster (n 28).

[31] See eg Stephen Holmes, 'Precommitment and the Paradox of Democracy' in Jon Elster and Rune Slagstad (eds), *Constitutionalism and Democracy* (CUP 1988); Elster (n 27); Jon Elster, *Ulysses Unbound: Studies in Rationality, Precommitment, and Constraints* (CUP 2000); Cass R Sunstein, *Designing Democracy: What Constitutions Do* (OUP 2003); Cass R Sunstein, 'Constitutionalism and Secession' (1991) 58 The University of Chicago Law Review 633.

[32] See Ferejohn and Sager (n 30) (distinguishing between internal and external commitments). In a similar vein, there is a debate regarding multi-track amendment procedures, whereby separate, more difficult tracks are assigned for particular issues. In this case it is assumed that the increased formal difficulty will spark more deliberation, promoting 'public reason' and allowing passions to cool down. See Dixon, 'Constitutional Amendment Rules: A Comparative Perspective' (n 29) 103.

[33] Ran Hirschl, *Towards Juristocracy: The Origins and Consequences of the New Constitutionalism* (Harvard UP 2004); Tom Ginsburg, *Judicial Review in New Democracies: Constitutional Courts in Asian Cases* (CUP 2003); Alec Stone Sweet, *Governing with Judges: Constitutional Politics in Europe* (OUP 2000); Martin Shapiro, *Courts: A Comparative and Political Analysis* (University of Chicago Press 1986).

of constitutional interpretation gives courts the *final word* over constitutional meaning. Put differently, these theories assume that once constitutional courts are conferred judicial review powers, the relevant constitutional system would function as the US system works—where courts are the centrepiece to understand constitutional change and (until very recently[34]) are seen as the locus for the protection of democracy against the tyranny of the majority and the enforcement of rights and liberties.[35] Importantly, their explanatory potential requires that, as an empirical matter, the constitutional text at hand remains stable across time. These pathbreaking works influenced comparative constitutional law in important ways. The amount of scholarship they have sparked is vast and important. The downside, however, is that comparative constitutional law as a field has been overly focusing on constitutional courts and judicial review (as the drivers of informal constitutional change), while largely overlooking other important phenomena that are essential to understand formal constitutional change.[36]

Moreover, there is a related strand of the literature that is pervaded by a normative assumption that sees apex courts as democracy builders and protectors of human rights.[37] These works, it can be argued, create normative expectations about the workings of constitutional orders (ie where there is constitutional review and formally rigid constitutions, courts should rise as powerful *progressive* actors)—so, when case studies do not quite meet such expectations, we end up getting accounts of failure or dysfunction.

Indeed, Mexico provides a good example of such a trend. After the fall of the seventy-plus-year hegemonic party regime in 1988, Mexico seemed to be

[34] See eg Linda Greenhouse, 'What in the World Happened to the Supreme Court?' [2022] *The Atlantic* <www.theatlantic.com/ideas/archive/2022/11/supreme-court-dobbs-conservative-majority/672089> accessed 13 September 2023; Reva Siegel, 'The Trump Court Limited Women's Rights Using 19th-Century Standards' *Washington Post* (25 June 2022) <www.washingtonpost.com/outlook/2022/06/25/trump-court-limited-womens-rights-using-19th-century-standards> accessed 13 September 2023; Jelani Cobb, 'The End of Affirmative Action' [2023] *The New Yorker* <www.newyorker.com/magazine/2023/07/10/the-end-of-affirmative-action> accessed 13 September 2023; Adam Liptak, 'Supreme Court Limits E.P.A.'s Power to Address Water Pollution' *The New York Times* (25 May 2023) <www.nytimes.com/2023/05/25/us/supreme-court-epa-water-pollution.html> accessed 13 September 2023.

[35] Ronald Dworkin, *Taking Rights Seriously: With a New Appendix, a Response to Critics* (Harvard UP 1978); Bruce Ackerman, 'The Rise of World Constitutionalism' (1997) 83 Virginia Law Review 771.

[36] For a general discussion on the role of courts in the era of new constitutionalism, see Alec Stone Sweet, 'Constitutional Courts' in Michel Rosenfeld and András Sajó (eds), *The Oxford Handbook of Comparative Constitutional Law* (OUP 2012).

[37] See eg Armin von Bogdandy and others (eds), *Transformative Constitutionalism in Latin America: The Emergence of a New Ius Commune* (OUP 2017); Rosalind Dixon, *Responsive Judicial Review: Democracy and Dysfunction in the Modern Age* (OUP 2023). For an excellent discussion of the existing literature, see Tom Gerald Daly, *The Alchemists: Questioning Our Faith in Courts as Democracy-Builders* (CUP 2017) 69–96.

following the judicialization of politics script. The weakened hegemonic party decided to formally empower the Supreme Court as a constitutional tribunal. As will be explained in detail in Chapter 7, the conventional wisdom of the time was that the absence of a hegemonic party coupled with the empowerment of the Supreme Court, in combination with the electoral reforms that eventually resulted in an era of divided government, would allow the system of separation of powers to work properly.[38] The general expectation was twofold: on the one hand, the once de facto flexible Constitution would become rigid and, on the other, the Court would become a powerful political actor as had happened, for example, in Colombia and South Africa.[39] Yet, none of this happened. As will be seen, most changes to the master-text Constitution have taken place since the transition to democracy in the 1990s (that is, in a period where no party has had the ability to amend the Constitution on its own) and, unlike its Colombian and South African counterparts, the role of the Mexican Supreme Court does not fit neatly into the judicialization of politics model. The high amendment rate is generally understood as a dysfunctional feature of the Mexican constitutional order[40] and, for some, the Supreme Court has failed to consolidate itself as a protector of human rights[41] or as a politically salient actor.[42] Varying degrees of judicial power and its relationship with

[38] Mariana Velasco-Rivera, 'Constitutional Rigidity: The Mexican Experiment' [2021] International Journal of Constitutional Law 1042, 1048.

[39] See eg Karina Ansolabehere, 'Jueces, Política y Derecho: Particularidades y Alcances de La Politización de La Justicia' (2005) 22 Isonomía: Revista de Teoría y Filosofía Del Derecho 39; Pilar Domingo, 'Judicial Independence: The Politics of the Supreme Court in Mexico' (2000) 32 Journal of Latin American Studies 705.

[40] See eg Francisca Pou Giménez and Andrea Pozas-Loyo, 'The Paradox of Mexico's Constitutional Hyper-Reformism: Enabling Peaceful Transition while Blocking Democratic Consolidation' in Richard Albert and others (eds), *Constitutional Change and Transformation in Latin America* (Hart Publishing 2019); Micaela Alterio, 'La Relación Entre Rigidez y Supremacía Constitucional: Un Análisis a La Luz de Las Reformas Constitucionales En México' (2017) 4 Revista del Centro de Estudios Constitucionales 209; Roberto Niembro, 'Conceptualizing Authoritarian Constitutionalism' (2016) 49 Verfassung und Recht in Übersee 339; Mauro Arturo Rivera León, 'Understanding Constitutional Amendments in Mexico: Perpetuum Mobile Constitution' (2017) 9 Mexican Law Review 3; María Amparo Casar and Ignacio Marván, 'Pluralismo y Reformas Constitucionales en México 1997–2012' in María Amparo Casar and Ignacio Marván Laborde (eds), *Reformar sin mayorías. La dinámica del cambio constitucional en México: 1997–2012* (Penguin Random House 2014); Jorge Carpizo, 'La Reforma Constitucional En México: Procedimiento y Realidad' (2011) 44 Boletín Mexicano de Derecho Comparado 543.

[41] See eg Ana Laura Magaloni, '¿Por qué la Suprema Corte no ha sido un instrumento para la defensa de derechos fundamentales?' in Arturo Zaldívar Lelo de Larrea and Eduardo Ferrer Mac-Gregor (eds), *La ciencia del derecho procesal constitucional. Estudios en homenaje a Héctor Fix-Zamudio en sus cincuenta años como investigador del derecho, t. I, Teoría general del derecho procesal constitucional* (Universidad Nacional Autónoma de México Instituto de Investigaciones Jurídicas 2008); Andrea Castagnola and Saúl López Noriega, 'The Supreme Court and the (No) Rights Revolution: An Empirical Analysis of the Court's Rulings 2000–2011' in Andrea Castagnola and Saúl López Noriega (eds), *Judicial Politics in Mexico: The Supreme Court and the Transition to Democracy* (Routledge 2016).

[42] See eg Andrea Castagnola and Saúl López Noriega, 'Are Mexican Justices True Arbiters among the Political Elites? An Empirical Analysis of the Court's Rulings from 2000–2011' in Andrea Castagnola

formal constitutional change may be explained in other ways. As will be seen in Chapter 7, the judicial embracement of a non-justiciability of constitutional amendments doctrine can serve as a guarantee to the political elite that as long as it can access the amendment mechanism, their interests and agendas will be shielded from any kind of review. Perhaps most importantly, such a doctrine has also been consequential for shaping those elites' beliefs about the scope and nature of the amendment power.

III. The Anti-Formalists

The second stream, which may be characterized as *anti-formalist*, recognizes that amendment rules might impact constitutional rigidity but maintains that there are other (more important) factors to take into account.[43] The *anti-formalist* stream can take the form both of quantitative and qualitative studies that question the impact of amendment mechanisms on constitutional rigidity. Scholars have identified different non-institutional factors that must be examined in order to better understand constitutional change dynamics: the 'amendment culture',[44] uncodified changes to amendment rules,[45] beliefs and normative attitudes towards the idea of formal amendment,[46] party system fragmentation,[47] the size of legislatures,[48] and the significance of constitutional amendments.[49] Like the *formalists*, the *anti-formalists* are also far from reaching consensus on the non-institutional or extra-constitutional determinants of constitutional rigidity.

and Saúl López Noriega (eds), *Judicial Politics in Mexico: The Supreme Court and the Transition to Democracy* (Routledge 2016). But see Andrea Pozas-Loyo, Camilo Saavedra-Herrera, and Francisca Pou Giménez, 'When More Leads to More: Constitutional Amendments and Interpretation in Mexico 1917–2020' [2022] Law and Social Inquiry 1 (arguing that the high amendment rate in Mexico has allowed the Supreme Court more opportunities for judicial interpretation and to effect constitutional change).

[43] See eg Elkins, Ginsburg, and Melton (n 1); Ginsburg and Melton (n 5); Jackson (n 5); Versteeg and Zackin (n 8); Albert (n 5); Negretto (n 8); Tsebelis (n 8); Jamie Cameron, 'Legality, Legitimacy and Constitutional Amendment in Canada' in David R Cameron and Richard Albert (eds), *Canada in the World: Comparative Perspectives on the Canadian Constitution* (CUP 2017) 122; Andrew Roberts, 'The Politics of Constitutional Amendment in Postcommunist Europe' (2008) 20 Constitutional Political Economy 99.
[44] Ginsburg and Melton (n 5); Albert (n 5).
[45] Albert (n 5) 127–36.
[46] Jackson (n 5).
[47] Negretto (n 8).
[48] Dixon and Holden (n 4).
[49] Tsebelis (n 8). Similarly, see Nuno Garoupa and Catarina Santos Botelho, 'Measuring Procedural and Substantial Amendment Rules: An Empirical Exploration' (2021) 22 German Law Journal 216.

At the *anti-formalist* extreme of the spectrum of the determinants of constitutional rigidity, we find Ginsburg and Melton.[50] In their study, they find that the existing metrics of amendment difficulty are poorly correlated.[51] Based on this finding, they suggest that in the end, institutional incentives may always be overcome by non-institutional (social or political) factors that drive behaviour.[52] Given the central role that Ginsburg and Melton give to the agency of individuals vis-à-vis institutional incentives, they end up doubting the possibility of creating cross-national indexes to measure constitutional rigidity. Moreover, they maintain that those extra-institutional forces should be conceptualized as *amendment culture*—defined as the 'shared attitudes about the desirability of amendment, independent of the substantive issue under consideration and the degree of pressure for change' and measured as the rate of amendment in the immediately preceding Constitution.[53] Amendment culture, from their perspective, is one of the most important factors determining amendment difficulty.[54] Amendment rules, in contrast, are a secondary factor. In fact, in their view, the *formalist approach*, as it solely focuses on institutions, will likely 'never fully capture the observed variation in patterns of amendment in different systems because certain societal attributes . . . are more important determinants of the level of resistance to constitutional amendments'.[55]

Somewhat farther away from the anti-formalist extreme of the spectrum, yet building on Ginsburg and Melton's work, one finds the work of Richard Albert, who argues that 'the difficulty of amendment is a function of more than the formal amendment rules themselves'.[56] In his view, in some cases, 'cultures of constitutional politics may predominate over the formal amendment rules'.[57] Albert identifies three types of amendment culture that have distinguishable effects on the difficulty of constitutional change: acceleration, redirection, and incapacitation.[58] Acceleration is understood as 'a reflection of a political or cultural inclination toward, or acceptance of, formal

[50] Ginsburg and Melton (n 5). See also Elkins, Ginsburg, and Melton (n 1) 100 (arguing, 'whether a constitution that requires a two-thirds vote of the legislatures to amend the constitution is more or less flexible than one that requires an ordinary legislative majority with a subsequent referendum by the public').

[51] Ginsburg and Melton (n 5) 697.

[52] ibid 686 (arguing '[t]he powerful force of institutional incentives can always be overcome by political or social factors that drive behavior. [. . .] amendment difficulty is subject to such extra-institutional forces').

[53] ibid 699.

[54] ibid 687.

[55] See ibid 699.

[56] Albert (n 5) 113–14.

[57] ibid 110.

[58] ibid 111.

amendment as an appropriate vehicle of constitutional change'.[59] The redirection of constitutional change 'by formal amendment toward other forms of change' is interpreted as an indication of a political and social culture that is reluctant to engage with formal amendment processes.[60] The final possible effect of an amendment culture is the incapacitation of formal amendment as a result of the combination between political and cultural forces and codified rules in a way that makes it virtually impossible to pursue the path established by the amendment rule.[61] Additionally, Albert identifies uncodified changes to amendment rules as factors that may exacerbate or ease difficulty (eg additional requirements established by ordinary laws or judicial interpretation).[62] In this context, Albert concludes that measuring amendment difficulty would be virtually impossible without a deep immersion in the law and politics of the jurisdiction under study.[63]

Similarly, in the case of Mexico, constitutional scholars associate a high amendment rate with 'constitutional fetishism'—a sort of magical thinking that leads political actors to believe that the solution to different types of social and economic problems lies in changing the constitutional text.[64] Akin to Albert, others argue that the increasing amendment rate is the product of a 'national culture' that has little respect for the Constitution.[65] These approaches do not explain the role of concrete political actors and the circumstances that may determine constitutional rigidity or flexibility across time.[66] For instance, the idea of 'constitutional fetishism' does not take into account things like the self-interest, political, and partisan motivations of the actors that have the legal power to activate the amendment mechanism. Elkins, Ginsburg, and Melton, by contrast, offer an explanation of the endurance and de facto flexibility of the Mexican Constitution during the PRI hegemonic rule that does take such factors into account.[67] They argue that constitutional amendments during that time served as a tool that provided political goods allowing for the co-optation

[59] ibid.
[60] ibid.
[61] ibid.
[62] ibid 127–36.
[63] ibid 137.
[64] Casar and Marván (n 40) 51 ('[T]he Mexican political elite has a lot of faith in the [Constitution's] ability to transform reality and, in that sense, reformers are moved by what may be called "constitutional fetichism"'. (Translation mine. All translations are mine unless otherwise indicated)).
[65] Carpizo (n 40) 584–85.
[66] Pou Giménez and Pozas-Loyo recognize the role of political parties in formal constitutional change after the PRI hegemonic rule, yet they do not seek to explain the causes of the frequency of amendments. Instead, they focus on how what they call hyper-reformism has served as an obstacle for the consolidation of democracy and the rule of law. Pou Giménez and Pozas-Loyo (n 40) 234–36. See also Alterio (n 40); Niembro (n 40).
[67] Elkins, Ginsburg, and Melton (n 1) 193–99.

of interest groups and the creation of the necessary loyalty to make bargaining possible.[68] However, their account does not explain why, after the fall of the hegemonic PRI, frequent amendments did not cease. By focusing on the dimension of constitutional culture and the choices and decisions made by key political actors, Chapter 5 and 6 are respectively devoted to answering that question. What is more, in line with the judicialization of politics expectations (and assumptions regarding the power of apex courts) of the time (shared by formalist and anti-formalists), Elkins, Ginsburg, and Melton assume that 'with the decline of the PRI supermajority, the primary mechanism of constitutional change . . . shifted from a formal constitutional amendment toward informal judicial amendment through interpretation'.[69] With the benefit of hindsight, in Chapter 7, I discuss the role the Supreme Court has played in determining amendment ease in the Mexican context.

In the US context, where Article V has generally been seen as the culprit for the alleged impossibility of formal constitutional change, Vicki Jackson argues that it is the *attitudes* towards formal amendment that likely determine the difficulty of textual change.[70] In her view, the low amendment rate in that country is not only the result of a stringent procedure but also of beliefs in the impossibility of amendments and normative attitudes of constitutional veneration.[71] Jackson illustrates this point by referring to the resistance of different public interest groups and political actors to amendment as a response to judicial interpretation in the wake of *Citizens United v Federal Election Comm'n*[72] (eg non-governmental organizations looking for ways to respond to the Court's decision not considering constitutional amendment as a viable option and relevant actors opposing the idea based on concerns that it would be impossible).[73] In her view, this is just an example of the belief in amendment difficulty that dominates legal discourse; the Constitution would be easier to amend if attitudes towards the idea of formal amendment changed. To be sure, Jackson does not deny that Article V affects amendment difficulty, but she underscores the importance of widely held beliefs that may or may not allow a political community to consider formal amendment as a feasible option.

[68] ibid 197 ('[C]onstitutional amendment during the PRI regime was frequent, and amendments provided political goods. The PRI used the Constitution to incorporate social insurgencies and political dissidents while limiting their effective power').

[69] ibid 198.

[70] Jackson (n 5).

[71] ibid 584.

[72] *Citizens United v Federal election Comm'n* [2010] US 558, 310.

[73] Jackson (n 5) 586–88.

From a political science perspective, Gabriel Negretto and George Tsebelis offer two key anti-formalist accounts. Negretto has done crucial work in bringing to the table otherwise hardly present actors in comparative constitutional amendment scholarship.[74] In particular, he considers *party system fragmentation* as a non-institutional variable to measure constitutional rigidity.[75] In a study of eighteen Latin American countries, he finds that party system fragmentation is the most significant variable to explain the amendment rate. When measuring formal stringency and party fragmentation together, Negretto finds that on average party fragmentation might increase the amendment rate when the amendment procedure is most flexible.[76] Moreover, he finds that the stringency level of amendment rules has a negative effect on the amendment rate when party fragmentation is above or equal to 2.5 of the effective number of parties (ENP).[77] Put differently, 'the frequency of amendments is likely to decrease when amendment procedures are rigid and party system fragmentation is high'.[78]

More recently, based on a study that covers ninety-four democracies, Tsebelis has presented a model that corroborates that constitutional rigidity leads to fewer amendments—though explicitly maintaining that 'institutional rigidity is a sufficient but not necessary condition for low amendment frequency'.[79] Tsebelis' model's explanatory variables are the 'core of the constitution' and 'amendment significance'.[80] The 'core of the constitution' variable is constructed by using the veto players approach to then reduce it into an index of constitutional rigidity—meaning the parts of the Constitution that in practice cannot be changed given the existing amendment rules and the preferences of the relevant actors.[81] The second variable, 'amendment significance', is developed based on an expert opinion survey. When evaluating the relationship between these two variables (using heteroskedastic regression), Tsebelis finds that the higher the significance of the amendment, the stronger the relationship between rigidity and the frequency of amendments.[82]

[74] Dixon (n 29).
[75] Negretto (n 8). For an analysis in this same line but at the sub-national level in the German context, see Werner Reutter and Astrid Lorenz, 'Explaining the Frequency of Constitutional Change in the German Länder: Institutional and Party Factors' (2016) 46 Publius: The Journal of Federalism 103.
[76] Negretto (n 8) 773.
[77] ibid.
[78] ibid 763.
[79] Tsebelis (n 8) 32.
[80] ibid 7.
[81] ibid.
[82] ibid.

The literature thus provides no conclusive answer as to what determines the level of rigidity of a constitution. Like the *formalists*, the *anti-formalists* reflect what each author believes are the most important factors influencing amending difficulty.[83] Ginsburg and Melton seem to be pessimistic towards the idea of finding a cross-national indicator to predict amendment difficulty because in their view, the amendment culture of the jurisdiction at hand may be more influential than the amendment rule itself. Negretto and Tsebelis seem to be more optimistic about the possibility of predicting constitutional rigidity, yet as will be seen in the following section, their approaches present shortcomings of a different nature.

IV. Pitfalls of the Formalist and Anti-Formalist Approaches to Constitutional Rigidity

The *anti-formalist* approach represents a step forward in the understanding of constitutional rigidity in that it considers factors other than just the institutional design. However, both the *formalist* and *anti-formalist* approaches share common pitfalls and explanatory limitations. The existing literature tends to conflate the normative and empirical dimensions of constitutional change. It also draws normative implications from the design of amendment rules that do not necessarily correspond to reality. Aggregated studies, despite their contributions to our understanding of different constitutional phenomena, can present explanatory limitations that risk overlooking important elements that may explain constitutional rigidity. Existing accounts fall short of revealing the factors that directly affect constitutional rigidity; the current literature does not offer a well-developed and empirically grounded theory of what makes a constitution difficult to change.

Conflation of the normative and empirical dimensions of constitutionalism

As noted earlier, the first pitfall lies in the conflation of the normative and empirical dimensions of constitutionalism. Scholarly debates about formal constitutional change usually assume that constitutional amendments have a direct link to the popular will. This assumption is reflected in the use of

[83] Bucur and Rasch (n 9) 166.

constitutional theory concepts and distinctions to explain empirically observed constitutional phenomena. For instance, Albert suggests that the acceleration effect (ie high amendment rates) of constitutional culture in several US states, despite the presence of stringent amendment rules in their constitutions, may be the result of citizens in those jurisdictions viewing 'amendments as an appropriate means of bringing about changes in governance'.[84] While the assertion may be true, it does not really explain what are the forces directly driving constitutional change and what exactly allows amendments to continue at a high rate despite the heightened formal difficulty. Asserting that stringent amendment rules have little or no effect in making formal constitutional change difficult because the people living under a particular constitution prefer amendments over other means of change obscures the fact that constitutional change in contemporary democracies is mainly a mediated phenomenon (ie as a general rule directly driven by political parties), while overlooking potential principal–agent problems in representation and the agency of self-interested political actors.[85] The conflation of the normative and empirical dimensions of constitutional change is by no means exclusive to Albert's work. In fact, it is a common feature in comparative constitutional change scholarship.[86]

[84] Albert (n 5) 114.

[85] To be sure, as noted above, Albert also identifies what he calls 'uncodified changes' to amendment rules as factors that may exacerbate or relax amendment difficulty. For instance, one of the examples he uses to illustrate these uncodified changes is Canada's Regional Veto Law, which grants provinces a functional veto in constitutional amendments (it requires the consent of 'the five major regions as well as [the] majority of all provinces' before introducing certain amendment proposals). Since these changes are brought about by political actors such as legislatures, executives, and/or courts, Albert rightly points at the political dimension of formal constitutional change. In his view, 'the federal government of the day offered the Regional Veto Law as an incentive to Quebec voters' to vote to remain in Canada in the 1995 Quebec referendum. However, when trying to offer a general explanation why these uncodified changes take place, he argues that where the amendment processes are too difficult or poorly designed to prevent disfavored outcomes or facilitate preferred outcomes, political actors may reimagine amendment rules to achieve their objectives. Somewhat paradoxically, Albert attributes the cause of uncodified changes to formal rules and, as a result, there is no discussion about the process by which Canada's Regional Veto Law was adopted, the political parties involved, and the motivations behind its adoption. ibid 129, 135.

[86] See eg Duncan Okubasu, 'The Implication of Conflation of Normal and "Constitutional Politics" on Constitutional Change in Africa' in Richard Albert, Xenophon Contiades, and Alkmene Fotiadou (eds), *The Foundations and Traditions of Constitutional Amendment* (Hart Publishing 2017) (arguing that the high amendment rate in African countries is problematic for African constitutionalism because it implies the conflation of constitutional and ordinary politics); Lael Weis, 'The Paradoxical Place of the Formal Amendment in Australian Constitutionalism' in Richard Albert, Xenophon Contiades, and Alkmene Fotiadou (eds), *The Foundations and Traditions of Constitutional Amendment* (Hart Publishing 2017) (arguing that the formal amendment process in Australia is the site of ordinary politics instead of a 'site for the emergence of the popular will').

Normative assumptions about amendment rules

Moreover, both *formalists* and *anti-formalists* typically assume that the design of amendment rules (eg voting thresholds and/or the number of steps in the procedure) has direct normative implications for the quality of amendment processes. For instance, Levinson and Jackson consider that formal amendments, like no other constitutional mechanism, are the best way of guaranteeing that the Constitution remains the legitimate product of the American people because they ensure deliberation, efficiency, and transparency.[87] First, Jackson argues that formal constitutional change ensures better deliberative processes because 'constitutional amendment focuses more political attention on the object of the amendment once it gains momentum. In its early phases, an amending process focuses proponents' attention on identifying the constitutional principle at stake. As it moves forward, and positions are articulated, areas of consensus on possible legislative solutions may emerge; greater identification of sources of opposition will also emerge'.[88] Furthermore, for Levinson and Jackson, when constitutional change is necessary, it should take place quickly. Informal constitutional change (eg judicial review), in this sense, is not ideal because it proceeds slowly and incrementally, allowing the past to prevail over present understandings.[89] Formal constitutional change, by contrast, is the best way to avoid the 'dead-hand' problem because it takes place at once through a known procedure that focuses attention on a particular text that results from a participatory process.[90] Finally, informal constitutional change runs against transparency because it is not and cannot be easily discernible. In this sense, Levinson argues that '[t]he degree of fundamental change is often covered up by being rationalized in incomprehensible legal jargon that requires inordinate faith in the lawyers and judges writing the opinions. If one believes that transparency is an important part of what Article IV of the Constitution identifies (but does not define) as a "Republican Form of Government," then the use of the judiciary as a "continuing constitutional convention" has real costs'.[91]

Levinson and Jackson's assumptions are not exclusive to constitutional scholarship. Prominently, Lutz suggests that amendments rules have definite, predictable, and meaningful consequences on the political process

[87] Levinson (n 6); Jackson (n 5) 602.
[88] Jackson (n 5) 595.
[89] ibid 598.
[90] ibid 602.
[91] Levinson (n 6) 164.

(ie amendment processes) regardless of the context.[92] In his view, '[t]he difficulty of the amendment process chosen by framers of constitutions seems related to the framers' relative commitment to the premises used by the Americans when they invented the formal amendment process: (1) popular sovereignty, (2) a deliberative process, and (3) the distinction between normal legislation and constitutional matter'.[93] The normative implication of Lutz's proposition is that, for example, an amendment rule that requires the approval of two-thirds of a bicameral congress and the approval of multiple state legislatures will result in an amendment process that is more deliberative and protective of popular sovereignty.

One can thus identify, from the analysis of the existing scholarship, four main assumptions associated with the heightened stringency of amendment formulas: deliberation insurance, transparency insurance, the protection of popular sovereignty and democratic legitimacy, and the protection of constitutional supremacy. To be sure, none of these assumptions are foreign to constitutional theory[94] and comparative constitutional studies.[95] As noted from the outset, constitutional amendments are often associated with or explained by borrowing from constitutional theory concepts and distinctions. Constitutional amendments are assumed to be different in nature from ordinary laws: they are seen as a direct reflection of the will of the people and, accordingly, associated with heightened deliberation and transparency. Constitutional amendment rules play a central role in ensuring that the resulting changes can in fact be characterized in these ways. Although it may be true that, from a theoretical standpoint, formal amendment may sound like an ideal way to deal with the dead-hand problem as well as to ensure deliberation and transparency, it is also true that, in actual practice (as the Mexican case illustrates), the hurdles imposed by the constitutional amendment formula in no way offer bullet-proof insurance for achieving such aims. Formal amendments in Mexico, despite the presence of a stringent amendment formula, are the result of highly centralized constitutional decision-making and poorly deliberative, fast-track, and opaque processes subject to little public scrutiny—which makes it hard to maintain that they channel the popular will.

[92] Lutz (n 3) 364–65.
[93] ibid 363.
[94] See eg Holmes (n 31); Holmes (n 27); Elster (n 31) 117–18; Ferejohn and Sager (n 30); Sager (n 30).
[95] See eg Lijphart (n 2); Richard Albert, 'The Expressive Function of Constitutional Amendment Rules' (2013) 59 McGill Law Journal 225 (arguing that amendment rules express special political commitments). Similarly, questions on the limits of the amendment power revolve around whether it is 'the people' who have spoken. See eg Yaniv Roznai, *Unconstitutional Constitutional Amendments: The Limits of Amendment Powers* (OUP 2017).

From this perspective, Mexico's constitutional amendment rate may sound like a Madisonian nightmare. One could argue that the Mexican Constitution has become too mutable, therefore it is not venerated and is unfit to facilitate democratic governance. In fact, this has been the main approach of scholarship offering accounts on Mexico's constitutional change dynamics.[96] For instance, Francisca Pou Giménez and Andrea Pozas-Loyo elaborate on the problems and obstacles that the high amendment rate might be creating for the consolidation of democracy and the rule of law in Mexico.[97] In their view, constitutional amendment in Mexico is not 'higher lawmaking' but 'just another incidence of ordinary politics' because the amendment mechanism does not require action by special actors outside the ordinary political process.[98] Roberto Niembro conceptualizes the ineffectiveness of the amendment rule as the manifestation of authoritarian constitutionalism—understood as the way in which the Constitution is used 'for practical and authoritarian ideological functions'.[99] Constitutional amendments, for instance, may be used for coordination or to elicit the cooperation of the powerless.[100] The problem that Niembro highlights is that provisions that are supposed to limit the exercise of power (eg the amendment mechanism) are ineffective and, therefore, the ruling elite is not effectively constrained by the Constitution.[101]

The question, however, is how useful it is to try to explain constitutional change in these terms when grappling with the question of constitutional rigidity. In the case of Mexico, the existing scholarship teaches us very little about why the Constitution, despite its formal rigidity, changes the way it does. Interpreting formal constitutional change through normative concepts and distinctions in radically different legal and political contexts obscures its main drivers and explanatory factors. What if, for example, the distinction between higher and ordinary law or the idea that constitutional amendment is the most

[96] Pou Giménez and Pozas-Loyo (n 39); Niembro (n 39); Micaela Alterio and Roberto Niembro, 'Constitutional Culture and Democracy in Mexico: A Critical View of the 100-Year-Old Mexican Constitution' in Mark A Graber, Sanford Levinson, and Mark V Tushnet (eds), *Constitutional Democracy in Crisis?* (OUP 2018); Héctor Fix-Fierro, Pedro Salazar, and Diego Valadés, 'Toward the Reorganization and Consolidation of the Text of the Constitution of the United Mexican States of 1917' (IIJ-UNAM 2015) <http://comparativeconstitutionsproject.org/wp-content/uploads/Introductory-Essay.pdf?6c8912> accessed 15 August 2024.

[97] Pou Giménez and Pozas-Loyo (n 40).

[98] ibid 229 ('it seems natural to associate the prospect of changing the Constitution with a moment of political discontinuity of some sort, in terms of inclusion participation, procedural adequacy, or at least in terms of public opinion mobilization. In Mexico, however, the constitutional reform is just another incidence of ordinary politics. Partly because Article 135 does not require action by special actors outside the ordinary political process [. . .] there are really no traces of "higher law making" ').

[99] Niembro (n 40).

[100] ibid 367.

[101] ibid 356.

important site for the popular will to emerge are simply not relevant to explaining and understanding constitutional change or assessing the quality of constitutionalism? If we are to learn how constitutions change and why they change the way they do, it is necessary to take the nuance of context seriously.

V. Unanswered Questions by Current Approaches

It is clear so far that it is not possible to predict the amendment rate just by looking at the design of amendment rules—let alone the quality of amendment processes or whether the new constitutional text will reflect popular sovereignty. Instead, in line with the *anti-formalists*, the answer to the question of what determines constitutional rigidity is highly context-dependent and to be found in non-institutional and/or political factors. This begs the question: what are the non-institutional or political determinants of constitutional rigidity? Ginsburg, Melton, and Negretto have made important contributions towards answering this question. Ginsburg and Melton, perhaps not explicitly, have brought to the surface the importance of public choice and public law to grapple with the question of constitutional rigidity. Negretto has brought political parties (specifically party system fragmentation) to the fore of the conversation. As noted above, political parties hardly receive attention in comparative constitutional amendment scholarship[102] which, as will be discussed in subsequent chapters, should be a central focus in studies grappling with both questions of constitutional change in general and rigidity in particular.

Yet, aggregated studies like these do not come without risks, such as giving partial or oversimplified accounts of the relevant context and, as a result, not capturing important factors. In the case of Ginsburg and Melton, despite underscoring the importance of social and political factors driving behaviour, their conceptualization of *amendment culture* ends up being undertheorized and thus not able to account for the actors whose behaviour is driven by different social and political factors and who have the legal power to activate the amendment mechanisms. Moreover, using Negretto's own data, when descriptively looking at particular cases, several questions arise that the model

[102] Dixon (n 29) 107 (arguing, 'the relationship between political parties and constitutional provisions is a topic which is generally under-developed in comparative constitutional scholarship; and the constitutional amendment literature does no better'); Richard H Pildes, 'Political Parties and Constitutionalism' in Tom Ginsburg and Rosalind Dixon (eds), *Comparative Constitutional Law* (Edward Elgar Publishing 2011).

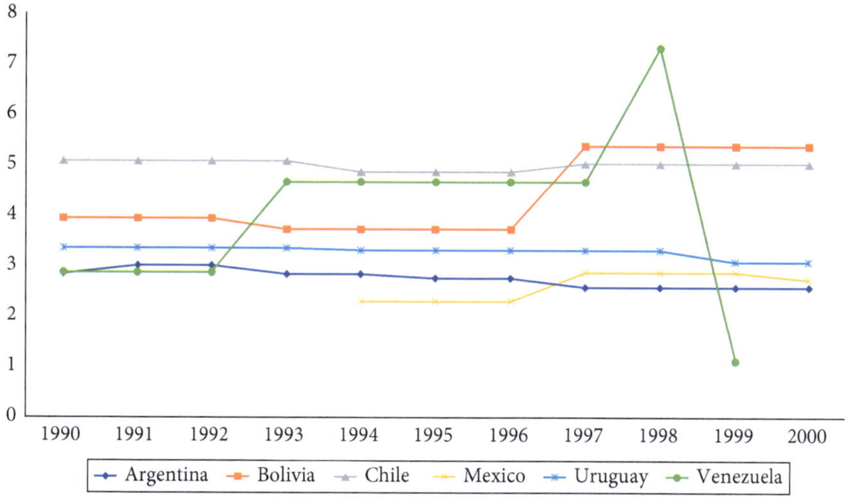

Figure 2.1 Political fragmentation: Latin American countries with rigid amendment procedures 1990–2000.

Source: Prepared by the author, working with Negretto's data <http://la-constitutionalchange.cide.edu/publications>.

is not able to answer.[103] Consider the following example. Figures 2.1, 2.2, and 2.3 show Argentina, Bolivia, Chile, Mexico, Uruguay, and Venezuela between 1990 and 2008. In Negretto's model, these Latin American countries fall under the highest level of rigidity between 1990 and 2008.[104] Figure 2.1 shows the level of political fragmentation, Figure 2.2 the amendment rate, and Figure 2.3 the number of amendments per year—all according to Negretto's data.

When looking at Argentina, Mexico, and Uruguay, we see that these countries stay close to each other on party system fragmentation but, despite having the same rigidity level, the difference in amendment rates is staggering. For example, how can one explain the difference of amendment rates between Argentina and Mexico in 1997–99 or between Uruguay and Mexico in 2000–03? Moreover, if one looks at Chile (the most fragmented country in the sample under the highest level of rigidity) between 1996 and 1997, contrary to Negretto's proposition, one can appreciate an increase in party system fragmentation as well as a visible increase in the amendment rate. Notably, Negretto's model presents ambivalent results. On the one hand, his study shows

[103] Data set on file with the author. I wish to thank Professor Gabriel Negretto for kindly sharing his data set with me.

[104] I excluded Peru because Negretto classifies it under the highest level of rigidity only during one year between 1990 and 2008.

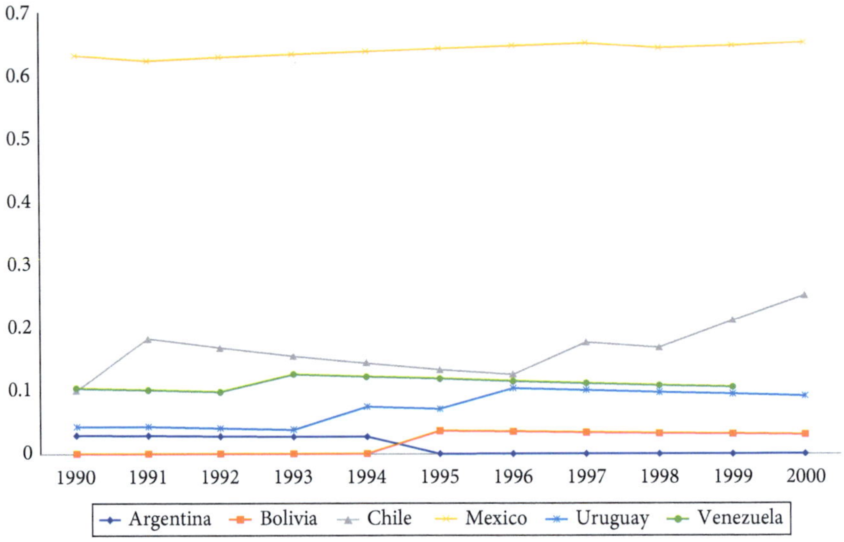

Figure 2.2 Amendment rate: Latin American countries with rigid amendment procedures 1990–2000.

Source: Prepared by the author, working with Negretto's data <http://la-constitutionalchange.cide.edu/publications>.

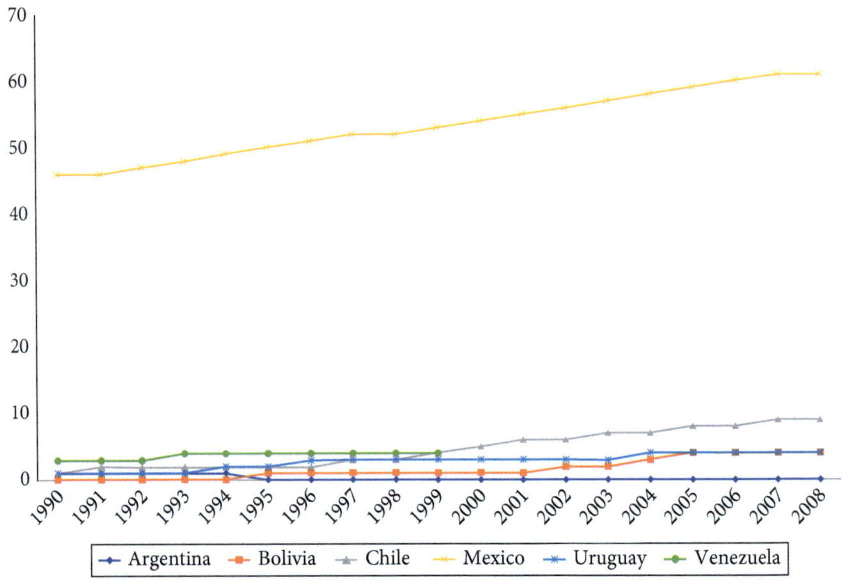

Figure 2.3 Number of amendments: Latin American countries with rigid procedures 1990–2008.

Source: Prepared by the author, working with Negretto's data <http://la-constitutionalchange

a positive effect of political fragmentation on the amendment rate, *caeteris paribus*. And on the other hand, he suggests that a country with high levels of political fragmentation and rigid amendment procedures might have a lower amendment rate than another one under the same rigidity model but with less fragmentation.

Using these results, one would find that Negretto's second proposition holds if we compare Chile and Mexico throughout 1994–2008 (see Figures 2.1 and 2.2). During this period, Mexico presents more amendments with less fragmentation than Chile. However, Negretto's model coefficients do not explain the staggering variation in the amendment rate between these two countries (see Figures 2.1 and 2.2). Nor do they explain why Argentina, with lower fragmentation than Mexico between 1997 and 2000 and under the same level of rigidity, remains so far below on its amendment rate.[105] Specifically in the case of Mexico, according to Negretto's proposition, as party system fragmentation increased, the country should have registered a decrease in the amendment rate. Yet what we see is that the rate remains significantly high. Why do the level of stringency of the amendment rule or the changes in political fragmentation have no visible impact on Mexico's amendment rate?

These unanswered questions exemplify the limits of this and other comparative quantitative studies that seek to theorize constitutional rigidity based on aggregated models. The fact that Negretto's model is unable to explain the significant differences in amendment rates despite similar levels of party system fragmentation and the same level of rigidity, or why the stringency of the amendment rule has had no visible impact on Mexico's amendment rate, suggests that part of the story of what makes constitutions difficult or easy to amend is not being captured by this approach. It also underscores the importance of and need for case studies and theory building.[106] This is precisely the path this book seeks to follow.

[105] This inconsistency is also observed when comparing Mexico and Uruguay between 2007 and 2008.

[106] James Jaccard and Jacob Jacoby, *Theory Construction and Model-Building Skills, Second Edition: A Practical Guide for Social Scientists* (Guilford Publications 2020); Eisenhardt and Graebner (n 25).

3

The Economy of Constitutional Change

I. Introduction

To overcome the current shortcomings in the literature that engages with the question of constitutional rigidity (and that are also applicable to scholarship on constitutional change in general), it is necessary to approach constitutional change differently. Accordingly, here I propose an analytical framework (which was developed based on my analysis of the Mexican case) that seeks to disrupt the conflation of the normative and empirical aspects of constitutional change. Specifically, it seeks to capture the descriptive dimension of constitutional change to shed light on its direct drivers (ie those actors who have the legal power to put in motion the mechanisms of constitutional change). In so doing, it puts aside the normative dimension of constitutional change—both the distinction between higher/ordinary law and constitutional/ordinary politics and assumptions regarding the impact of formal rules on the quality of constitutional amendment processes. To be sure, I do not negate the importance of these categories and ideas; however, when it comes to identifying the factors that explain constitutional change, it is necessary to do away with them to focus on its direct drivers. In order to do so, the analytical framework offered here adopts what Ran Hirschl calls a strategic-realist approach.[1]

The strategic-realist approach views constitutional amendment as politics by other means.[2] This approach is interdisciplinary and descriptive. As such, it draws from positive constitutional economics,[3] collective action theory,[4]

[1] Ran Hirschl, 'The Strategic Foundations of Constitutions' in Denis J Galligan and Mila Versteeg (eds), *Social and Political Foundations of Constitutions* (CUP 2013) 157.

[2] ibid 157.

[3] Stefan Voigt, *Explaining Constitutional Change: A Positive Economics Approach* (Edward Elgar 1999). For the normative formulation of constitutional economics, see James M Buchanan and Gordon Tullock, *The Calculus of Consent* (University of Michigan Press 1961); James M Buchanan, 'The Domain of Constitutional Economics' (1990) 1 Constitutional Political Economy 1; FA Hayek, *Law, Legislation and Liberty, Volume 1: Rules and Order* (University of Chicago Press 1978); FA Hayek, *Law, Legislation and Liberty, Volume 3: The Political Order of a Free People* (University of Chicago Press 2011).

[4] Elinor Ostrom, 'Collective Action Theory' in Carles Boix and Susan C Stokes (eds), *The Oxford Handbook of Comparative Politics* (OUP 2009) 186–208.

The Politics of Constitutional Rigidity. Mariana Velasco-Rivera, Oxford University Press.
 DOI: 10.1093/9780191981876.003.0003

and constitutional law, theory, and history. Like the positive branch of constitutional economics[5] and the constitutional theory of partisan entrenchment,[6] the strategic-realist approach seeks to identify the actors who make those choices and the political conditions that facilitate or prevent formal constitutional change.[7] It seeks to explain the origin of formal constitutional change and views politics from a rational choice perspective—that is, as a 'process of exchange through which individuals seek to advance their interests'.[8] Accordingly, it operates on the premise that, as Hirschl puts it, 'constitutions are human-made institutions; their establishment, amendment or abolition is carried out by identifiable actors—not abstract ideas or amorphic organic pressures, but real people who make concrete decisions and choices'.[9] It also assumes that, when choosing constitutionalization, rather than acting in a self-defeating way, said identifiable actors act motivated by self-interest.[10] This idea is present, either implicitly or explicitly, in comparative studies that explain the political construction of judicial power,[11] constitutional renegotiation,[12] and constitution-making[13] but rarely appears in the study of constitutional amendments.[14]

The strategic-realist approach is also descriptive. Unlike scholars in the social sciences (eg positive constitutional economists and collective action theorists), I am less interested in predicting outcomes or trajectories than I am in shedding light on the factors that drive constitutional change. As suggested in Chapter 2, the explanatory limitations of existing aggregated models that seek to measure constitutional rigidity call for in-depth case studies that capture the rich context in which formal constitutional change takes place. Only in this way can we be in a position to understand why there are countries like

[5] Voigt (n 3).

[6] Jack M Balkin and Sanford Levinson, 'Understanding the Constitutional Revolution' (2001) 87 Virginia Law Review 1045.

[7] Hirschl (n 1) 165.

[8] Tom Ginsburg, 'Public Choice and Constitutional Design' in Daniel A Farber and Anne Joseph O'Connell (eds), *Research Handbook in Public Choice and Public Law* (Edward Elgar 2010) 261. See also Balkin and Levinson (n 6).

[9] Hirschl (n 1) 165.

[10] ibid 166.

[11] Tom Ginsburg, *Judicial Review in New Democracies: Constitutional Courts in Asian Cases* (CUP 2003); Ran Hirschl, *Towards Juristocracy: The Origins and Consequences of the New Constitutionalism* (Harvard UP 2004).

[12] Zachary Elkins, Tom Ginsburg, and James Melton, *The Endurance of National Constitutions* (CUP 2009).

[13] Gabriel Negretto, *Making Constitutions: Presidents, Parties, and Institutional Choice in Latin America* (CUP 2013); Alexander Hudson, *The Veil of Participation: Citizens and Political Parties in Constitution-Making Processes* (CUP 2021).

[14] But see Gabriel Negretto, 'Replacing and Amending Constitutions: The Logic of Constitutional Change in Latin America' (2012) 46 Law & Society Review 749; Voigt (n 3).

Mexico where the stringency of the amendment rule and party system fragmentation (in Negretto's terms) have no visible impact on the amendment rate. The analytical framework offered in this chapter seeks to contribute to such an endeavour by offering a basic framework that will hopefully make the systematic study of constitutional change feasible. The rest of this book focuses on Mexico as a case study, exploring the interplay of the three basic elements of the framework offered here.

Following the strategic-realist approach, the framework posits that to understand constitutional change in general, and constitutional rigidity (or flexibility) in particular, political parties and party systems should occupy a central role in any such study. The reason for this is because as a general rule constitutional change is a mediated phenomenon—that is, in contemporary constitutional democracies, political parties (and/or individual members of parties) are the actors that have the legal power to activate most if not all mechanisms of constitutional change (eg the constitutional amendment process, as well as accessing mechanisms of constitutional judicial review). As such, political parties can be understood as direct drivers of constitutional change. Moreover, they are not monoliths but organizations formed by individuals who make concrete decisions and choices: when it comes to constitutional change, it is assumed that these individuals are seeking to entrench their values, beliefs, interests, and agendas across time through the different mechanisms of entrenchment offered by a given constitutional order (eg constitutional amendment, ordinary legislation, and judicial review). As such, constitutional change (formal or informal) is understood as a function of political entrenchment. Importantly, the choices made by the relevant actors will be largely informed by the country's constitutional culture. Political parties, party systems, constitutional culture, and the choices made by key political actors to entrench their interests are the main elements of what I call an economy of constitutional change.

In light of the above, the analytical framework presented in this chapter is based on four basic propositions to be taken into consideration to understand and explain constitutional change in general and amendment difficulty in particular: (i) in contemporary constitutional democracies political parties and party systems should have a central role when it comes to explaining the dynamics of constitutional change, particularly constitutional amendments; (ii) a country's constitutional culture (understood as the beliefs, understandings, assumptions, and attitudes of the relevant actors regarding constitutional change) inevitably impacts the ways in which constitutions change; (iii) the modes of constitutional change will be to different extents determined by the choices of key political actors among the *available* means of entrenchment in a given constitutional order; and (iv) the availability of the mechanisms of entrenchment will be determined by the interplay of (i), (ii), and (iii) in an economy of change whereby constitutional change (formal and informal) is a function of political entrenchment.[15] The rest of the chapter expands on each of these propositions.

II. Political Parties and Party Systems

As noted earlier, political parties are rarely present in comparative constitutional law scholarship—at least not as central factors to explain constitutional rigidity.[16] For example, Elkins, Ginsburg, and Melton's theory of constitutional renegotiation, which seeks to explain notions of constitutional formation, adjustment, and endurance, understands constitutions as 'bargains that embody agreement among relevant parties'.[17] But instead of pinning down the term 'relevant parties' as political parties, Elkins, Ginsburg, and Melton leave the term at an abstract level—possibly so that their model captures instances of constitutional replacement that are not necessarily led by political parties. Similarly, constitutional economics models like Stefan Voigt's implicitly recognize the central role of political parties but work at a rather abstract level that ends up portraying parties as monoliths—thus, somewhat paradoxically, ignoring human agency.[18] Still, Elkins, Ginsburg, Melton, and Voigt's reliance on the idea of constitutions as contracts (not in the sense of social contract theory) and on bargaining theory points to the fact that constitutions reflect specific agreements between a finite number of contracting parties.[19]

[15] In using the word 'determined', my intention is not to suggest a strict causal relationship between these factors and constitutional rigidity. On the one hand, as noted above, there might be other factors that affect constitutional rigidity that are not included in the analytical framework offered here. On the other hand, the relationship between rigidity and the factors presented here may in some cases be bidirectional or bilateral: not only can these three factors be determined by, for example, history, economics, and law but also perhaps by the constitutional rule of change. My aim is more modest. What I want to show instead is that including the analysis of political parties, party systems, constitutional culture, and the choices made by key actors, to which the academic literature has paid insufficient attention, puts us in a much better position to explain constitutional rigidity.

[16] See eg Rosalind Dixon, 'Constitutional Amendment Rules: A Comparative Perspective' in Tom Ginsburg and Rosalind Dixon (eds), *Comparative Constitutional Law* (Edward Elgar 2011) 96–111; Richard H Pildes, 'Political Parties and Constitutionalism' in Tom Ginsburg and Rosalind Dixon (eds), *Comparative Constitutional Law* (Edward Elgar 2011) 254–64.

[17] Elkins, Ginsburg, and Melton (n 12) 66.

[18] Voigt refers to 'parties' in the contractual sense. Yet, the level of abstraction in which he portrays his model of constitutional change allows us to infer that it implicitly captures political parties as the actors that have the legal power to activate amendment mechanisms. See Voigt (n 3).

[19] ibid 107.

The framework offered here draws on that idea but goes a step further by identifying the relevant parties (ie political parties) and trying to capture their multi-member nature in constitutional democracies.

Political parties are constituted by rational, self-interested individuals whose actions, preferences, and choices are shaped by the constitutional culture in which they operate. This approach seeks to account for the shared unwritten norms and practices that shape and drive the behaviour of political actors and interactions among contracting parties in formal amendment process settings.[20] Moreover, it is particularly mindful of the discourse of key political actors to place and enforce such norms and practices, as well as their choices among institutional mechanisms to advance and protect their agendas and interests. Doing so sheds light on the interaction between politics and amendment rules and captures the limits of the latter as a constraint on the exercise of power. As will be seen in Chapters 4, 5, and 6, the constitutional amendment frequency in Mexico is largely a result of very strong party discipline and cross-party cooperation.

Once political parties are understood as central to constitutional amendment dynamics—specifically, to understanding why or why not the amendment mechanism is accessible—the need to focus on intra- and interparty dynamics naturally follows. Since parties are not monoliths but organizations made up of individuals, we must understand the internal party dynamics as well as interparty dynamics. In particular, we must look at party unity/cohesion or disunity, party discipline, and party centralization or decentralization. Where there is cohesion and discipline and/or party centralization, access to the amendment mechanism is more likely. That is, the party leadership can whip party members into passing a constitutional amendment. Where there is no party unity/cohesion or party discipline and/or party centralization, the amendment mechanism is likely to be less accessible. To understand why party members are more or less disciplined in a given jurisdiction, it is necessary to examine parties' internal organization such as candidate selection for general elections and its implications for legislative behaviour.[21] As reported by Hazan, the way in which candidates are selected is largely not regulated by law in most countries—that is, parties are allowed to determine their own rules for candidate selection.[22] Research shows that

[20] In particular, the approach seeks to understand the conditions that have led to political parties to trust and cooperate with each other. See Ostrom (n 4) 198–202.

[21] Reuven Y Hazan, 'Candidate Selection: Implications and Challenges for Legislative Behaviour' in Shane Martin, Thomas Saalfeld, and Kaare W Strøm (eds), *The Oxford Handbook of Legislative Studies* (OUP 2014) 214.

[22] ibid 214.

such rules have important implications for legislative behaviour[23] (eg party discipline and party cohesion).[24] Therefore, since as a general rule access to the amendment mechanism is limited to legislators only, candidate selection rules necessarily have implications for its availability as a mechanism of entrenchment and more generally for how constitutions change. Inasmuch as candidate selection influences legislative behaviour, it is particularly relevant to understand the impact of such rules in the use of entrenchment mechanisms by those who get elected. Understanding how these rules work will be central to understanding why some mechanisms of entrenchment are available and some are not.

But, of course, internal party rules and dynamics are not enough to understand why there is access (or not) to the amendment mechanism. Where there is more than one political party with representation in the relevant legislative body, it is also important to grasp the interparty dynamics, particularly coalition politics.[25] Coalition politics is central to understanding the access (or lack thereof) to the amendment mechanism.[26]

As will be seen in Chapters 4 and 6, political parties in Mexico are highly centralized, disciplined, and capable of building coalitions for cross-party entrenchment. As such, they have regularly been able to access the constitutional amendment mechanism. Importantly, such an ability emerged in a particular context. Naturally, the internal and interparty dynamics will vary across countries, and with them the access to the different means of constitutional change. Accordingly, studies that aim to explain constitutional rigidity/flexibility need to provide an account that captures the party-politics dimension in the jurisdiction at hand.

[23] Ulrich Sieberer, 'Party Unity in Parliamentary Democracies: A Comparative Analysis' (2006) 12 The Journal of Legislative Studies 150; Thorsten Faas, 'To Defect or Not to Defect? National, Institutional and Party Group Pressures on MEPs and Their Consequences for Party Group Cohesion in the European Parliament' (2003) 42 European Journal of Political Research 841; Simon Hix, 'Electoral Institutions and Legislative Behavior: Explaining Voting Defection in the European Parliament' (2004) 56 World Politics 194.

[24] Note that determining whether it is party cohesion or party discipline is an empirical question. If it is cohesion that explains legislative behaviour, it is likely that constitutional principles and values are being protected and in tune with the public interest.

[25] See eg Kaare Strøm, Wolfgang C Müller, and Daniel Markham Smith, 'Parliamentary Control of Coalition Governments' (2010) 13 Annual Review of Political Science 517.

[26] See eg Michael Laver and Norman Schofield, *Multiparty Government: The Politics of Coalition in Europe* (University of Michigan Press 1998).

III. Constitutional Culture

Of course, one cannot make sense of these practices without considering the constitutional culture of the relevant case study: a country's past experiences and practices might shed light on path-dependency patterns. Accordingly, the framework offered in this book draws from the anti-formalist scholarship that stresses the importance of constitutional culture as a factor to understand constitutional change (such as Ginsburg and Melton or Albert and Jackson). Importantly, it does not attempt to measure amendment culture (like Ginsburg and Melton) but instead seeks to explore in what ways constitutional history reflects and informs current constitutional understandings and practices. As discussed in Chapter 2, aggregated studies are unlikely to capture those norms, practices, and conventions. In other words, the claim here is that accounts of constitutional culture are needed not as a measurable variable in a Ginsburg and Melton sense but as Vicki Jackson-style accounts that are informed by constitutional history so as to shed light on path-dependency patterns.[27]

Constitutional culture is here understood as the beliefs, understandings, assumptions, and attitudes of the relevant group (eg political parties, the relevant legal community, or the society at large) regarding constitutional change.[28] Here, the relevant group is part of an interpretative community able to construct constitutional meaning[29] in their day-to-day interpretation of the

[27] Vicki C Jackson, 'The (Myth of Un)Amendability of the US Constitution and the Democratic Component of Constitutionalism' (2015) 13 International Journal of Constitutional Law 575.

[28] I am aware of how slippery the concept of constitutional culture is. Mindful of that and the debates regarding the concepts of 'legal families', 'legal culture', and 'legal traditions', I am defining 'constitutional culture' as narrowly as possible. Additionally, my definition of constitutional culture shares some similarities with what Oran Doyle understands as first- and second-order preferences to explain de facto unamendability. See Oran Doyle, 'The Difficulty with Amendment Difficulty' (on file with author). For a discussion regarding the debates on the concepts of 'legal culture' and 'legal tradition', see Jaakko Husa, 'Legal Culture vs. Legal Tradition: Different Epistemologies?' (2012) Maastricht European Private Law Institute Working Paper 2012/18 <https://papers.ssrn.com/abstract=2179890> accessed 15 August 2024. See also Lawrence Meir Friedman, *The Republic of Choice: Law, Authority, and Culture* (Harvard UP 1990); H Patrick Glenn, *Legal Traditions of the World: Sustainable Diversity in Law* (OUP 2014); Csaba Varga, *Comparative Legal Cultures* (NYU Press 1992); Pierre Legrand, 'The Impossibility of "Legal Transplants"' (1997) 4 Maastricht Journal of European and Comparative Law 111; David Kenny, '"It's Just the Vibe of the Thing": Mapping the Role of Culture in Comparative Constitutional Law' (2023) <www.tcd.ie/law/researchpapers/David.Kenny-It's_just_the_vibe_of_the_thing.pdf> accessed 25 October 2024.

[29] For Jack Balkin, constitutions are changing all the time even when the text does not change. That constant change takes place through what he calls 'constitutional construction'—ie a dialectical process whereby the political branches act based on their assertions about what the constitution permits them to do. Judges, through interpretation, also contribute to constitutional construction. Accordingly, the ways in which constitutions work are shaped by the beliefs and assumptions held by the relevant political actors. See Jack M Balkin, 'Framework Model and Constitutional Interpretation' in David Dyzenhaus and Malcolm Thorburn (eds), *Philosophical Foundations of Constitutional Law* (OUP 2016) 241–42.

Constitution (in this particular case, the different means of entrenchment).[30] While in some countries certain mechanisms could be understood as inaccessible, in others the opposite may be the case. Importantly, the understandings, beliefs, and attitudes of the relevant group are informed by, but not limited to, the country's own constitutional history and experience. In light of what I have argued above, as a general rule, the relevant group to consider when talking about amendment difficulty would be those who have the power to activate the amendment mechanism—namely, the political parties in the jurisdiction at hand. Once again, take, for example, the cases of the US and Mexico.

As explained by Jackson, in the US the idea of amending the Constitution is simply an off-the-wall[31] possibility because the relevant legal community considers it out of reach.[32] Even though Jackson's argument is not focused on political parties, her work illustrates well what I mean by beliefs, understandings, assumptions, and attitudes towards certain entrenchment mechanisms. Jackson argues that the two-thirds requirement to pass a constitutional amendment as per Article V of the Constitution cannot be per se what makes the US Constitution difficult to amend if considered against the historical backdrop of congressional overrides of presidential vetoes in that country. In other words, the fact that Congress has been able to join together to override presidential vetoes at a rate of 15.9 per cent shows that the two-thirds requirement of each House is not, by itself, an unsurmountable obstacle to proposing constitutional amendments.[33] Jackson argues that what increases the difficulty of amendment in the US 'is a widespread view that constitutional change *cannot* be sought through amendment, as a practical matter, and [that] as a normative matter amendments *should* not be the vehicle for legal change'.[34] For example, she shows how the relevant legal community ruled out the possibility of a constitutional amendment, while showing a clear preference for the development of new jurisprudence through judicial interpretation, to respond to the Supreme Court in the aftermath of *Citizens United*.[35] Put simply, assuming the process would be difficult, the relevant community is constructing the

[30] ibid.
[31] ibid.
[32] Jackson (n 27).
[33] According to Jackson, as of 2015, 'a 2013 study finds that looking only at "regular vetoes" since 1961, thirty seven out of 233 vetoes were overridden—for a rate of 15.9 percent. If two-thirds of both Houses of Congress can join together to override Presidential vetoes at these rates, then perhaps the requirement that two-thirds of each House join in proposing amendments may not, by itself, be quite so large an obstacle to proposing amendments as might be thought; and as noted, most amendments proposed by Congress have been ratified by the states'. ibid 580.
[34] ibid 584.
[35] ibid 584–89.

difficulty of amendment based on beliefs and attitudes against formal constitutional change (and in favour of other methods of change like adjudication and judicial appointments) that are independent of the formal requirements established by Article V. Jackson also shows how the beliefs against amendment translate into normative arguments that at the same time reinforce the former.

By contrast, as will be seen in Chapter 5, for the relevant actors (ie political parties) in Mexico, constitutional amendment is an on-the-wall possibility because it has been consistently and effectively used throughout constitutional history (ie for more than 150 years).[36] Additionally, as opposed to the US, judicial review and judicial appointments have gained relevance as mechanisms of entrenchment only in the last three decades. In fact, as will be argued in Chapter 7, the deference of the Mexican Supreme Court when it comes to constitutional review of constitutional amendments (ie through the non-justiciability of constitutional amendments and constitutional restrictions doctrines) is a crucial factor explaining the attitudes in favour of amendments and, thus, the frequent use of the amendment mechanism. In short, by consistently refusing to substantively review the constitutionality of constitutional amendments, the Supreme Court has played an insurance policy function[37] that incentivizes the continuous resort to the amendment mechanism. Supreme Court doctrines are likely informing and influencing beliefs, understandings, assumptions, attitudes, and the choices of political actors regarding the different entrenchment mechanisms, in particular constitutional amendments. This is so for a simple reason: constitutional amendment allows the modification of the master text of the Constitution and guarantees the insulation of cross-party agreements, effectively removing them from the sphere of judicial oversight (or any kind of oversight, for that matter).

Relatedly and in contrast to the experience of the US concerning the normative arguments against constitutional amendment as an appropriate means to bring about legal change, the Mexican case is the opposite. As will be seen in Chapter 7, the notion of a 'permanent constituent power', coined by Felipe Tena Ramirez, posits that once the original constituent power is exhausted, a materially unlimited *permanent* constituent power emerges.[38] Under this view, and reminiscent of the constitutional theory approaches that conflate

[36] Mariana Velasco-Rivera, 'Constitutional Rigidity: The Mexican Experiment' (2021) 19 International Journal of Constitutional Law 1042.

[37] Tom Ginsburg, *Judicial Review in New Democracies: Constitutional Courts in Asian Cases* (CUP 2003); Hirschl (n 11); Rosalind Dixon and Tom Ginsburg, 'The Forms and Limits of Constitutions as Political Insurance' (2017) 15 International Journal of Constitutional Law 988.

[38] Velasco-Rivera (n 36) 1059.

the normative and descriptive dimensions of constitutional change, the permanent constituent power is an iteration of popular sovereignty that manifests through the amendment mechanism. This makes, on the one hand, the amendment procedure the most democratically legitimate form to bring about constitutional change and, on the other, the resulting constitutional amendments unquestionable.[39] At the same time, the concept of a permanent constituent power becomes a tool to legitimize frequent amendments. As such and in contrast to the US, the concept of a permanent constituent power facilitates the availability of the amendment mechanism.

These understandings and attitudes are informed by the constitutional history of the jurisdiction at hand. Accordingly, whether a mechanism of constitutional change is available will in part be determined by these understandings and attitudes. These can change over time. For example, should the non-justiciability doctrine be reversed in Mexico, it is reasonable to believe that this would shape perceptions about the suitability of constitutional amendments to advance changes with the purpose of placing them out of the court's jurisdiction.[40]

IV. Choices by Key Political Actors

Yet, the question about how constitutional change takes place will ultimately depend on choices made by key political actors.[41] That is, for different reasons, key political actors will decide to use a specific institutional mechanism for constitutional change over others (eg choosing to use the constitutional amendment mechanism over ordinary legislation). Of course, the choices made by key political actors will be directly influenced by both the party system and political parties' dynamics (as previously described) and by the constitutional culture (as defined here) of the jurisdiction at hand but will

[39] For a discussion on the origins and evolution of the notion of a 'permanent constituent power' in Mexico, see Mariana Velasco-Rivera and Joel I Colón-Ríos, 'On the Legal Implications of a "Permanent" Constituent Power' (2023) 12 Global Constitutionalism 269.

[40] In the US, by contrast, due to the skittishness the Supreme Court has exhibited in questions regarding the amending power, it is less likely that considerations about judicial scrutiny of constitutional amendments would play a central role in decision-makers' reasoning when deciding to advance a constitutional amendment. For a discussion on the stance of the US Supreme Court regarding this issue, see Richard S Kay, 'Formal and Informal Amendment of the United States Constitution' (2018) 66 The American Journal of Comparative Law 243, 259.

[41] For a study emphasizing the importance of political leaders as a variable to explain constitutional change in the form of government, see Bernd Hayo and Stefan Voigt, 'Endogenous Constitutions: Politics and Politicians Matter, Economic Outcomes Don't' (2013) 88 Journal of Economic Behavior & Organization 47.

also be influenced by other factors. Such additional factors may include but are not limited to: how respectful of the constitutional order and the rule of law are the relevant actors (ie political parties and their leaders); the popularity of the relevant key political leaders (eg the president, prime minister, party leaders); whether they are subject to re-election; the electoral calendar; and considerations regarding the subject matter of the amendments. For example, in systems where constitutional amendments are proposed by political parties (ie the government in parliamentary systems) but subject to referendum, the government would need to assess whether a given issue would, in fact, be likely to be ratified by the public before activating the amendment mechanism.[42] Such an assessment will likely prove consequential as to which constitutional change mechanism would be selected, regardless of whether the government prefer to amend the master text of the Constitution.

Events around a set of amendments adopted in Mexico in 2022–23 illustrate the importance of choices made by key political actors as a factor determining which mechanism of constitutional change is used. As the reader knows by now, formal constitutional amendments have been the preferred mode of change in Mexico for over a century. But an episode in 2023 clearly shows that the agency of the relevant political actors is essential to maintain the amendment mechanism available for direct political entrenchment. In February of that year, the Mexican Federal Congress passed a set of amendments to electoral law overhauling the electoral watchdog—the Instituto Nacional Electoral (INE).[43] Together with another set of amendments passed in December 2022, the changes to electoral law undermined the agency's independence by, among other things, slashing the size of the agency's civil service by 85 per cent.[44] The move seriously challenged the capacity of the agency to guarantee the organization of free and fair elections in 2024.[45] These changes to ordinary legislation (dubbed as Plan B) were pursued as the second-best option to overhaul

[42] See Oran Doyle, *The Constitution of Ireland: A Contextual Analysis* (Bloomsbury Publishing 2018) 170 (arguing that the government in Ireland is in the driver's seat when it comes to proposing constitutional amendments).

[43] 'Mexico Hobbles Election Agency That Helped End One-Party Rule' *The New York Times* (22 February 2023) <www.nytimes.com/2023/02/22/world/americas/mexico-election-law.html> accessed 29 May 2023.

[44] Instituto Nacional Electoral, 'Resumen Ejecutivo Implicaciones Plan B de la Reforma Electoral' (nd) <https://centralelectoral.ine.mx/wp-content/uploads/2023/01/Resumen-ejecutivo-implicaciones-reforma-electoral-1.pdf> accessed 15 August 2024.

[45] Mariana Velasco-Rivera, 'Mexican Democracy (and the Supreme Court) at a Crossroads' [2023] Verfassungsblog <https://verfassungsblog.de/mexican-democracy-and-the-supreme-court-at-a-crossroads> accessed 27 May 2023; Vázquez F, 'Del #YoDefiendoalINE al "plan B" de la reforma electoral' *Gatopardo* (24 February 2023) <https://gatopardo.com/podcast-gatopardo/del-yodefiendoaline-al-plan-b-de-la-reforma-electoral> accessed 29 May 2023.

the electoral agency after MORENA, the party in government, failed to meet the qualified majority threshold to pass a constitutional amendment. Such failure came after the PRI's refusal to collaborate with the government to push the amendment through Congress.[46] In so doing, PRI broke with what, in Chapters 5 and 6, I call the rule of cooperation—namely, an unwritten rule of cross-party cooperation to meet the otherwise stringent constitutional requirements to amend the Constitution. Rather than the amendment rule's stringent requirements, constitutional rigidity, in this case, was determined by a specific political calculation by a key political actor.

V. The Economy of Constitutional Change and Political Entrenchment

The previous three factors can be understood as the key elements of an *economy of constitutional change*. In the economy of constitutional change, constitutional change is a *function of political entrenchment*. That is, constitutional change is the product of the formal or informal insulation of interests, values, and beliefs of and by the relevant actors (eg political parties, interest groups, etc) through the institutional means available (eg constitutional amendment, ordinary legislation, judicial appointments, etc) in a given constitutional order.[47] In this way, constitutions offer different institutional means

[46] Note that the amendment mechanism was not completely inaccessible during the López Obrador administration. The PRI was a reliable partner of the party in government, MORENA, to pass a wide variety of constitutional amendments during the first half of López Obrador's term. The PRI's choice not to cooperate in this particular case was against the backdrop of unprecedented mass protests against the government's attempt to amend the constitution to undermine the INE just months before the governor's election in the State of Mexico—a PRI electoral stronghold with decisive weight for presidential elections. The 2024 presidential race was roughly a year away. See Guadalupe Irízar, Natalia Vitela, and Martha Martínez, 'Y tras la marcha . . . rechaza PRI aprobar reforma electoral' *Reforma* (Mexico, 15 November 2022) <www.elnorte.com/y-tras-la-marcha-rechaza-pri-aprobar-reforma-electoral/ar2504372> accessed 27 February 2023.

[47] The idea of political entrenchment as one of the main drivers of constitutional change builds on what Jack Balkin and Sanford Levinson call partisan entrenchment. Their theory of constitutional change explicitly jettisons Ackerman's concept of constitutional moments, arguing that constitutional change does not always occur in the same way. In particular, Balkin and Levinson argue that political parties are among the most important institutions for translating and interpreting the popular will. As such, political parties 'are influenced by and provide a filter for the views of various interest groups and social movements'. The 'people', therefore, rather than being an entity that appears in one extraordinary moment as a consensual voice, are all the individuals and interest groups, with competing and even contradictory views and values, which they seek to protect by putting their party in power. Given how rare Article V constitutional amendments are in the US, other means of entrenchment like judicial appointments are more prevalent. For instance, assuming an acquiescent Senate, winning the White House allows the party in power to fill the federal judiciary with members of its own party. Life tenure makes judges 'temporally extended representatives of particular parties, and hence, of popular understandings about public policy and the Constitution'. This temporal extension of partisan representation is what Balkin and Levinson mean by 'partisan entrenchment'. Jack M Balkin and Sanford Levinson,

or tools for individuals to further their interests and agendas and protect them across time, and the availability of those means or tools for political entrenchment will depend, at the very least, on the three key elements of the economy of constitutional change present in a jurisdiction at a given time—namely, political parties, party systems, constitutional culture, and the choices by key political actors.

The fact that political entrenchment can take place through different types of mechanisms provided in a constitutional order means that it can be direct or indirect. Direct political entrenchment takes place when the master text of the Constitution changes—that is, through constitution-making[48] or constitutional amendment. Indirect political entrenchment takes place through any institutional means available within the constitutional order (eg ordinary legislation, executive orders, judicial appointments, judicial review, etc).[49]

The assumption here, suggested by the previous discussion of the factors that comprise the economy of constitutional change, is that the relevant actors

'Understanding the Constitutional Revolution' (2001) 87 Virginia Law Review 1045, 1066–67, 1079. Similarly, Robert Post and Reva Siegel's theory of democratic constitutionalism offers a model where informal constitutional change (ie constitutional interpretation) comprises, first and foremost, the formal or informal entrenchment of interests, values, and beliefs of different groups through the institutional means available in a given constitutional order (eg constitutional amendment, judicial review, and judicial appointments). Robert Post and Reva Siegel, 'Roe Rage: Democratic Constitutionalism and Backlash Essay' (2007) 42 Harvard Civil Rights–Civil Liberties Law Review 373. These ideas, in particular that of partisan entrenchment, shed light on the direct drivers of constitutional change in the US context. However, I do not share what seems to be Balkin and Levinson's implicit core assumption regarding the link between political parties and the popular will. Balkin and Levinson seem to replace the idea of the 'people' in Ackerman's work with that of political parties as an effective vehicle to translate the popular will. While in theory political parties should be effective vehicles to translate the popular will, given the decline and transformation of political parties and their impact on representative democracies, such an assumption would not hold in practice. (I thank David Kenny for pointing this out to me.) For a discussion on the decline and transformation of political parties and their effects on representative democracy, see eg Heiko Giebler and others, 'Decline or Change? Party Types and the Crisis of Representative Democracy' in Wolfgang Merkel and Sascha Kneip (eds), *Democracy and Crisis: Challenges in Turbulent Times* (Springer 2018) 145–76; Russell J Dalton, David M Farrell, and Ian McAllister, *Political Parties and Democratic Linkage: How Parties Organize Democracy* (OUP 2011); Pippa Norris, *Democratic Deficit: Critical Citizens Revisited* (CUP 2011); Russell J Dalton, *Democratic Challenges, Democratic Choices: The Erosion of Political Support in Advanced Industrial Democracies* (OUP 2004).

[48] This would be in line with Ginsburg and Hirschl's theories on the emergence of judicial review (see Ginsburg (n 11) and Hirschl (n 11)). However, these theories are only able to explain judicial review in T1. They are not able to explain longer periods of time in that they do not include the possibility of frequent constitutional amendments.

[49] See Jack M Balkin and Sanford Levinson, 'Understanding the Constitutional Revolution' (2001) 87 Virginia Law Review 1067–68 (arguing, 'Partisan entrenchment is an especially important engine of constitutional change. When enough members of a particular party are appointed to the federal judiciary, they start to change the understandings of the Constitution that appear in positive law. If more people are appointed in a relatively short period of time, the changes will occur more quickly. Constitutional revolutions are the cumulative result of successful partisan entrenchment when the entrenching party has a relatively coherent political ideology or can pick up sufficient ideological allies from the appointees of other parties').

will seek to use what they consider to be the most effective entrenchment mechanism to advance their interests and political agenda. In the abstract, by definition, direct political entrenchment (ie constitution-making and constitutional amendment) is more effective than indirect entrenchment, at least in terms of immediacy: once a given policy or agenda is entrenched in the constitutional text, it becomes the parameter in light of which apex courts will review the constitutionality of all ordinary laws and government action. Unlike formal constitutional change, constitutional change brought about by indirect means of entrenchment like judicial interpretation is less effective in that it may take years or decades to materialize, it can be harder to identify (among other things, this kind of change is not accessible to the layperson due to legal jargon[50]), and it may be struck down through judicial review, as is the case for ordinary legislation or executive orders.

Within direct entrenchment, constitutional amendment will generally be more effective than adopting a new Constitution. For instance, constitutional amendment allows compartmentalizing policy issues. Constitution-making processes, by contrast, are more costly in that everything is up for grabs.[51] Constitutional amendments may also give visibility to policy choices that may amass votes for future elections. The different mechanisms of political entrenchment can be understood as what in economic theory is known as close-substitute goods. Yet, assuming that, for the reasons stated above, the relevant actors will by default prefer amending the Constitution, the question is whether such a mechanism of direct entrenchment is available. The fact that direct means of entrenchment (eg constitutional amendment) are by definition more effective does not mean they will be available to the relevant political actors.

Indeed, the relevant actors to look at will vary depending on the type of entrenchment mechanism in question. When dealing with direct political entrenchment, specifically constitutional amendment, *particular attention must be given to political parties.* This is so for a simple reason: in contemporary constitutional democracies, formal constitutional change is largely a mediated phenomenon. In contemporary constitutional democracies, the actors that, as a general rule, have the legal power to activate the amendment mechanism are

[50] Sanford Levinson, *Our Undemocratic Constitution: Where the Constitution Goes Wrong (and How We the People Can Correct It)* (OUP 2006) 164.

[51] See Elkins, Ginsburg, and Melton (n 12) 74–75 (Elkins, Ginsburg, and Melton consider that replacing a constitution is more costly than amending it mainly for three reasons: '[1] there may be more issues over which to bargain, requiring more time and energy for negotiation; [2] previously settled issues may be raised again, rendering bargaining results less predictable; and, [3] the costs of failure may be much more severe because in a strict sense, replacement may be illegal'.

political parties.[52] By contrast, in the case of informal constitutional change through individual constitutional complaints or other constitutional review mechanisms, particular attention must be given to those bringing the lawsuits.[53] Since this book is about constitutional amendment, and constitutional rigidity in particular, special attention is given to political parties and the party system in Mexico.

The availability of institutional means for political entrenchment is not guaranteed by their formal existence. Instead, the availability of the entrenchment mechanisms depends on institutional and non-institutional factors. The most obvious institutional factor is their formal existence in the constitutional order. In addition to that, for instance in the case of informal constitutional change through judicial review, a formal factor determining its availability would be the applicable standing rules. A non-institutional factor would be, for example, the likelihood of success in the court in light of its ideological composition before deciding to bring a case to court. When it comes to constitutional amendment, in addition to institutional factors such as the formal provision of an amendment rule in the Constitution as well as its requirements, the basic non-institutional factors determining its availability are, as argued above, the political parties and party system, constitutional culture, and, importantly, the choices by key political actors.[54] A necessary implication of this proposition (ie that the availability of the amendment mechanism depends on institutional and non-institutional factors) is that the difficulty of amendment is determined not only by the requirements imposed by the amendment rule but also by the interaction between formal and informal factors.

[52] In the US constitutional law context, this idea is present in Balkin and Levinson's work. They argue that political parties are among the most important institutions for translating and interpreting the popular will. As such, political parties (ideally) 'are influenced by and provide a filter for the views of various interest groups and social movements'. Balkin and Levinson (n 6) 1066.

[53] For a study on how the interaction between citizens and officials produces informal constitutional change in the US context, see Reva B Siegel, 'Constitutional Culture, Social Movement Conflict and the Constitutional Change: The Case of the de Facto ERA—2005–06 Brennan Center Symposium Lecture' (2006) 94 California Law Review 1323.

[54] For a study emphasizing the importance of political leaders as a variable to explain constitutional change in the form of government, see Hayo and Voigt (n 41).

4
Political Parties and Formal Constitutional Change in Contemporary Mexico

I. Introduction

Despite its formal rigidity, the Mexican Constitution has been amended incessantly since its adoption in 1917. Perhaps most strikingly, the vast majority of amendments have taken place since 1988, the year when the hegemonic PRI lost the power to amend the Constitution on its own. If one relies on the formalist and anti-formalist streams of the literature discussed in Chapter 2, the amendment reality in Mexico would be hard to explain because, for instance, party system fragmentation, in combination with formal hurdles, is expected to make constitutions more difficult to change.[1] This has clearly not been the case in Mexico. This chapter seeks to start building an answer as to why that is the case through the lenses of what I call the economy of constitutional change. In particular, it seeks to shed light on the first dimension of Mexico's economy of constitutional change: the political parties and party system.

Section II of the chapter shows that the constitutional amendment processes between 1997 and 2024 have been characterized by two elements: *fast-track approvals* in both chambers of Congress and a *lack of opposition* in state legislatures. These findings challenge not only the well-established proposition that formal hurdles determine constitutional rigidity[2] but also that formal hurdles like the ones imposed by Mexico's amendment mechanism (eg supermajority voting requirements, number of veto players, and veto points) increase the quality of constitutional amendment processes by promoting transparency

[1] See Gabriel Negretto, 'Replacing and Amending Constitutions: The Logic of Constitutional Change in Latin America' (2012) 46 Law and Society Review 749, 760.

[2] Sanford Levinson, *Our Undemocratic Constitution: Where the Constitution Goes Wrong (and How We the People Can Correct It)* (OUP 2006); John Ferejohn, 'The Politics of Imperfection: The Amendment of Constitutions' (1997) 22 Law and Social Inquiry 501, 523; Rosalind Dixon, 'Constitutional Amendment Rules: A Comparative Perspective' in Tom Ginsburg and Rosalind Dixon (eds), *Comparative Constitutional Law* (Edward Elgar Publishing 2011) 96–111; Rosalind Dixon and Richard Holden, 'Constitutional Amendment Rules: The Denominator Problem' in Tom Ginsburg (ed), *Comparative Constitutional Design* (CUP 2012) 195–218.

The Politics of Constitutional Rigidity. Mariana Velasco-Rivera, Oxford University Press.
 DOI: 10.1093/9780191981876.003.0004

and deliberation.[3] They also challenge the scholarship that predicted that the demise of the hegemonic PRI would allow the constitutional system of separation of powers and checks and balances to work properly—even more so in an era of divided government.[4] Most importantly, the findings suggest that the factors driving the dynamics of formal constitutional change in Mexico are very strong party discipline, cross-party cooperation, and centralization of constitutional decision-making. Section III offers examples of constitutional amendment processes that took place during the period under study to illustrate the bargaining and horse-trading dynamics created by the previously mentioned factors. Those processes not only provide a glimpse into the workings of centralized constitutional decision-making in the context of constitutional amendments but also exemplify the ways in which amendments have served to fulfil different political agendas and needs.

II. Constitutional Amendment in Mexico Post-1988

Even though, in 1988, the PRI lost the ability to amend the Constitution on its own, the constitutional text did not cease to be amended. The amendment rate steadily increased while the political landscape became more plural. This was unexpected. The political fragmentation and the eventual transition to democracy were expected to lead to a new regime with a functional constitutional system of separation of powers and effective constitutional veto points, which would naturally entail a decrease in constitutional amendments. For instance, according to Jeffrey Weldon, vertical and horizontal mechanisms of accountability in Mexico did not function properly because the constitutional system

[3] See eg Donald Lutz, 'Toward a Theory of Constitutional Amendment' in Sanford Levinson (ed), *Responding to Imperfection: The Theory and Practice of Constitutional Amendment* (Princeton UP 1995) 237–74; Levinson (n 2); Stephen M Griffin, 'The Nominee Is . . . Article V' in Sanford Levinson, William N Eskridge, and Murphy Institute of Political Economy (eds), *Constitutional Stupidities, Constitutional Tragedies* (New York UP 1998) 51–53; Kathleen M Sullivan, 'Constitutional Constancy: Why Congress Should Cure Itself of Amendment Fever Address' (1995) 17 Cardozo Law Review 691; Vicki C Jackson, 'The (Myth of Un)Amendability of the US Constitution and the Democratic Component of Constitutionalism' (2015) 13 International Journal of Constitutional Law 575.

[4] Jeffrey Weldon, 'Political Sources of Presidencialismo in Mexico' in Scott Mainwaring and Matthew Soberg Shugart (eds), *Presidentialism and Democracy in Latin America* (CUP 1997) 225-258; Ignacio Marván Laborde, *Y Despés Del Presidencialismo? Reflexiones Para La Formación de Un Nuevo Régimen* (1st edn, Oceano 1997); María Amparo Casar, 'Executive-Legislative Relations: The Case of Mexico (1946–1997)' in Scott Morgenstern and Benito Nacif (eds), *Legislative Politics in Latin America* (CUP 2002) 114-144; Benito Nacif, 'The Fall of the Dominant Presidency: Lawmaking under Divided Government in Mexico' in Roderic Ai Camp (ed), *The Oxford Handbook of Mexican Politics* (OUP 2012) 234-264.

was co-opted by one party within which decision-making was highly centralized. Mexico's constitutional system would only function properly whenever the PRI hegemonic regime ceased to exist. For Weldon, the PRI hegemonic regime relied on four necessary conditions:

> (1) a presidential system based in the constitution; (2) a unified government, where the ruling party controls the presidency and both houses of Congress; (3) discipline within the ruling party; and (4) a president who is the acknowledged leader of the ruling party.[5]

In that regime, access to the amendment mechanism was ensured by party discipline—an unwritten rule enforced by corporatist politics that resulted in the lack of incentives to exercise the veto points established in the Constitution. Constitutional entrenchment rules were in place and formally observed, but the power of the president was effectively unbound. Since Weldon's conditions are necessary, it follows, if any of them ceased to exist, the equilibrium of *presidencialismo* would begin to break down and eventually disappear. Accordingly, the fall of the PRI as a hegemonic party should have ended the centralization of decision-making that characterized the old PRI regime and, therefore, the amendment rate should have dropped. In the context of the political debilitation of the PRI, these expectations were reasonable. From 1997 onwards, as an even more plural political landscape emerged, some observers even expected legislative deadlock due to the conditions of divided government.[6] Yet, when the political conditions changed in 1989 and the hegemonic party regime unravelled, at least when it came to the workings of the constitutional amendment mechanism, vertical and horizontal mechanisms of accountability did not begin to function properly. While some signs suggesting that the mechanisms of checks and balances were in fact starting to work as intended (eg public confrontation between power branches, the exercise of the presidential veto, increasing cases being brought before the Supreme Court, and the rejection of judicial nominations)[7] were seen as the PRI lost power, the amendment rate did

[5] Weldon (n 4) 227.

[6] Note that regarding constitutional amendments, I understand the divided government as starting in 1988 when the PRI lost the needed qualified majority to amend the Constitution in the Chamber of Deputies, and not in 1997, when that party lost the majority of seats in that same chamber. But see Ulises Carrillo and Alonso Lujambio, 'La Incertidumbre Constitucional. Gobierno Dividido y Aprobación Presupuestal En La LVII Legislatura Del Congreso Mexicano, 1997–2000' (1998) 60 Revista Mexicana de Sociología 239 and María Amparo Casar and Ignacio Marván, *Reformar sin Mayorías, La Dinámica del Cambio Constitucional en México: 1997–2012* (Taurus 2014) 31.

[7] See María Amparo Casar, 'Executive–Legislative Relations: The Case of Mexico (1946–97)' in Scott Morgenstern and Benito Nacif (eds), *Legislative Politics in Latin America* (CUP 2002) 142 (arguing, 'From 1978 to 1996, Mexico enacted six electoral reforms. These reforms have helped to move Mexico

not drop, but increased. Figure 4.1 shows the increasing number of constitutional amendments by presidential term in the period between 1917 and 2024.

Predictions and accounts like Lutz's or Weldon's are not able to explain Mexico's constitutional change reality. On the one hand, Lutz's theory overlooks the role of political parties and party systems altogether. Weldon's assumption, on the other hand, is that unwritten rules, political norms, and practices that developed during the PRI regime, in particular party discipline, would disappear once the PRI regime disappeared. As will be seen in Chapters 5 and 6, the constitutional change dynamics that followed the fall of the PRI suggest the existence of a regime that operates based on long-standing pre-understandings regarding the function of the amendment mechanism—what I will call the cross-party entrenchment regime (CPER). But before explaining how the CPER emerged, it is important to first focus on the dynamics that gave rise to that regime and its core features (ie the ability to cooperate across party lines, party discipline, and the consequent centralization of constitutional decision-making).

Moreover, as discussed in Chapter 2, according to Lutz and others, a level of stringency like that of Article 135 of the Mexican Constitution should provide an amendment process with an increased level of difficulty that promotes deliberation and gives constitutional change an extraordinary nature.[8] Constitutional amendment episodes in Mexico are far from extraordinary or deliberative. Rather, constitutional amendments have been markedly increasing since 1988.

toward a true electoral democracy by limiting fraud and improving the chances for opposition electoral victories. The result has been a substantial change in the structure of political opportunity and, consequently, a depletion of the president's partisan powers. As a result, characterizations of the postclassical period will likely depict the end of Mexico's subservient legislature'). See also Benito Nacif, 'The Fall of the Dominant Presidency: Lawmaking under Divided Government in Mexico' in Roderic Ai Camp (ed), *The Oxford Handbook of Mexican Politics* (OUP 2012) 234 and Armand B Peschard-Sverdrup and Sara Rioff, *Mexican Governance: From Single-Party Rule to Divided Government* (Centre for Strategic and International Studies 2005).

[8] See Lutz (n 3) 264 (Donald Lutz classifies Article 135 of the Mexican Constitution at the second highest level of amendment difficulty for requiring a qualified majority (two-thirds) in both chambers of Congress and the majority of state legislatures. He argues that the amendment process entails a 'complex decision-making process, which emphasizes the deliberative process and the distinction between constitutional and normal legislative matters'). Similarly, see Jon Elster, 'Don't Burn Your Bridge before You Come to It: Some Ambiguities and Complexities of Precommitment Symposium: Precommitment Theory in Bioethics and Constitutional Law: General Issues' (2002) 81 Texas Law Review 1751, 1783 (arguing, 'By requiring constitutional amendments to be passed by two successive parliaments, one makes it less likely that an ephemeral majority might run away with the constitution. The same effect can be achieved by requiring a supermajority of three-fifths, two-thirds or three-fourths. Yet these two devices—delays and supermajorities—also have other justifications, which point to a difficult tension at the core of the constitution making process. On the one hand, one would wish for constitutional amendments to emerge from calm and deliberative reflection. Delays can prevent the constitution from being changed under the influence of short-lived passions. On the other hand, one would wish for constitutional changes to result from popular mobilization') and Bruce Ackerman, *We the People: Foundations* (Harvard UP 1991) 6–7, 285–86, 300–07 (discussing constitutional changes that are the result of popular mobilization).

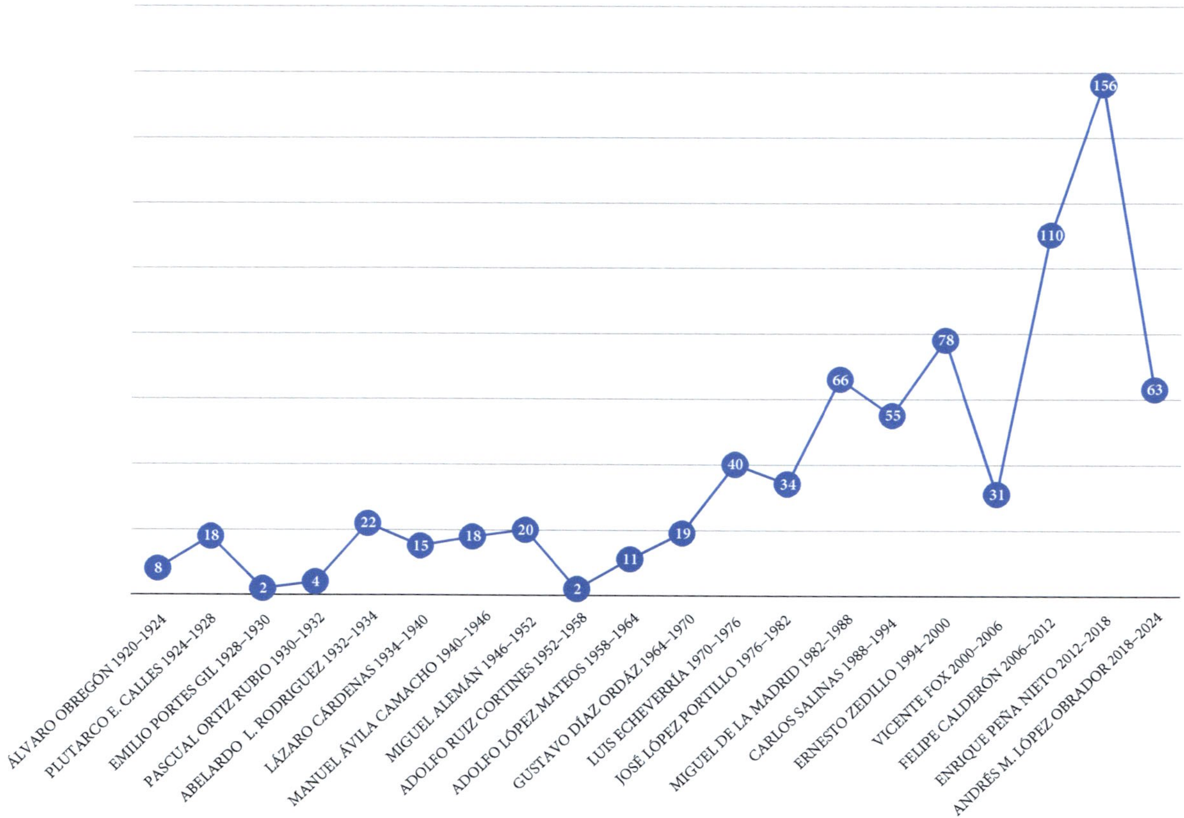

Figure 4.1 Constitutional articles amended by presidential term 1917–2024.

Source: Prepared by the author, working with data from Cámara de Diputados <www.diputados.gob.mx/LeyesBiblio/ref/cpeum_per.htm>. The figure for 2018–24 includes all amendments between 1 December 2018 and 31 July 2024.

What is more, these processes are characterized by two features: *fast-track approvals* in both chambers of Congress (ie a Chamber of Deputies and a Senate cromprised of 500 and 128 members, respetively) and the *lack of opposition* in state legislatures when passing constitutional amendments. Incorporating the role of political parties and party systems may prove instructive to better understand both the workings of the latter and of constitutional change dynamics. Against this backdrop, in what follows, I present three aspects of constitutional amendment dynamics in Mexico (ie the *volume of amendments* between 1917 and 2024; the *fast-track pattern* in the adoption of constitutional amendments; and the *lack of opposition* by state legislatures) that, in turn, provide a window to discover three distinctive features of that country's party system: the possibility of cross-party cooperation, strong party discipline, and the centralization of decision-making in constitutional amendment processes.

Volume of constitutional amendments: a sign of cross-party cooperation

Figure 4.1 clearly shows an increasing trend in the amendment rate throughout the last century: between 1917 and 2024, 772 constitutional amendments were adopted.[9] Figure 4.2 shows the percentage of amendments that were adopted from that total before and after 1988. Looking at Figures 4.1 and 4.2, we learn several things about formal constitutional change and constitutional politics in Mexico. When it comes to the question of constitutional rigidity, the number of amendments during the period between 1917 and 1988 is not surprising in light of the hegemonic party rule that the country was under in that period.

By contrast, the number of constitutional amendments adopted since 1988 is almost twice as high as those adopted in the previous seven decades: 64 per cent of the constitutional amendments adopted (ie 493 of the total 772 amendments) since the enactment of the Constitution took place after 1988. This fact is noteworthy because, as noted earlier, in 1988 the PRI lost the ability to amend the Constitution on its own. That is to say, the amendment mechanism

[9] This number accounts for the constitutional amendments adopted until July 2024. Importantly, this figure refers to the number of constitutional articles modified in each presidential administration, which is different from the number of amendment decrees. Amendment decrees normally include the modification of more than one article and clauses within articles. Therefore, the number of decrees would always be lower than the number of modifications (ie articles and/or clauses) to the text of the Constitution. This section focuses on the number of articles modified to give a better grasp of the magnitude of the increasing amendment rate. See Cámara de Diputados, 'Reformas Constitucionales por Periodo Presidencial' <www.diputados.gob.mx/LeyesBiblio/ref/cpeum_per.htm> accessed 2 August 2024.

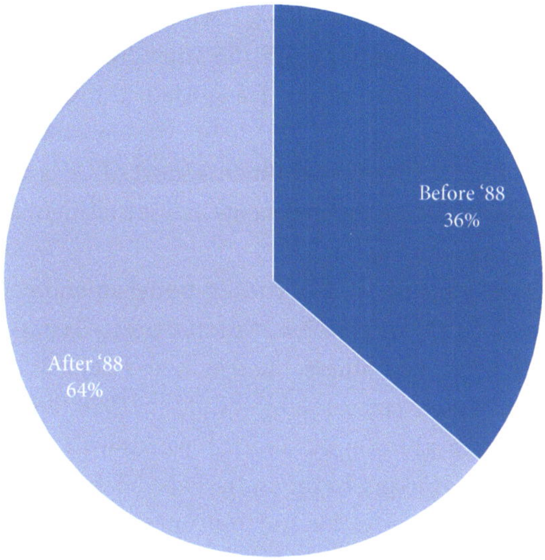

Figure 4.2 Percentage of constitutional amendments before and after 1988.
Source: Prepared by the author, working with data from Cámara de Diputados <www.diputados.gob.mx/LeyesBiblio/ref/cpeum_per.htm>.

could not be accessed without the cooperation of at least two political forces. It follows that all constitutional amendments since 1988 have taken place via the cooperation of least two political parties. Therefore, the most important lesson to be drawn in this context is that one of the core features of Mexico's party system since 1988 is the ability to cooperate across party lines.

Taking a closer look at the increasing number of amendments after 1988 against the backdrop of the PRI hegemonic years is helpful to get a better grasp of the magnitude of cross-party cooperation. Between 1988 and 2024, a total of 493 constitutional articles were modified, 133 between 1988 and 2000 and 360 between 2000 and 2024. In thirty years, the Constitution was amended more times than during the previous seven decades (493 vs 279). Furthermore, even the lowest number of amendments in a presidential term after 1988 is still high compared to the PRI hegemonic days. The thirty-one amendments adopted during the Fox administration are more than those adopted in the nine administrations between 1929 and 1970, and only fall short by three of those adopted during López Portillo's (1976–82). Furthermore, during the Calderón administration alone (2006–12), 110 amendments were passed, only 30 fewer than the reforms adopted during the Echeverría (1970–76), López Portillo (1976–82), and De la Madrid (1982–88) administrations together (140), which happen to be the three presidents that most amended the Constitution during the old regime. Between 2012 and 2018, during the PRI Peña Nieto administration, the Constitution went through 156 amendments; that is, seven more than Echeverría, López Portillo, and De la Madrid together. Finally, during the López Obrador administration (2018–24), the Constitution went through sixty-three amendments (three amendments short of De la Madrid, the president who introduced the most amendments in one presidential administration during the PRI hegemonic regime).[10]

The increased length and detail of constitutional amendments also speak to the ability of cross-party cooperation. As reported by Pozas-Loyo, Saavedra-Herrera, Pou-Giménez, and others, the length and detail of the Constitution have markedly increased since 1988.[11] While in 1988, by the end of De la Madrid's term, the Constitution was 34,916[12] words without counting the preamble or transitory provisions, by the end of Peña Nieto's presidency in 2018, it was 74,667 words.[13] If the preamble and transitory provisions are included, the increase is more staggering. While by the end of De la Madrid's presidency the word count was 48,919 words, by the end of Peña Nieto's it was 125,064.[14] Put differently, the Constitution more than doubled in size in three decades. This could very well be the result of a path-dependency pattern, as Pozas-Loyo and Pou-Giménez have argued.[15] In their view, length and frequency are related. Reforms create the need for further amendments: 'the hyper-detailed nature of the regulation makes in turn further additional and piecemeal reforms

[10] It is important to note that this figure reflects the number of articles amended until July 2024; that is, two months before the end of López Obrador's term in October of that year. As of August 2024, a set of eighteen amendment initiatives that would modify 37 per cent (ie 51 out of 136 articles) of the Constitution were being considered by Congress and were likely to be passed before the end of his term. See Julio Rios-Figueroa, 'Mexico 2024: The Battle for the Constitution' (ConstitutionNet, 29 February 2024) <http://constitutionnet.org/news/voices/mexico-2024-battle-constitution> accessed 4 August 2024; Mariana Velasco-Rivera, 'A Democratic Mandate to Overhaul Mexico's Judiciary?' (Verfassungsblog, 24 July 2024) <https://verfassungsblog.de/a-democratic-mandate-to-overhaul-mexicos-judiciary> accessed 4 August 2024.

[11] Andrea Pozas-Loyo, Camilo Saavedra-Herrera, and Francisca Pou-Giménez, 'When More Leads to More: Constitutional Amendments and Interpretation in Mexico 1917–2020' (2023) 48 Law and Social Inquiry 1, 6; Héctor Fix-Fierro, Diego Valadés, and Daniel Márquez, 'Toward the Reorganization and Consolidation of the Text of the Constitution of the United Mexican States of 1917: Introductory Essay' in *Constitución Política de los Estados Unidos Mexicanos. Texto Reordenado y Consolidado. Con las Reformas y Adiciones hasta el 10 de julio de 2015* (IIJ-UNAM 2016) 2–4.

[12] Fix-Fierro, Valadés, and Márquez (n 11) 3–4; Pozas-Loyo, Saavedra-Herrera, and Pou-Giménez (n 11) 6–7.

[13] Working with information available in the Supreme Court's database on historical legislation. Available at <www.scjn.gob.mx/normativa-nacional-internacional> accessed 11 October 2024.

[14] ibid.

[15] Francisca Pou-Giménez and Andrea Pozas-Loyo, 'The Paradox of Mexico's Constitutional Hyper-Reformism: Enabling Peaceful Transition while Blocking Democratic Consolidation' in Richard Albert and others (eds), *Constitutional Change and Transformation in Latin America* (Hart Publishing 2019) 221–42.

necessary, both because it becomes obsolete sooner, and because it naturally touches on countless provisions'.[16]

Importantly, length and detail may also be understood as a clear indication of the political parties' ability to negotiate the scope, nature, and language of modifications. Put differently, path dependency could simply not take place without the political will to cooperate across party lines to bring the relevant changes forward. Length and detail could also be understood as an indication that the negotiating parties try to be as specific as possible to protect their interests in the best way possible. In this way, the large volume and increasing length of constitutional amendments may be understood as a reflection of the emergence of new dynamics of political interaction in a context of increasing political fragmentation. Should this be the case, the increasing length and detail of the Constitution since 1988 suggest that the amendment mechanism became an attractive and accessible tool for political entrenchment. The number of amendments, despite the fragmentation of political power, makes it clear that the amendment mechanism remained available in Mexico's economy of constitutional change and that it has been an effective means for political entrenchment. As observed by other scholars, since the fall of the hegemonic PRI, constitutional amendments have tended to be the result of broad coalitions by the three main political parties: PRI, PAN, and PRD.[17] This means that an important feature to explain the dynamics of formal constitutional change in Mexico from 1988 onwards has to do with the distribution of power in Congress.[18] Tables 4.1 and 4.2 show that for most of the time between 1997 and 2015 the PRI could comfortably reach the qualified majority required by Article 135 (ie 334 votes out 500 and 86 out of 128 in the Chamber of Deputies and the Senate, respectively) only by cooperating with the PAN. That changed from 2015 to 2024 as the party system became more fragmented. As shown in Table 4.2, in that period, the biggest party in the Chamber of Deputies needed to cooperate with at least two parties in the opposition to meet the qualified majority required by the amendment rule. Similarly, from 2018 to 2024 MORENA, as the biggest party in the Senate, needed the cooperation of at least two other parties. As seen in figure 4.1, despite party fragmentation both Peña Nieto's PRI and López Obrador's MORENA were well able to access

[16] ibid 232.

[17] María Amparo Casar and Ignacio Marván (eds), *Reformar sin Mayorías. La dinámica del cambio constitucional en México: 1997–2012* (Penguin Random House 2014) 13–85; George Tsebelis and Edwin Atilano-Robles, 'Why Are Constitutional Amendments in Mexico So Frequent?' (2024) 16 Journal of Politics in Latin America 300.

[18] The process of political pluralization started in 1988. Before then, the PRI had won over 70 per cent of seats in the Chamber of Deputies. Casar and Marván (n 6) 31, graph 2.

Table 4.1 Distribution of seats in Congress 1997–2015

Number of seats in the Chamber of Deputies 1997–2015							
Legislature	**Period**	**PAN**	**PRI**	**PRD**	**Rest**	**PRI+PAN**	**PRI+PAN pct**
LVII	1997–2000	122	239	125	14	361	72.2
LVII	2000–2003	206	211	50	33	417	83.4
LIX	2003–2006	152	224	96	28	376	75.2
LX	2006–2009	206	106	127	61	312	62.4
LXI	2009–2012	143	237	69	51	380	76
LXII	2012–2015	114	213	101	72	327	65.4
Number of seats in the Senate 1997–2015							
Legislature	**Period**	**PAN**	**PRI**	**PRD**	**Rest**	**PRI+PAN**	**PRI+PAN pct**
LVII	1997–2000	33	77	16	2	110	85.9
LVIII–LIX	2000–2006	46	60	16	6	106	82.8
LX–LXI	2006–2012	52	33	26	17	85	66.4
LXII	2012–2015	38	52	22	16	90	70.3

Source: George Tsebelis and Edwin Atilano-Robles, 'Why Are Constitutional Amendments in Mexico So Frequent?' (2024) 16 Journal of Politics in Latin America 300.

the amendment mechanism. The former, as will be seen, largely thanks to the *Pacto por México* between PRI, PAN, and PRD discussed in Section III; while the latter was able to do so thanks to stable coalition it formed with PT, PVEM, and PES, but also thanks to the cooperation of the PRI, PAN, and PRD. What is more, both presidents and their predecessors were not just able amend the constitution, but the processes through which the constitution was amended were characterized by fast-track approvals and the lack of opposition by state legislatures.

Fast-track approvals in Congress

In this section, I analyse the 120 constitutional amendment processes that took place from 1997 to July 2024. To carry out this analysis, I measured the time it takes (in days) for a constitutional amendment bill to go through each of the relevant steps and stages of the constitutional amendment process provided by Article 135 and to comply with the applicable congressional rules before being adopted. Table 4.3 shows the different steps of the constitutional amendment process.

Table 4.2 Distribution of seats in Congress 2015–24

Number of seats in the Chamber of Deputies 2015–24											
Legislature	**Period**	**PAN**	**PRI**	**PRD**	**PT**	**PVEM**	**PES**	**MORENA**	**Rest**	**PAN+PRI**	**PRI+PAN pct**
LXIII	2015–2018	104	199	50	0	38	11	49	39	303	61.8
		PAN	**PRI**	**PRD**	**PT**	**PVEM**	**PES**	**MORENA**	**Rest**	**MORENA+Allies**	**MORENA+Allies pct**
LXIV	2018–2021	77	47	12	42	11	23	250	29	326	66.4
LXV	2021–2024	112	68	12	34	39	0	200	34	273	54.7
Number of seats in the Senate 2015–24											
Legislature	**Period**	**PAN**	**PRI**	**PRD**	**PT**	**PVEM**	**PES**	**MORENA**	**Rest**	**PAN+PRI**	**PRI+PAN pct**
LXIII	2015–2018	34	55	6	19	5	0	0	9	89	69.5
		PAN	**PRI**	**PRD**	**PT**	**PVEM**	**PES**	**MORENA**	**Rest**	**MORENA+Allies**	**MORENA+Allies pct**
LXIV	2018–2021	25	13	3	6	6	4	61	9	77	60.2
LXV	2021–2024	19	13	4	6	8	4	57	17	75	58.6

Source: Prepared by the author, working with data from Sistema de Información Legislativa. Note: MORENA allies are here understood as PT, PVEM and PES.

Table 4.3 Steps of the constitutional amendment process

1	Presentation of the amendment bill to either of the chambers of Congress. (The chamber where the amendment proposal is initially presented is known as the chamber of origin. The chamber that studies the amendment subsequently is known as the reviewing chamber.) In this step, the *Junta de Coordinación Política* of the relevant chamber intervenes to determine whether a proposal is included in the legislative work schedule. If included, the proposal is allocated to the relevant legislative committees for assessment.
2	A legislative committee(s) report assessing the proposal is produced to recommend adoption, or adoption with modifications (hereinafter committee report). The committee report is the result of a process that mirrors the proceedings in the floor. The committee(s) votes on the report; if passed, it is submitted to the floor of the chamber of origin.
3	Once on the floor of the chamber, proposals may only be deliberated and voted on after two readings of the committee report in two consecutive sessions, one of which may be obviated if so decided by the floor. Once the two-readings requirement is met, the floor opens for deliberation and discussion of the report by the chamber of origin.
4	The floor votes the proposal which may be passed with or without modifications or dismissed if it fails to meet the qualified majority requirement. If modified, the report returns to the legislative committee(s) to incorporate the modifications and thereafter a new report is presented to the floor. If passed, the amendment proposal is submitted to the reviewing chamber.
5	Reception of the amendment proposal at the reviewing chamber. The proposal is processed in the same way as in the chamber of origin.
6	The legislative committee report containing the amendment proposal as approved by the chamber of origin is deliberated in the relevant committee(s). The committee(s) votes on the report. If passed, it is submitted to the floor of the reviewing chamber. The report may recommend the adoption of the amendment with or without modifications.
7	Once on the floor of the chamber, proposals may only be deliberated and voted on after two readings of the committee(s) report in two consecutive sessions, one of which may be obviated if so decided by the floor. Once the two-readings requirement is met, the floor opens for deliberation and discussion of the report.
8	The floor votes to pass the amendment in question with or without modifications. If the qualified majority is not met, the bill is dismissed. If the floor votes to pass the proposal with modifications, the bill returns to the chamber of origin to repeat steps 2–4.
9	If approved by both chambers of Congress, the bill is submitted for ratification by the majority of the 32 state legislatures.
10	If the majority of state legislatures ratify the amendment, a formal declaration of adoption is issued (*declaratoria de reforma constitucional*).
11	Once adopted, the amendment is submitted to the president for publication.
12	Publication in the government gazette, the *Diario Oficial de la Federación* (DOF). With this publication, amendments are officially enacted.

Source: Prepared by the author, working with Articles 72 and 135 of the Constitution; Ley Orgánica del Congreso General de los Estados Unidos Mexicanos, Reglamento de la Cámara de Diputados; Reglamento de la Cámara de Senadores.

Table 4.4 Stages of the constitutional amendment process

1	The time it takes for the legislative committee(s) to present the report to the floor from the moment the amendment bill was introduced.
2	The time it takes for the full chamber to open the floor for deliberation and discussion from the moment the report is presented.
3	The time it takes to approve a legislative committee(s) report from the moment the floor is open for deliberation and discussion.
4	The time between the moment of approval in the chamber of origin and reception of the amendment bill by the reviewing chamber.
5	The time it takes for the legislative committee(s) to present the report from the moment the bill is received by the reviewing chamber.
6	Same as 2 but in the reviewing chamber.
7	Same as 3 but in the reviewing chamber.
8	The time between the submission of the of the bill for the ratification of state legislatures and adoption (*declaratoria de reforma*).
9	The time between the *declaratoria de reforma* and the enactment of the amendment.

Source: Prepared with author's own data.

These twelve steps, at the same time, form nine stages. Table 4.4 shows the different stages that the constitutional amendment process entails. Stages 1, 2, 3, 5, 6, 7, and 8 are the deliberative moments of the process. Given that committee sessions (which take place in stages 1 and 5) are public only by agreement, the only moments where as a general rule proceedings are *public* are at stages 2, 3, 6, and 7. Strictly speaking, however, in terms of the latter four stages, proper deliberation could only take place during stages 3 and 7, which is where legislators may voice their views. Stages 2 and 6 consist of formal proceedings that require two readings (*primera y segunda lectura*). In other words, given that stages 1 and 5 can take place beyond the public eye, only stages 3 and 7 can be understood as having been designed to be where heightened publicity and transparency happen. A similar logic should apply to stage 8. However, since no constitutional amendment has ever been rejected by the state legislatures, a detailed analysis of the amendment processes at that level is, for the purposes of this study, unnecessary. I will return to a broader discussion about the role of state legislatures below.

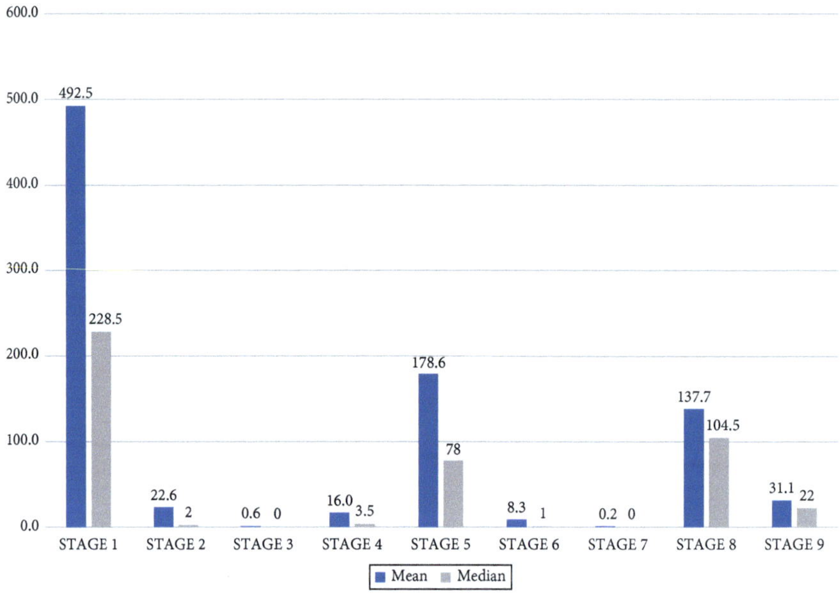

Figure 4.3 Number of days for a constitutional amendment bill to go through each stage of the amendment process.
Source: Calculated working with author's own data.

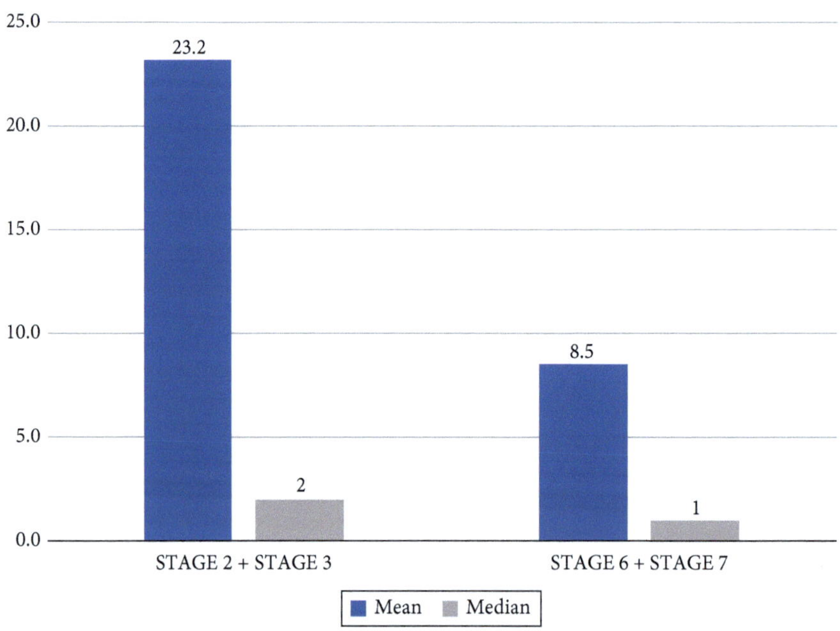

Figure 4.4 Number of days an amendment bill takes to be approved by the relevant chamber from the moment the committee report is submitted to the floor.
Source: Calculated working with author's own data.

Figure 4.3 shows stages 1–9.[19] Stages 2, 3, 6, and 7 show the time a legislative committee report on an amendment proposal spends on the floor of each chamber of Congress before being passed. These stages, at the same time, are supposed to be where the deliberative part of the amendment process takes place. Figure 4.4 shows the total number of days a legislative committee report spends on the floor of each chamber before being passed (ie stage 2 plus stage 3; and stage 6 plus stage 7).

In contrast with what the theory tells us, amendment processes' timeframes of approval in Congress between 1997 and 2024 show a *fast-track* trend in the approval of the legislative committee reports, which is manifested in very short public deliberations. The median number of days the chamber of origin and the reviewing chamber take to approve a committee report from the moment it is presented to the floor is 2 and 1, respectively (see Figure 4.4). More specifically, stages 3 and 7 in Figure 4.3 show the time an amendment proposal spends being *actively* deliberated before being voted—that is, these stages measure how long it takes for the relevant chamber to approve a committee report from the moment the floor opens for deliberation and discussion of the proposal. Crucially, the data shows that the median number of days that both the chamber of origin and the reviewing chamber take to approve a committee report from the moment the floor opens for deliberation and discussion of a proposal is 0. This means that committee reports are generally approved on the same day the floor opens for deliberation.

As noted in Table 4.3, if the proposal is modified by the reviewing chamber, the proposal goes back to the chamber of origin to follow steps 2–4. From the total 120 amendment procedures included in the data set, in thirty-eight occasions a proposal was modified by the reviewing chamber. In this subset, the median number of days the relevant chamber takes to approve a committee report from the moment it is presented to the floor is 1. Notably, the median number of days the relevant chamber takes to approve a committee report from the moment the floor opens for discussion is 0. Additionally, in seven instances during the process of approving a modified proposal, the chamber of origin approved additional modifications, which in turn had to be approved by the reviewing chamber. In these cases, the trend repeats: the median number of days the relevant chamber takes to approve a committee report from the moment it is presented to the floor is 0. The median and the average number of

[19] I calculated the median to control for outliers.

days it takes for the relevant chamber to approve a report from the moment the floor opens for discussion is 0.

The fast-track trend identified here suggests that legislative committee reports are presented when the needed majorities are secured. Once the legislative committee presents its report to the chamber in question, in the vast majority of cases the 'deliberation' and approval happen on the same day the floor opens for deliberation and discussion. Based on this findings, it is clear that constitutional amendments are the result of rash approvals rather than careful consideration. From this point of view, floor sessions where public legislative deliberation is supposed to take place are hardly more than rubber-stamping ceremonies.

Stages 1 and 5, on the other hand, show the time it takes for the legislative committee to present the report to the floor of the relevant chamber since the reception of the bill. The median numbers of days that an amendment bill spends in the legislative committee at the chamber of origin and the reviewing chamber are 228.4 and 78, respectively. Note that these numbers do not necessarily correspond to the time a bill is under study by the committee. More research is needed to determine the time it effectively takes to draft a committee report and how long deliberations are in the legislative committees. Yet, the sharp difference between stages 1 and 5 and stages 2, 3, 6, and 7 suggests that constitutional bargaining and decision-making take place beyond the public eye.

Moreover, when looking at stages 1–9—that is, the time it takes to enact an amendment, measured from the moment the initiative is presented to publication—the median number of days is 625.7. One could think that such extended periods involve careful consideration and deliberation of amendment proposals. Such a conclusion, however, would be mistaken. Even though the amendment processes (from initiative to publication) may go beyond legislative periods, the *fast-track* trend in public deliberation and voting is present in the vast majority of cases, as shown by the median number of days in the deliberate stages (ie stages 2, 3, 6, and 7) of the process discussed above. Other than careful consideration and thoughtful deliberation, explanations for amendment proposals going beyond legislatures likely have to do with the distribution of power in Congress, or whether a given proposal was convenient for the parties cooperating. Political interests, needs, and priorities vary with time and so does the will of parties to cooperate with each other to push amendments through.

The amendment to Article 88 of the Constitution, which established a framework to grant the president the power to leave the country for up to seven days without previous approval of Congress, is a case in point.[20] Even though it took several years for it to be enacted, counting from the moment the amendment initiative was presented, the whole process at the Congress level (ie both chambers) took place on the same day the legislative committee report was presented to the full chamber of origin.[21] Both President Ernesto Zedillo and President Vicente Fox faced obstacles put by Congress to travel abroad to fulfil their foreign policy agendas. In 2002, the Fox administration proposed a constitutional amendment on the issue, but the PRI and PRD representatives strongly defended the matter as something Congress should have the power to decide.[22] The initiative remained on standby until June 2008 when, already under Felipe Calderón's administration, the amendment was passed in *both chambers* of Congress (by 295 votes in the Chamber of Deputies and 77 in the Senate) the very next day the legislative committee presented its report to the floor in the Chamber of Deputies and was ratified by seventeen state legislatures on 13 August.[23]

The previous unwillingness of PRI and PRD representatives to pass the amendment, followed by its expedited adoption, suggests that something happened that made direct entrenchment suddenly available. During the Fox administration, the PRI had more seats than the PAN (the party in government) in the Chamber of Deputies—which gave the PRI more leverage to determine the constitutional agenda. This changed in 2006–09, when after the 2006 general election the PRI representation in Congress shrank[24] and the PAN retained the presidency. The new PAN administration was interested in bringing its policy agenda forward and although the PRI had lost strength in Congress, it kept its strongholds at the local level. Thus, should the PAN want to reform the Constitution, a coalition with the PRI remained necessary.[25] In

[20] Constitution of 1917, as amended, Art 88, Diario Oficial de la Federación (29 August 2008).

[21] Constitution of 1917, as amended, Art 88, Diario Oficial de la Federación (28 May 2021). The article establishes the following: 'The President of the Republic can leave the national territory for up to seven days, previously notifying his reasons to the Senate or the Permanent Committee, as applicable, as well as the outcome of his activities. For absences larger than seven days, the President shall request a permit from the Senate or the Permanent Committee.' (Translation by Costitute Project.)

[22] Andrea Becerril, 'Descartan Senadores y Diputados Modificar el Artículo 88 para Facilitar los Viajes de Fox' *La Jornada* (13 April 2002) <www.jornada.unam.mx/2002/04/13/006n1pol.php?print ver=0> accessed 11 October 2024.

[23] Cámara de Diputados, 'Reformas Constitucionales por Periodo Presidencial' <www.diputados.gob.mx/LeyesBiblio/ref/cpeum_per.htm> accessed 11 October 2024.

[24] In the Chamber of Deputies the PAN representation soared from 152 to 206 and the PRD from 96 to 127, while the PRI decreased from 224 to 106. See Table 4.1.

[25] The relationship with the PRD (the second biggest majority in the Chamber of Deputies) was rather complicated. The general election of July 2006, the first general election after the transition to democracy in 2000, soured the relationship between the PRD and the PAN. PRD candidate Andrés Manuel López Obrador lost the election to PAN candidate Felipe Calderón Hinojosa by a very small margin of fewer

fact, this reform was passed by the votes of the PRI and PAN in both chambers of Congress.[26] Looking at this case individually, the cooperation of the PRI to pass an amendment that only benefited the PAN would not make sense. However, as will be seen later in this chapter, the PRI had also been bringing forward its agenda (eg, the amendments related to the reallocation of the power to adjudicate inter-state border disputes regulated in Article 76).

An alternative explanation to the findings presented in this section could be that fast-track processes may be the result of the fact that the constitutional amendments being adopted are mostly not substantive or significant. Or one could argue that perhaps the majority of cases in which fast-track processes take place are related to 'statutory' constitutional provisions which due to their nature require regular updates.[27] However, looking at the subject matter and scope of constitutional reforms in the last thirty years, it is clear that this is not the case. Examples of the subject matter of amendments go from the reallocation of the power to adjudicate inter-state border disputes, to transparency and access to information, to education, to energy, to antitrust, to telecommunications, to the right to culture. The importance of the subject matter of amendments has not impeded fast-track approvals. There are extreme cases where the drafting, presentation, discussion, and approval of the legislative committee's report in both chambers happens on the same day the amendment initiative is presented. This is the case, for example, for the amendment to Article 4 of the Constitution to include the 'right to sports' and the 'right to nutritious, quality and sufficient food' in October 2011.[28] One could attribute

than 235,000 votes out of over 40 million votes (ie, roughly a 0.58% margin). Against the backdrop of a fraught electoral campaign trail that was marked by, as put by Joseph Klesner, 'lavish media spending and the use of negative attack ads [*campañas negativas*]' and such a small margin, López Obrador challenged the results before the Electoral Tribunal alleging wide-spread fraud. Additionally, he led mass rallies in Mexico city demanding a full vote recount (the rallying cry was '*voto por voto, casilla por casilla*', which can be translated into 'vote by vote, polling station by polling station'). In September of that year, the Electoral Tribunal, based on a recount of 9% of the polling stations, certified the final count and handed the victory to Felipe Calderón. See Joseph L Klesner, 'The 2006 Mexican Election and Its Aftermath: Editor's Introduction' (2007) 40 PS: Political Science & Politics 11; Joseph L Klesner, 'The July 2006 Presidential and Congressional Elections in Mexico' (2007) 26 Electoral Studies 803.

[26] The PRD parliamentary group voted against the reform in both chambers of Congress. See <http://legislacion.scjn.gob.mx/Buscador/Paginas/wfProcesoLegislativoCompleto.aspx?q=b/EcoMjefuFeB6DOaNOimNPZPsNLFqe0s7fey1FqricrFd7Va3YSUY/21obIl3mqS2AzZtJ1gyK3A6ET+CAqGw==> accessed 11 October 2024.

[27] Tom Ginsburg and James Melton, 'Does the Constitutional Amendment Rule Matter at All? Amendment Cultures and the Challenges of Measuring Amendment Difficulty' (2015) 13 International Journal of Constitutional Law 686, 711.

[28] Additionally, there are more extreme cases like the Energy Reform of 20 December 2013 and the amendment to give the federal Congress the exclusive power to allocate competences on criminal matters related to enforced disappearance enacted on 10 July 2005, where stages 1– 7 of the amendment process took only two days.

the expedited process to the fact that, for politicians, including socioeconomic rights in the Constitution could mean nothing more than scoring political points by adopting what could hardly be unpopular measures. However, structural amendments are not exempted from such trends. Take, for example, the Energy Reform of 2013. There, the Constitution was amended to open the oil industry to private and foreign companies after almost eight decades since the nationalization of the industry in 1938.[29] After the initiative was presented, it took seventy-two hours for both chambers of Congress to pass it and seven days to get the approval of the majority of state legislatures.

The Energy Reform was part of the *Pacto por México* (Pact for Mexico), a written agreement between President Peña Nieto and the (not democratically elected) presidents of the PRI, PAN, and PRD—later joined by the Partido Verde Ecologista de México (PVEM)—which went public the day after the former took office on 1 December 2012. The pact, which will be examined in more detail below, ensured that these political parties would respectively vote in favour of several constitutional reforms in Congress. Such an expedited process—despite the complexity of the amendment—reflects the absence of thorough and considered scrutiny by Congress and the state legislatures. What is more, the deal made between the heads of the political parties, in practice, raises normative questions about the role of popularly elected representatives in Congress and their independence in relation to their party leaders. In other words, what is the purpose of electing representatives if they are ready to do as they are told by individuals who are not democratically elected? The Energy Reform suggests a greater degree of centralization of decision-making in that the needed majorities were secured even before activating Article 135.

Against this backdrop, given that since 1988 no political party has had the needed majority to amend the Constitution on its own, the fast-track trend suggests two things: on the one hand, real interparty negotiations and deliberation about the scope and nature of amendments do not take place on the floor of the two chambers of the legislative body but behind closed doors. On the other hand, the difference between stages 1 and 5 compared with 3 and 7 suggests a high degree of centralization in constitutional decision-making: decisions are not made by the legislative body in charge but by smaller groups (eg by popularly elected representatives who are members of the legislative commissions

[29] See Juan Montes, Laurence Iliff, and David Luhnow, 'Mexico Congress Passes Historic Energy Bill' *Wall Street Journal* (12 December 2013) <www.wsj.com/articles/SB10001424052702303932504579254013051981266> accessed 11 October 2024; Dan Molinski and Anthony Harrup, 'Mexican Government Presses Ahead With Energy Overhaul' *Wall Street Journal* (22 February 2016) <www.wsj.com/articles/mexican-government-presses-ahead-with-energy-overhaul-1456181673> accessed 11 October 2024.

or by the leadership of the parties). Given the time initiatives spend in legislative committees (stages 1 and 5) and the time it takes to approve an amendment from the moment the floor is open for deliberation (stages 3 and 7), we can assume that as a general rule: (a) the real work is done in formal and informal settings during stages 1 and 5, (b) decisions are taken in these stages, and (c) stages 3 and 7 are characterized by strong party discipline. We cannot assume the same about expedited processes like the Energy Reform (discussed in more detail in Section II), where the needed majorities were secured even before activating Article 135—which at the same time implies greater centralization of decision-making. Regardless of the degree of centralization, what we learn from these cases is that committee reports are most likely presented to the relevant floor when the needed majorities are secured. In this way, deliberations on the floor of the chambers are, at best, the public positioning of what has been already decided.

These findings speak against Lutz's prediction, as well as pervasive assumptions in the literature, regarding the quality of amendment processes based on the design of rules. The data suggests that far from ensuring public deliberation, the design of amendment rules has little effect on the quality of debate, deliberation, and transparency of constitutional amendment proposals and processes.[30] In a democracy, deliberation is normally understood as what precedes and informs a decision. At the same time, deliberation is traditionally understood to take place in the legislative body. If the decision to adopt a constitutional amendment, let alone its scope and nature, is made outside such a body by party leaders even before activating the amendment mechanism, as in the case of the Energy Reform, then it is hard to say that true legislative deliberation exists.[31] But even when it comes to the majority of cases, where needed majorities seem to be secured at the legislative committees before the proposals are submitted to the floor, it is also hard to say that authentic public

[30] For a discussion on the assumptions around the impact of amendment rules on the quality of amendment processes, see Chapter 2.

[31] This question is not only applicable to cases like Mexico but is also relevant to the whip system in parliamentary democracies like that in Ireland. The drawbacks of the whip system were already being pointed out pre-independence as the party's popularity waned. As documented by Martin O'Donoghue, Eoin MacNeill, a nationalist politician, wrote in a letter in 1916 that Irish MPs were 'hopeless . . . because no able, honest man could sell his soul to his leaders in the way in which the Irish Party rank and filer is expected to do'. The system and its critics persist to this day. In 2013, Eoghan Murphy, a Fine Gael politician, said that too strong a whip system left a TD (member of parliament) a 'legislator in name but not in practice'. Martin O'Donoghue, 'A Short History of the Party Whip System in Irish Politics' (24 April 2024) <www.rte.ie/brainstorm/2024/0424/1445249-irish-politics-party-whip-system-reform-overview> accessed 12 September 2024. For a discussion on the centralization of the Irish Parliamentary Party, see Martin O'Donoghue, *The Legacy of the Irish Parliamentary Party: In Independent Ireland, 1922–1949* (Liverpool UP 2019).

legislative deliberation exists. To be sure, one could argue that these findings are in line with what Jon Elster presents as some of the necessary steps in a constitution-making process. That is, early constitutional bargaining needs to happen privately to then be subject to substantive public deliberation.[32] Still, the Mexican case lacks the latter in that, as shown by the data, the stages where public deliberation is supposed to happen are extremely short. This suggests that real constitutional decision-making happens behind closed doors, which fails to meet the purpose of formally having a demanding process that is supposed to secure transparent and deliberative processes.

James Fearon has stressed the importance of public deliberation for the legitimacy of political decisions. In his view, public deliberation makes it necessary to 'put on the table the various reasons and arguments that different individuals had in mind, and thus to ensure that no one could see the result as arbitrary rather than reasonable and justifiable'.[33] It also helps losers understand whether they should treat a decision as legitimate; it allows them to determine whether the majority thought of and carefully weighed the minority's arguments against it.[34] Publicity is necessary because argumentation is different in private and public settings. In public settings, politicians have to speak in terms of principles rather than plain bargaining. Fast-track processes preclude the possibility of knowing the reasons and arguments that were considered to justify the need for amendments. In this way, as will be discussed in Chapter 7, in the CPER, transparency suffers because it is very difficult (if not impossible) to scrutinize decisions.

[32] See Jon Elster, 'Deliberation and Constitution Making' in Jon Elster and Adam Przeworski (eds), *Deliberative Democracy* (CUP 1998) 97, 111 (arguing, 'the effect of an audience is to replace the language of interest by the language of reason and to replace impartial motives by passionate ones. The presence of a public makes it especially hard to appear motivated merely by self-interest. Even if one's fellow assembly members would not be shocked, the audience would be. In general, the civilizing force of hypocrisy is a desirable effect of publicity' (citation and emphasis omitted).

[33] James D Fearon, 'Deliberation as Discussion' in Jon Elster and Adam Przeworski (eds), *Deliberative Democracy* (CUP 1998) 62.

[34] See ibid. On the importance of public discussion for the legitimacy of political decisions, Fearon maintains that 'if we all deliberated privately, the losers in a vote would not know exactly what reasons and arguments the winners had judged to be stronger in deciding the merits of the case. Thus, it would not be clear why the decision would be legitimate *for them*, if they had no grounds for understanding why the majority thought this is the most reasonable thing to do. Now, if people were assumed to be unboundedly rational calculators, then they could simply *infer from losing* a vote that a majority must have judged arguments x, y, and z to be stronger, and the effect would be the same if they had held a discussion. But if people are boundedly rational . . . then losing the vote may leave the losers perplexed as to exactly why they should view the decision as legitimate. Further without public discussion, the losers could not have a complete confidence that members of the majority had thought of and carefully weighed the minority's arguments against the decision. Hence discussion rather than private deliberation would be necessary to put on the table the various reasons and arguments that different individuals had in mind, and this to ensure that no one could see the result as arbitrary rather than reasonable and justifiable, even if not what he or she happened to see as *most* justifiable').

Lack of opposition by state legislatures: rubber-stamping constitutional amendments

After the approval of Congress, Article 135 of the Constitution requires the ratification of the majority of state legislatures. This stage of the amendment process is also supposed to be deliberative. On average, ratification takes 137.7 days. This result might sound like a reasonable time for the considered and thorough deliberation of amendment proposals. However, the most important fact to understand the role of state legislatures in the constitutional amendment process is that to this day, not once in history has an amendment been rejected at this stage of the constitutional amendment process.[35] From this point of view, the ratification stage of the process has been reduced to a rubber-stamping stage. That is to say, the historical role of state legislatures has been limited to blindly validating decisions resulting, as seen above, from processes that lack transparency and public deliberation. The rubber-stamping of constitutional amendments by state legislatures suggests a very strong centralization of constitutional decision-making. In practice, state legislatures have effectively renounced their role as veto players in the amendment process and submitted to the decisions made at the top of their parties.

The absence of opposition by state legislatures naturally raises questions about the workings of federalism in Mexico. In theory, the ratification of amendments by state legislatures in federal systems should pose a significant hurdle increasing the difficulty of formal constitutional change.[36] However, state legislatures in Mexico have not been characterized by making efforts to challenge federal policies, even in cases when their own powers are formally restricted or undercut. Indeed, Article 73, the constitutional provision establishing the federal Congress' exclusive legislative powers, has been amended eighty-five times since 1917,[37] which makes it the most amended article in the Constitution. To be sure, the amendment trend concerning Article 73 has been one of centralization. Article 124 of the Constitution reserves residual powers to the States. It follows that any power added to Article 73 originally

[35] Casar and Marván (n 17) 38, fn 30.

[36] More research is needed to better understand the real impact of the involvement of sub-national units in levels of constitutional rigidity. For a study suggesting that sub-national units have a limited impact on the difficulty of federal constitutional amendment processes, see Andrea Katz and Dominque Alvarado-Holden, 'Constitutional Change and Federalism' in Oran Doyle and Mariana Velasco-Rivera (eds), *Edward Elgar Research Handbook on Constitutional Change* (Edward Elgar Publishing forthcoming).

[37] Constitution of 1917, Art 73, as amended, Diario Oficial de la Federación (28 May 2021). Data from Cámara de Diputados, 'Reformas Constitucionales por Artículo' <www.diputados.gob.mx/LeyesBiblio/ref/cpeum_art.htm> accessed 17 September 2024.

belonged to them. Article 73 has been increasingly aggrandized to give the federation the power to regulate a wide range of policy sectors and industries and decide the terms based on which States and municipalities should operate within those areas.[38] For instance, in 1942, Article 73-XXIX was introduced to empower the federal Congress with fiscal authority on sectors and industries such as foreign trade, electricity, tobacco, gasoline, and beer and to establish a revenue-sharing system (to be specified in secondary law) over that income.[39] Said article has gone from a relatively small one listing such areas and industries[40] to twenty-six sections.[41] The latter cover a wide variety of policy sectors and industries such as education, health, urban planning, tourism, access to information, data protection, elections, fishing, and aquaculture.[42]

Against this backdrop, the historical trend of the participation of state legislatures in constitutional amendment processes is not surprising. Assuming the presence of strong party discipline across all levels of government, the absence of opposition by state legislatures reveals the power the PRI retained after losing the presidency in 2000. Between 2000 and 2015, the PRI retained control of the majority of States: in 2000, the PRI governed nineteen states; seventeen in 2003, eighteen in 2009, and twenty-one in 2012.[43] Such a dominant position meant the PRI remained the most powerful actor in the context of formal constitutional change: without its cooperation, no constitutional

[38] José María Serna de la Garza, *The Constitution of Mexico: A Contextual Analysis* (Hart Publishing 2013) 139–40; Raúl Manuel Mejía Garza and Laura Patricia Rojas Zamudio, *Federalismo(s): El rompecabezas actual* (Fondo de Cultura Economica 2018).

[39] Constitution of 1917, Art 73, sec XXIX, as amended, Diario Oficial de la Federación (24 October 1942).

[40] In 1942, Art 73, sec XXIX consisted of a list of five items, one of which contained a list of six items and a two-sentence paragraph.

[41] Constitution of 1917, Art 73 sec XXIX, as amended, Diario Oficial de la Federación (28 May 2021).

[42] Perhaps the starkest example of the States' willingness to relinquish their autonomy is the forgoing of their fiscal authority. Díaz-Cayeros has shown that Mexico's revenue authority centralization shows levels of centralization found in many unitary states. Mexico's fiscal federalism is based on what has been described as 'a massive abdication of power': the *Sistema de Coordinación Fiscal* (System of Fiscal Coordination). Such a system, which strictly speaking has no constitutional basis but has been interpreted as contained in the implicit powers of the federal Congress clause, is based on the *Pactos de Coordinación Fiscal*, which are written agreements whereby the States surrendered their authority to collect and control taxes in exchange for transfers under different modalities by the federal government—chiefly *participaciones*, which are unconditional, and *aportaciones*, which are discretional. Alberto Díaz-Cayeros, *Federalism, Fiscal Authority, and Centralization in Latin America* (CUP 2006) 4; Juan F González Bertomeu, 'Constitutional Politics of Federalism in Latin America' in Mark Tushnet and Dimitry Kochenov (eds), *Research Handbook on the Politics of Constitutional Law* (Edward Elgar Publishing 2023) 237; Francisca Pou-Giménez, 'The Constitution of Mexico' in Conrado Hübner Mendes, Roberto Gargarella, and Sebastián Guidi (eds), *The Oxford Handbook of Constitutional Law in Latin America* (OUP 2022) 220; Tulia Gabriela Falleti, *Decentralization and Subnational Politics in Latin America* (CUP 2010) 221.

[43] Leticia Robles, 'PRI Perdió Control de 54% Del País; Tenemos Que Saber Qué Pasó: Beltrones' *Excélsior* (7 June 2016) <www.excelsior.com.mx/nacional/2016/06/07/1097284> accessed 26 September 2024.

amendment could pass. In this way, the constitutional amendment rate shows that the PRI did not lose its power to determine the country's constitutional fate until 2016 when, for the first time since its founding, it lost control of the majority of the territory, being able to keep the governorship of fifteen states only.[44] Since then, the PRI's territorial power steadily decreased to the benefit of MORENA and its allies. As a result of MORENA's landslide victory in the general election of 2018, in addition to winning the presidency, it won control of nineteen state legislatures[45] and five out of the nine governorships that were up for grabs. After the elections of 2024, MORENA territorial power extended to twenty-four governorships and to being the dominant party in twenty-seven state legislatures.[46] Thus, there is no reason to believe that the rubber-stamping role of state legislatures will change any time soon.

The rubber-stamping role of state legislatures in the amendment process does not mean that all state legislatures always agree with what is decided at the Congress level. There are records showing cases where a handful of state legislatures have voted against ratification of (eventually adopted) amendments. For instance, legislative records show that between 1997 and 2017, there were three occasions (2007, 2008, and 2013) in which state legislatures voted against the adoption of an amendment: in 2007, the legislature of Coahuila voted against the electoral reform establishing a system to distribute airtime for political campaigns; in 2008, the legislature of Querétaro voted against an amendment to Article 116 adding an age requirement to be a state governor; and finally, in 2013, the legislatures of Michoacán, Morelos, Oaxaca, and Zacatecas voted against an amendment to Article 24 that defined the concept of 'freedom of worship' as the 'freedom of ethical convictions, conscience and religion' and forbid acts of public worship with political purposes.[47] Although one could

[44] ibid ibid.

[45] Esther Sánchez, 'Morena Es Mayoría En 19 de 26 Congresos Locales' *El Universal* (Mexico, 4 July 2018) <www.eluniversal.com.mx/estados/mayoria-de-morena-en-19-de-26-congresos-locales> accessed 26 September 2024.

[46] Tom Phillips and David Agren, 'Mexico Election: Historic Landslide Victory for Leftist AMLO' *The Guardian* (2 July 2018) <www.theguardian.com/world/2018/jul/02/mexico-election-leftist-amlo-set-for-historic-landslide-victory> accessed 26 September 2024; Carlos S Maldonado, 'Morena, el "Tsunami" Político de México: De Dominar 4 a 24 Estados en Seis Años' *El País México* (3 June 2024) <https://elpais.com/mexico/elecciones-mexicanas/2024-06-03/morena-el-tsunami-politico-de-mexico-de-dominar-4-a-24-estados-en-seis-anos.html> accessed 26 September 2024; Sugeyry Gándara, 'Conquistan Más Congresos: Morena y Aliados Ya Son Mayoría En 27 Legislaturas Estatales, Claves Para El "Plan C"—SinEmbargo MX' *Sin Embargo* (14 June 2024) <www.sinembargo.mx/14-06-2024/4513193> accessed 26 September 2024.

[47] See Cámara de Diputados, 'Proceso Legislativo Reforma Constitucional 26 de septiembre de 2008 (requisitos para ser gobernador)' <www.diputados.gob.mx/LeyesBiblio/proceso/lx/113_DOF_26sep08.pdf> accessed 25 September 2024; Cámara de diputados, 'Proceso Legislativo Reforma Constitucional 13 de noviembre de 2007 (reforma electoral)' <www.diputados.gob.mx/Leye

read these episodes as a positive sign of the willingness of state legislatures to act independently and be a check on power in constitutional amendment processes, the fact is that, historically, they have never represented a real obstacle to the adoption of amendments. The practical implication of this situation is that once both chambers of Congress have reached the required majorities, the vote of state legislatures to adopt a constitutional amendment is a given. To this day, state legislatures pose no threat to those wanting to access direct political entrenchment. Just like ordinary legislation, constitutional amendments are practically enacted once both chambers of Congress have passed it.

In sum, against the backdrop of an increasing number of constitutional amendments, fast-track processes and rubber-stamping ratification are two factors that help explain why in the context of changing political conditions from a hegemonic party to a multi-party system, the amendment mechanism remained available in Mexico's economy of constitutional change. Both fast-track processes in Congress and the rubber-stamping of proposed amendments at the state level suggest that constitutional decision-making is highly centralized (in the best-case scenario, decisions are made behind closed doors in the legislative commissions[48]) which, in the context of a multi-party system, would not be possible without cross-party deal-making ability and strong party discipline.

III. Tracking Cross-Party Entrenchment

This section seeks to illustrate the bargaining and horse-trading logic behind constitutional amendments. In so doing, I look at different reform processes to shed light on how political parties have entrenched their interests and agendas. Since 1988, one can find at least three trends: (i) cross-party cooperation to fulfil separate policy agendas; (ii) the proliferation of independent agencies giving Congress, especially the Senate, a role in the appointment processes; and (iii) low politics amendments.

sBiblio/proceso/lx/055_DOF_13nov07.pdf> accessed 25 September 2024; Cámara de diputados, 'Proceso Legislativo Reforma Constitucional 19 de julio de 2013 (libertad de culto como "libertad de convicciones éticas, de conciencia y de religión" restringe actos de culto público con fines políticos)' <www.diputados.gob.mx/LeyesBiblio/proceso/cpeum/CPEUM_209_DOF_19jul13.pdf> accessed 25 September 2024.

[48] As we will see in the next section with the *Pacto por México*, this is not always the case.

Cross-party cooperation to fulfil separate policy agendas: the *Pacto por México*

This trend of amendments responds to constitutional bargaining across time. Apart from striking deals regarding the content of particular amendments, parties' deal-making ability includes the possibility of making agreements regarding big policy issues according to their individual agendas. That is, party X agrees to vote in favour of passing an amendment party Y wants; in exchange, party Y votes in favour of an amendment party X wants. These mechanics are beneficial to all as all relevant parties are, eventually, able to access direct political entrenchment. I will illustrate this trend through a discussion of the amendments adopted between December 2012 and 2017 which can only be understood in the context of the *Pacto por México*.

The *Pacto por México*, as noted earlier, was a written agreement between President Peña Nieto and the (non-democratically elected) leaders of the PRI, PAN, and PRD. The agreement was signed the day after Peña Nieto took office on 1 December 2012. Just like six years before, the presidential election was highly competitive and not free from electoral corruption scandals. With 38 per cent of the vote, visible social unrest against his presidency, and without a majority in neither of the chambers of Congress, Peña Nieto needed to legitimize his office. Entering into a cross-party agreement to bring forward structural reforms that were portrayed as essential to finally move Mexico towards progress was the perfect means to that end. The pact and the amendments achieved positive international coverage,[49] perhaps proving to the government they had made the right choice at least in terms of optics. In February 2014, Peña Nieto appeared on the cover of *TIME* magazine with the legend, 'Saving Mexico. How Enrique Peña Nieto's sweeping reforms have changed the narrative in his narco-stained nation'.[50] The PRI succeeded in selling the party as a brand-new one, far from its authoritarian past.

The *Pacto por México* was negotiated between October and November 2012 by seven individuals representing the three main political parties and the presidential transition team.[51] It consisted of five big tent agreements (ie rights and liberties; economic growth, employment, and competitiveness; public safety and

[49] See eg 'Keep It Up' *The Economist* (9 August 2014) <www.economist.com/leaders/2014/08/09/keep-it-up> accessed 18 July 2024.

[50] Michael Crowley, 'TIME Magazine Cover: Saving Mexico' *TIME* (24 February 2014) <https://content.time.com/time/covers/pacific/0,16641,20140224,00.html> accessed 18 July 2024.

[51] Gustavo Madero and Santiago Creel from PAN; Jesus Zambrano and Jesus Ortega from PRD; and Luis Videgaray and Miguel Angel Osorio Chong from PRI, representing the transition team.

justice; transparency, accountability, and anti-corruption; and democratic governance) that, at the same time, translated into ninety-five specific points of agreement, from which sixty-three required a modification to the Constitution. The latter included the education reform; the energy reform; and the transformation of the federal district into a state. These three amendments, at the same time, were consistent with the three main political parties' agendas, the PRI, PAN, and PRD.

The negotiations took place behind closed doors and without prior notice to elected party members.[52] Importantly, one of the rules within the negotiating group—publicly acknowledged afterwards—was to work in a discreet manner[53] in order to 'find a common ground between the interests of the different political forces, and after reaching that point in the negotiation group, turn to their parties to build consensus and ensure the passage of the reforms'.[54] In this instance, this approach allowed for the centralization of constitutional decision-making. The negotiations aimed at striking deals first in the small group, then turning to the parties to 'build consensus' once the amendment initiatives were formally submitted to Congress.

An important feature to explain why the *Pacto* worked has to do with the distribution of power in Congress that allowed for the formation of the broad coalition behind the passage of the different amendments that comprise it. From 2000 to 2015, the PRI and PAN, if cooperating with each other, were close to having the qualified majority to amend the Constitution. Between 2012 and 2015, the PRI and PAN respectively held 214 and 113 seats in the Chamber of Deputies. That is, if working in coalition, these parties held 327 votes out of the 334 needed for the required qualified majority to amend the Constitution, assuming the attendance of all members.[55] In the Senate, between 2012 and 2018, the PRI and PAN had ninety-three seats combined; that is, seven more than the eighty-six needed to reach a qualified majority. This numerical advantage technically meant that, when working in coalition, during 2012–15 (since the Chamber of Deputies renovates every three years) these parties needed six additional votes to amend the Constitution.

One could ask: why bother entering into a process of multilevel bargaining like the *Pacto por México* if only seven additional votes were needed? We must

[52] Claudia Guerrero, 'Fraguan el Pacto durante Dos Meses' *Reforma* (Mexico, 28 November 2012).

[53] '¿Cómo Se Logró? Pacto Por México' <http://pactopormexico.org/como> accessed 9 May 2017 (rule number 6); this can now be found at <https://archive.is/PIExY> accessed 3 October 2024.

[54] ibid.

[55] Article 135 requires two-thirds of the members present in each chamber of Congress. This means that the total number of votes will vary depending on attendance. For example, in the Senate, when in full attendance, the required qualified majority is 86 out of 128, but if there is less than full attendance, the total number of votes to meet the required qualified majority will change accordingly (eg if there are 127 Senators in attendance, the required votes would be 85).

not forget we are talking about a politically plural context. Strictly speaking, the PAN had no obligation to work with the PRI. Indeed, should the former have decided to play the role of opposition and work with the PRD and smaller parties, they would have been able to block the PRI in both chambers of Congress. From that point of view, should the PRI want to bring forward its agenda, the incentives were high to seek for a stable coalition. The previous written agreement reflecting important policy items for each of the signatories made the passage of the respective amendments at different moments in time workable. In this sense, the previous written agreement served at least two separate functions. On the one hand, it gave stakeholders something to hold on to and a reason to trust each other over time by providing them with a credible commitment. On the other, the agreement had a legitimizing function. By becoming part of it, each major party legitimizes each other by giving an image of having the political will to work beyond partisan lines and collaborate with each other in favour of the country.[56] This is a golden function, particularly in a context where one or more of the relevant parties lacks credibility or is facing a legitimacy crisis. As will be seen in Chapter 6, agreements like the *Pacto por México* have played a consequential role in shaping Mexico's constitutional democracy. In the 1990s, agreements akin to the *Pacto por Mexico* that were also led by the PRI served a crucial function to legitimize the party instead of completely dislodging it after losing its hegemony, on the one hand, and to create what I call the CPER, on the other.

The way in which the *Pacto por México* was negotiated in its early stages could also be read as an example of the private bargaining that takes place in constitution-making according to Elster.[57] However, as suggested by the fast-track trend identified in this chapter, in Mexico it would be hard to argue that constitutional amendments are subject to substantive public deliberation. A case in point to illustrate the low interest legislators have in closely scrutinizing the content of amendment proposals is the fact that they have no problem publicly acknowledging that they would vote as they are told. In the context of the constitutional reform proposals that were to be presented shortly after by the signatories of the *Pacto por México*, Luis Alberto Villareal, the PAN coordinator in the Chamber of Deputies, stated:

[56] For an extensive study on the importance of collaboration within and among branches of government to protect rights and constitutional democracy, see Aileen Kavanagh, *The Collaborative Constitution* (CUP 2023).

[57] Elster (n 32).

> they [the initiatives] would come already agreed upon [. . .] even though we would be analysing them, there is a permanent will to comply with the agreements that our national chiefs and our parties have agreed upon.[58]

This public statement illustrates the general attitude of representatives vis-à-vis decisions taken by party leaders that, at the same time, facilitated the centralization of constitutional decision-making to allow swift access to the amendment mechanism. This is further illustrated by the following two examples, which were part of the *Pacto por México*: the Public Education Reform and the Energy Reform of 2013.

Education Reform of 2013

This amendment went through both chambers of Congress in three public sessions (two in the Chamber of Deputies and one in the Senate) that consisted of the official positioning of the parties without much deliberation. The different stages of the amendment process were dealt with at a remarkable speed. It took one day for two legislative committees to analyse the initiative and draft their reports and one floor session for the Chamber of Deputies to approve it. Moreover, it took only a few hours for the relevant committee in the Senate to write its report and to be approved in a plenary session.[59] As for the last stage of the amendment process, it took forty days to get the approval of twenty-three state legislatures.[60]

The public education reform can be divided into three main changes: (i) the mandatory evaluations of teachers for admission, promotion [. . .] and continuation in the professional service;[61] (ii) the constitutionalization of the Sistema Nacional de Evaluación Educativa (National System for the Evaluation of Education) and the transformation of the Instituto Nacional para la Evaluación de la Educación (National Institute for the Evaluation of Education) (INEE) into an independent agency (formerly a decentralized government agency) and its corresponding procedure to appoint the board

[58] Erika Hernández, 'Reformas por Pacto, en 2 semanas—PAN' *Reforma* (Mexico, 3 December 2012).

[59] Note that the amendment bill was sent back to the Chamber of Deputies because of modifications made to the fifth transitory article.

[60] The state legislatures giving their approval were Aguascalientes, Baja California, Baja California Sur, Campeche, Chiapas, Chihuahua, Coahuila, Colima, Durango, Guerrero, Hidalgo, Jalisco, Estado de México, Nayarit, Puebla, Querétaro, Quintana Roo, San Luis Potosí, Sinaloa, Tamaulipas, Veracruz, Yucatán, and Zacatecas. See Cámara de Diputados, 'Reformas Constitucionales por Orden Cronológico, Proceso Legislativos' (26 February 2013) <www.diputados.gob.mx/LeyesBiblio/ref/cpeum_crono.htm> accessed 11 October 2024.

[61] Constitution of 1917, Art 3-III, as amended, Diario Oficial de la Federación (26 February 2013).

members;[62] and (iii) the obligation of the State to guarantee the quality of education.[63]

Even though it was presented as a transformative reform, it did not establish anything new. Instead, the amendment directly entrenched policies that were introduced by the PAN since 2002.[64] The INEE had been created a decade before during President Fox's administration and a system of evaluation for the admission and promotion of teachers was implemented in 2008, during the Calderón administration. This system was a result of the Alianza por la Calidad de la Educación (Alliance for the Quality of Education) (ACE) between President Calderón and the head of the Sindicato Nacional de Trabajadores de la Educación (National Education Workers Union), Elba Esther Gordillo.[65] The alliance was formalized by a written agreement on 15 May 2008. Among other things, the agreement included the implementation of full-day schools, admission tests, and performance evaluations for prospective and already-serving teachers. The set of policy measures introduced in the context of the ACE was massively challenged in courts: 70,000 *amparo* suits (ie individual constitutional complaints) were filed by teachers claiming the violation of labour rights—in particular, job security as provided by Article 123-B of the Constitution. On 17 December 2012, a Circuit Court decided in favour of all teachers challenging the measure. This meant 70,000 teachers across the country would not be subject to the mandatory evaluation scheme adopted in 2008.[66] The ruling in these cases had the potential to render the policy in question completely ineffective. Even though according to *amparo* proceedings rules, decisions do not have general effects, but only benefit the claimants,[67]

[62] Constitution of 1917, Art 3, sec 9, as amended, Diario Oficial de la Federación (26 February 2013).
[63] Constitution of 1917, Art 3, sec 3, as amended, Diario Oficial de la Federación (26 February 2013).
[64] This was repeatedly stated by PAN representatives in both chambers of Congress during the amendment process. As representative Ernesto Alfonso Robledo Leal put it, 'this reform constitutionalizes public policy measures the PAN implemented in the last 12 years to achieve quality education for all'. Cámara de Diputados, 'Diario de Debates' (19 December 2012). See also Cámara de Diputados, 'Diario de Debates' (21 December 2012) <http://cronica.diputados.gob.mx> accessed 11 October 2024; Cámara de Senadores, 'Diario de Debates' (20 December 2012) <www.senado.gob.mx/64/diario_de_los_debates> accessed 13 October 2024.
[65] Secretaría de Educación Pública, 'Alianza por la Calidad de la Educación' 1-24 (2008) <www.conafe.gob.mx/transparencia1/libro-blanco/2-anexos-edu-inicial/anexo21/Alianza%20por%20la%20Calidad%20de%20la%20Educacion.pdf> accessed 11 October 2024. (Before this alliance, teachers were subject to evaluations on a voluntary basis and with different incentive schemes through the 'Programa Nacional de Carrera Magisterial' (see Secretaría de Educación Pública, 'Programa Nacional de Carrera Magisterial' <www.gob.mx/sep/documentos/antologia-de-gestion-escolar-programa-nacional-de-carrera-magisterial> accessed 13 October 2024).
[66] Octavio Velez, 'Amparan a Maestros contra Evaluación' *La Jornada* (Mexico, 17 December 2012) <www.jornada.com.mx/2012/12/17/politica/007n3pol> accessed 11 October 2024.
[67] 'Ley de Amparo, Reglamentaria de los artículos 103 y 107 de la Constitución Política de los Estados Unidos Mexicanos', Art 78, Diario Oficial de la Federación (2 April 2013).

also according to such rules, this set of cases created a binding precedent for all lower federal courts. Accordingly, any teacher who did not want to take an evaluation could potentially file an *amparo* and could be fairly certain to win in court. Two days after the Circuit Court's decision, the Chamber of Deputies passed the constitutional amendment adopting mandatory evaluation.[68]

Against this backdrop, the constitutional amendment adopting the mandatory evaluation scheme served to shield the education policy that had been brought forward by PAN administrations since 2000. In particular, it allowed the court decisions against the system of evaluation established in the context of the ACE to be overridden. In a context where there is no constitutional doctrine allowing the judicial review of constitutional amendments, its constitutionalization ensured the policy in question would continue to be implemented and shielded it from judicial scrutiny. Importantly, the amendment was naturally not framed (or understood by the public) as a move to override the relevant court decisions, even though the practical effect was precisely that. Rather, it was framed and advertised as an unprecedented effort to improve the quality of public education. Unless proven otherwise, it is clear that the Education Reform of 2013 was at least in part intended to shield PAN's widely unpopular policies from a setback in court.

Shortly after the amendment was enacted, it proved to work perfectly. In March 2013, several collective *amparos* were filed against the constitutional amendment arguing the violation of constitutional labour rights. Yet, the cases were first dismissed by district judges, then by Circuit Courts, and, finally, by the Supreme Court on the basis that the courts did not have jurisdiction to declare invalid a constitutional amendment.[69] As will be discussed in Chapter 7, the Court's non-justiciability doctrine has been likely informing the political parties and government preference for the amendment mechanism to entrench government policies, therefore contributing to the availability of the amendment mechanism in Mexico's economy of constitutional change. Although this reform may seem to be only serving the PAN's agenda, there

[68] Redacción Animal Político, '70 Mil Profes Se Amparan Contra Evaluación Universal' (Animal Político, 17 December 2012) <www.animalpolitico.com/2012/12/70-mil-profes-se-amparan-contra-evaluacion-universal> accessed 11 October 2024.

[69] See SCJN, 14 August 2013, Solicitud de Ejercicio de la Facultad de Atracción [SEFA] 222/2013; SCJN, 14 August 2013, SEFA 227/2013; SCJN, 14 August 2013, SEFA 228/2013; SCJN, 21 August 2013, SEFA 224/2013; SCJN, 21 August 2013, SEFA 225/2013; SCJN, 21 August 2013, SEFA 229/2013; SCJN, 28 August 2013, SEFA 221/2013; SCJN, 28 August 2013, SEFA 226/2013. See also La Redacción, 'Niega La Corte Amparos a Maestros Por La Reforma Educativa' *Proceso* (Mexico, 14 August 2013) <www.proceso.com.mx/350089/niega-la-corte-amparos-a-maestros-por-la-reforma-educativa> accessed 11 October 2024.

were more reforms in the pipeline. One year later, a bigger and indeed transformative reform would take place.

Energy Reform of 2013

The Energy Reform fundamentally changed Mexico's energy sector. Often referred to as the most important reform since the enactment of the Constitution of 1917, the modifications to Articles 25, 27, and 28 of the Constitution opened the industry to private and foreign investment after seventy-five years since President Lázaro Cárdenas nationalized it. Given the declining productivity of the state-owned petroleum company Petróleos Mexicanos (Pemex), there was consensus regarding the need for modernization to make it efficient, productive, and competitive. However, there was no consensus as to how such change should take place. The amendment in question was nonetheless adopted at a remarkable speed: after the amendment initiative was presented, it took seventy-two hours for both chambers of Congress to pass it and seven days to get the approval of the majority of state legislatures.

The question of the oil ownership was, and remains, particularly controversial. Amending the Constitution in this particular instance was, for the longest time, simply a good that was not available in Mexico's economy of constitutional change. This was not because of the formal rigidity of the Constitution but because the question of oil property carries significant historical and political weight in the country's constitutional culture—not to mention its importance for state finances. As Duncan Wood and Jeremy Martin put it,

> [o]il, Pemex and national sovereignty are intricately connected. [. . .] President Cárdenas's historic decision imbued citizens of Mexico with a sense of ownership of the nation's oil and a fervent shared desire to keep Pemex in state hands. For years, oil—and specifically, the constitutional elements associated with it—was a third-rail political issue. No politician dared touch it, and the arrangement had developed quite favorably for the federal coffers.[70]

The conundrum was that constitutional constraints needed to be lifted to allow Pemex to collaborate with foreign companies to be able to exploit oil resources in deep waters and boost its productivity, but it was politically impossible to

[70] Duncan Wood and Jeremy Martin, 'Of Paradigm Shifts and Political Conflict: The History of Mexico's Second Energy Revolution' in Duncan Wood (ed), *Mexico's New Energy Reform* (Wilson Center 2018) 19 <www.wilsoncenter.org/sites/default/files/media/documents/publication/mexicos_new_energy_reform.pdf> accessed 11 October 2024.

even suggest foreign investment. Any change appearing to reverse Cárdenas' achievement was doomed to be seen as an attempt to sell a national treasure to foreign companies.[71] The need for deep constitutional transformation of the sector came to a tipping point in 2012. In that year, the 'easy oil' in Cantarell Field sagged,[72] and the moratorium preventing international companies in the US from exploiting hydrocarbons near the Gulf of Mexico's maritime boundary drawn under the West Gap Treaty[73] was about to expire.[74] As Miriam Grunstein points out,

> the Mexican government was well aware of the significant risks it would face if the moratorium were to end before Pemex underwent substantial reform. Without coordinating with international companies, Pemex [would not be able to] prevent Mexican oil near the maritime boundary from flowing to U.S. territory and being exploited by the international companies operating there.[75]

In other words, the government needed to lift the constitutional constraints preventing the modernization of Mexico's energy sector, and it needed it fast. The *Pacto por México* included a commitment to bring an Energy Reform that 'maintains the property and control of the "hydrocarbons" and the property of Pemex in the hands of the Nation. At all times, the Nation will receive the totality of the hydrocarbons production'.[76] In hindsight, given Pemex's collaborative needs, such a commitment was not realistic. Yet, had it been formulated in different (and realistic) terms, the PRD would have never agreed to be part of the *Pacto por México*. Predictably, when the time came to present the reform initiatives (there were three in total), the PAN and the PRI did not honour the

[71] Duncan Wood, 'The Administration of Decline: Mexico's Looming Oil Crisis' (2010) 16 Law and Business Review of the Americas 855, 872.

[72] Jesse Bogan, 'With Easy Oil Gone, Pemex Sobers Up' *Forbes* (7 May 2009) <www.forbes.com/2009/05/07/pemex-petrobras-mexico-business-energy-oil.html> accessed 11 October 2024.

[73] 'Treaty Between the Government of the United Mexican States and the Government of the United States of America on the Delimitation of the Continental Shelf in the Western Gulf of Mexico Beyond 200 Nautical Miles', US–Mexico (9 June 2000), S Treaty Doc No 106-39.

[74] See Miriam Grunstein, 'Unitized We Stand, Divided We Fall: A Mexican Response to Karla Urdaneta's Analysis of Transboundary Petroleum Reservoirs in the Deep Waters of the Gulf of Mexico' (2011) 33 Houston Journal of International Law 345, 352 (arguing, '[the Western Gap Treaty] fully demarcated the maritime boundaries between the United States and Mexico, and it established a temporary moratorium on the exploitation of any hydrocarbons found near that maritime boundary this moratorium was originally scheduled to expire January 17, 2011, but it was recently extended to prohibit oilfield development in the "buffer zone" until at least 2014'). See also Wood (n 71).

[75] Grunstein (n 74) 354.

[76] 'Acuerdos, Pacto por México', *Compromiso* 54 <http://pactopormexico.org/acuerdos> accessed 9 May 2017.

commitment to maintain the property and control of oil exclusively in hands of the State. The PRD considered that, on the one hand, an amendment to the Constitution was unnecessary to make the oil industry productive, and instead proposed a number of legislative reforms. On the other hand, according to the PRD, given the fundamental importance of the issue, a constitutional amendment on this matter should in any case be subject to a *consulta popular* (referendum)—a mechanism that had recently been adopted (even though the secondary legislation was still yet to be enacted).[77]

Broadly speaking, both the PRI and the PAN proposed to open the industry and lift the ban on contracting with private companies[78] and transform Pemex into a 'productive state-owned company' able to compete with private companies on a level playing field. But even though the PRI and PAN had similar interests, without the PRD, the support of the PAN alone was not enough to pass the reform in both chambers of Congress. Acting in tandem, the PRI and PAN were seven votes short of passing the amendment in the Chamber of Deputies (ie they had 327 votes in total). In the end, the amendment was not passed by the vote of the three main signatories of the *Pacto por México* but by the PRI, PAN, and PVEM.

Before the adoption of the amendment, paragraphs 4 and 6 of Article 27 of the Constitution established that oil was the property of the nation and prohibited granting concessions on petroleum and solid, liquid, or gaseous hydrocarbons. Paragraph 4 of Article 28 established an exclusive right of the state to exploit the oil economic sector. After the amendment, both provisions stayed the same, except for the fact that Article 27, paragraph 7, also allowed the participation of private companies as follows:

> In the case of petroleum and solid, liquid or gaseous hydrocarbons found underneath the surface, dominion by the Nation shall be inalienable and imprescriptible, and no concessions shall be granted. In order to obtain revenue for the State and contribute to the long-term development of the Nation, the State shall explore for and exploit oil and other hydrocarbons through assignment to productive state-owned companies, or through contracts to be

[77] Armando Estrop, 'Se rompe el Pacto . . . Por la Izquierda' *Reporte Indigo* (28 November 2013) <www.reporteindigo.com/reporte/se-rompe-el-pacto-por-la-izquierda> accessed 3 November 2023.

[78] Senado de la República, LXII Legislatura, 'Dictamen de las Comisiones Unidas de Puntos Constitucionales, de Energía y Estudios Legislativos con Proyecto de Decreto por el que se Reforman y Adicionan los Artículos 25, 27 y 28 de la Constitución Política de los Estados Unidos Mexicanos' (9 December 2013) 167–68 <www.scribd.com/document/190255142/proyecto-reforma-energetica-pdf#from_embed> accessed 11 October 2024.

> executed with them or private parties, in accordance with the implementing law. To fulfill the purpose of said allocations and contracts, the productive state-owned companies may enter into contracts with private parties. In any event, subsoil hydrocarbons shall remain property of the Nation and it shall be so expressed in the allocation and contracts.[79]

Maintaining the Article 27 ban on granting concessions and the exclusive right of the State to exploit oil resources was crucial to try to lower the political costs of opening the industry to foreign companies. Additionally, the bill included twenty-one transitional provisions (containing over 6,000 words) addressing aspects that either had to be in the main text or in ordinary legislation;[80] for example, the creation of an administrative agency in charge of policing the activities in the hydrocarbon sector for industrial security and environmental protection. They also provided detailed organizational guidelines for Pemex as a productive state-owned company. These detailed organizational guidelines had a specific purpose: excluding Pemex union leader, PRI senator, long stalwart, and corruption icon[81] Carlos Romero Deschamps from the board of directors. As reported by the media, this was the condition of the PAN to fully support the amendment.[82] In another example of cross-party cooperation, the agency in charge of policing activities in the hydrocarbon sector, according to PRD senator Dolores Padierna, was created as per the request of the PVEM.[83]

Given that the amendment did remove the constitutional constraints for private and foreign investment, unsurprisingly, PRD and Partido del Trabajo (PT) senators denounced the Energy Reform as a privatizing measure and

[79] Constitution of 1917, Art 27, sec 7, as amended, Diario Oficial de la Federación (20 December 2013).

[80] For a discussion of the transitory articles of the Energy Reform, see Guillermo García Sánchez, 'The Fine Print of the Mexican Energy Reform' in Duncan Wood (ed), *Mexico's New Energy Reform* (Wilson Center 2018) 17–35 <www.wilsoncenter.org/sites/default/files/media/documents/publication/mexicos_new_energy_reform.pdf> accessed 11 October 2024.

[81] Dolia Estevez, 'The 10 Most Corrupt Mexicans of 2013' *Forbes* (3 November 2023) <www.forbes.com/sites/doliaestevez/2013/12/16/the-10-most-corrupt-mexicans-of-2013> accessed 11 October 2024.

[82] La Redacción, 'Sacan Al Sindicato de Romero Deschamps Del Consejo de Pemex' Proceso (Mexico, 9 December 2013) <www.proceso.com.mx/360011/sacan-al-sindicato-de-romero-deschamps-del-consejo-de-pemex> accessed 11 October 2024.

[83] Senator Dolores Padierna (PRD) stated: 'I wanted to speak just before Senator Ninfa Salinas from [PVEM] because this committee report is including a special budget that the former did not include. The budget is for a National Agency for the Industry's Safety, Environmental Protection and the Hydrocarbons Sector [Agencia Nacional de Seguridad Industrial y Protección del Medio Ambiente y del Sector de Hidrocarburos], which is precisely the PVEM's agency yet now to be funded with public resources. [. . .] These are the agreements, these are the negotiations, these are the costs of the Energy Reform that is going to harm the country. A few are going to win while the rest of the country will lose'). See Senado de la Republica, 'Diario de Debates' (10 December 2013) 961 <www.senado.gob.mx/64/diario_de_los_debates/documento/2572> accessed 13 October 2024.

announced their intention to sabotage the committees' sessions to prevent the approval of the committee reports to be submitted for debate. Anticipating the difficulty and foreseeable delay to agree on a text in the committees in charge of the reports, the chairs of the three Senate committees presented a pre-negotiated committee report in two different moments. These moves were easy to make because the chairs of the committees were PRI (two) and PAN (one) members. First, before the committee sessions began, Senator Penchyna (PRI) and Senator Enrique Burgos (PRI) presented a 'pre-bill' which, according to media reports, was the result of a parallel undisclosed negotiation table between the president, the PRI, and the PAN.[84] Outraged, PRD senators decided to occupy the Senate floor to prevent the committee session from proceeding. They were then persuaded to let the session take place in exchange for bringing the *Ley Federal de Consulta Popular* (Referendum Statute)[85] out of deadlock in the Chamber of Deputies and its immediate approval.[86] Yet, this agreement did not prevent them from slow-walking the committee session by presenting more than 160 modificatory motions. On 9 December 2013, after a nine-hour session and very little progress because of the numerous motions made by the PRD, the PRI provoked a tie in one of the committees to end the session and send the bill for debate.[87] After not being able to break the tie because of the absence of the fifth committee member (PAN's senator, Sonia Mendoza), the 'pre-bill' was set to be sent for debate the next day.

Subsequently, the chairs of the committees submitted a modified version of the bill. This version of the bill, submitted overnight, was clearly not reviewed or discussed by the rest of the committees' members. According to legislative records, this modification was published in the legislative gazette at 4:30 am, hours before the debate on the floor was scheduled to start at 11:30 am.[88] Naturally, no one would have been able to analyse a 300-page document before the public deliberation took place. In the end, it did not matter that the actions of the chairs of the committees were against procedural legislative

[84] Rafael Cabrera, 'PRI Consigue Que Reservas de La Reforma Energética Se Discutan Directo En El Pleno Del Senado' (Animal Político, 10 December 2013) <www.animalpolitico.com/2013/12/pri-consigue-que-reservas-de-la-reforma-energetica-se-discutan-directo-en-el-pleno-del-senado> accessed 11 October 2024.

[85] 'Ley Federal de Consulta Popular', Diario Oficial de la Federación (14 March 2014).

[86] Cabrera (n 84).

[87] In the Legislative Studies Committee, composed of five members, PRI senator Miguel Angel Chico voted in favour of a motion made by PRD senator Dolores Padierna. See Cabrera (n 84).

[88] Different senators from the PRD condemned how the legislative committee proceeded. For instance, PRD senator Angélica de la Peña affirmed: 'the government made concession to the "anti-Cárdenas" right in the middle of the night to be able to impose their political project'. See Cámara de Senadores, 'Diario de Debates' (10 December 2013) <www.senado.gob.mx/64/diario_de_los_debates/documento/2572> accessed 13 October 2024.

rules or how many modificatory motions the PRD made to delay the vote. The amendment was set to be passed by the PRI, PAN, and PVEM, which together had enough votes to reach the required two-thirds majority in both chambers of Congress. In fact, the amendment wended through both chambers of Congress in seventy-two hours,[89] and was approved by the majority of state legislatures seven days later. By 20 December 2013, the Energy Reform was already enacted.

The *Pacto por México* seemed to have fallen through after the adoption of the Energy Reform. However, the PRD eventually resumed its cooperation. This was exemplified in 2015, when Congress passed a constitutional amendment transforming the capital of the country into a State. This amendment, included in the *Pacto por México*, materialized a long-standing item on the PRD's agenda.[90]

The proliferation of independent agencies

In the last three decades, Mexico saw what has been described as a process of '*despresidencialización*' (de-presidentialization) of public administration.[91] Agencies that formerly were part of the executive branch were increasingly decentralized and turned into *órganos constitucionales autónomos* (independent agencies) (OCAs).[92] Putting aside the diverse array of functions OCAs perform (eg human rights ombudsman function, regulation of telecommunications and broadcasting services, guarantee access to public and protection of

[89] Sonia Corona, 'México Cambia su Historia Energética a Contrarreloj' *El País* (Madrid, 13 December 2013) <https://elpais.com/internacional/2013/12/12/actualidad/1386888542_011957.html> accessed 3 November 2023.

[90] Mexico City had been a PRD strong-hold for two decades. Yet, as it was not a State, its political power was rather limited—it did not have representation in the federal Congress. Although politically it was very important for the party, it did not necessarily respond to a long-standing demand of the citizens from Mexico City, as suggested by the voting turnout of 28 per cent in the election of the constituent assembly. Redacción Animal Político, 'En la CDMX Ganan Morena y el Abstencionismo (Animal Político, 6 June 2016) <www.animalpolitico.com/2016/06/en-la-cdmx-gana-morena-y-pierden-prd-e-independientes> accessed 11 October 2024.

[91] José Roldán Xopa, 'De la Desconcentración Administrativa a la Autonomía Constitucional. Los Órganos Reguladores en su Nuevo Escenario' in María del Carmen Pardo and Guillermo M Cejudo (eds), *Trayectorias de Reformas Administrativas En México: Legados y Conexiones* (El Colegio de México 2016) 439, 459; Mauricio I Dussauge Laguna, 'Organismos Constitucionales Autónomos y Reforma Administrativa En México' in María del Carmen Pardo and Guillermo M Cejudo (eds), *Trayectorias de reformas administrativas en México: Legados y Conexiones* (El Colegio de Mexico 2016) 477–521.

[92] For a study shedding light on the formation process of these bodies as a result of political struggles between different actors trying to shape them in their own interest, see Cristopher Ballinas Valdes, *Political Struggles and the Forging of Autonomous Government Agencies* (Palgrave Macmillan 2011).

privacy rights), the shared characteristic among them is the congressional participation in the appointment systems—in particular, the Senate. For the purposes of this work, this trend is important on two counts.

This trend offers a glimpse of the workings of Mexico's economy of constitutional change. The creation of these independent agencies results in a power-sharing arrangement where the major political parties gain influence in appointment processes. As Christopher Ballinas put it,

> each modification represents a new power equilibrium and not necessarily an improvement on government processes. (. . .) [The] competences and prerogatives of these agencies is not the result of a careful technical and legal assessment, but the result of political interests of those who create [the agencies].[93]

In a context where the cooperation between parties is possible, the multiple positions to fill and the staggered systems of appointments to these agencies open the possibility for horse-trading appointments on a regular basis. What is more, the constitutional amendments through which the former administrative agencies have been transformed into independent agencies have been used as a means to replace their members. This creates a great opportunity to capture these organs. This is the case, for example, for the telecommunications and education constitutional reforms of 2013, which ordered the replacement of all sitting members in the antitrust (COFECE), telecommunications (IFT), and education (INEE) agencies.[94] Similar to constitutional amendments, congressional confirmation (either in the Senate or the Chamber of Deputies—depending on the agency) requires a two-thirds majority. This means that, given the dominance of the PRI and PAN in the Senate, these two parties were in control of the appointments to all of these agencies and thus capable of entrenching their interests in the relevant policy areas. Indeed, as reported by the media, the PAN and the PRI commonly took turns to appoint

[93] Christopher Ballinas, 'El Laberinto de la Soledad de los Órganos Autónomos' (NEXOS, 1 July 2018) <www.nexos.com.mx/?p=38371> accessed 11 October 2024.

[94] The sixth and seventh transitory clauses of the telecommunications reform establish the transition regime for the COFECE and IFT. These clauses ordered the replacement of all sitting members in a period of eighty days. The education reform orders the replacement of the members of the INEE in its second transitory clause. See 'Decreto por el que se Reforman y Adicionan Diversas Disposiciones de los Artículos 60, 70, 27, 28, 73, 78, 94 y 105 de la Constitución Política de los Estados Unidos Mexicanos, en Materia de Telecomunicaciones' Diario Oficial de la Federación (11 June 2013) 2–13; and 'Decreto por el que se Reforman los Artículos 3o. en sus Fracciones III, VII y VIII; y 73, Fracción XXV, y se Adiciona un Párrafo Tercero, un Inciso d) al Párrafo Segundo de la Fracción II y una Fracción IX al Artículo 3o. de la Constitución Política de los Estados Unidos Mexicano' Diario Oficial de la Federación (26 February 2013).

their preferred candidates in exchange for future appointments. In the words of Movimiento Ciudadano (MC) senator Marta Tagle (2015–18),

> the participation of the legislative branch in appointment processes [. . .] is supposed to produce the appointment of a person that meets the legal requirements to be appointed while verifying its qualifications and guaranteeing that the appointee is not subject to any political agreement that may harm his/her independence. However, nothing of this happens in the appointment processes that take place in the Senate either because it submits to the Executive or because it looks to appoint someone close and/or committed to those who actually appointed him/her.[95]

To some extent, the proliferation of this kind of agency can be understood as a direct reaction to a Supreme Court decision in 2007 that struck down the legal reforms giving the Senate a limited role in the appointment processes of members of two administrative agencies (*órganos desconcentrados*)—that is, the power to object to the appointments made by the president.[96] Interestingly, the year following this decision marks the beginning of the trend of constitutional reforms transforming administrative agencies into independent ones. Ten years after that decision, the number of independent agencies had increased from three to ten. The policy areas include monetary policy, elections, public education, telecommunications, antitrust, access to public information, evaluation of social policy, statistics and geography, and the public prosecutor office.[97] All these areas require congressional participation, in particular of the Senate,[98] and interaction with the president in the appointment processes.[99]

[95] Marta Tagle, '#BlogTMx: Indispensable abrir las designaciones públicas' Transparencia Mexicana (19 April 2017) <www.tm.org.mx/mt-designaciones> accessed 11 October 2024. See also Jenaro Villamil, '#FiscalCarnal, el Costo de la Simulación' Proceso (Mexico, 29 November 2016) <www.proceso.com.mx/464495/fiscalcarnal-costo-la-simulacion> accessed 11 October 2024; Newsweek Mexico, 'Una Corte sin Cuotas ni Cuates' *Newsweek* (4 October 2015) <https://newsweekespanol.com/2015/10/una-corte-sin-cuotas-ni-cuates> accessed 11 October 2024; Francisco Resendiz, 'Propuesta para Cofetel, un Pago de Cuotas: Senadores' *El Universal* (Mexico, 26 June 2006) <https://archivo.eluniversal.com.mx/nacion/139934.html> accessed 11 October 2024.

[96] SCJN, 6 June 2007, Acción de Inconstitucionalidad [AI] 26/2006. See also Roldán Xopa (n 98) 452-454; Carlos Avilés and Angelina Mejía, 'Ordenan Restituir a Funcionarios de Cofetel' *El Universal* (Mexico, 15 May 2007) <http://archivo.eluniversal.com.mx/nacion/151008.html> accessed 27 May 2017.

[97] For an overview of the different bodies and the reasons that were given to justify its creation, see Irene Cuéllar, *Órganos Constitucionales Autónomos: El Porqué de su Autonomía* (Tesis de Licenciatura, CIDE 2018) 18–23.

[98] José Roldán Xopa, 'De la Desconcentración Administrativa a la Autonomía Constitucional: Los Órganos Reguladores en su Nuevo Escenario' in María del Carmen Pardo and Guillermo M Cejudo (eds), *Trayectorias de Reformas Administrativas En México: Legados y Conexiones* (El Colegio de México 2016) 258, 263.

[99] Eight out of ten appointment processes require Senate confirmation. See Tagle (n 95).

Knowing that they could not shift the appointment power balance through legal modifications without such an attempt being struck down by the Supreme Court, once again we see the relevant political parties opting for direct political entrenchment to shield their policy choices from judicial review.

The multiple agencies allow the parties to share power in that they have to negotiate appointments. José Roldán Xopa has argued that the increasing number of independent agencies is due to the mutual distrust between political actors who opt for constitutional reforms in order to secure the stability of their agreements.[100] However, as we have seen in the previous examples, parties seem to work on the opposite premise: they trust and cooperate with each other. Had they no trust in each other and no willingness to share the multiple posts created by these agencies, there would be no incentives to reform the Constitution to take the appointment power away from the president. In a context of distrust, they would prefer to maintain these agencies under presidential control—which would allow the party in power to have full control of the appointments (ie political entrenchment would operate in the same way as Balkin and Levison's partisan entrenchment theory). It is because they trusted and cooperated with each other that these reforms were possible. I will return to this point in Chapter 6.

Low politics constitutional amendments

Balkin and Levinson, in the context of a discussion around *Bush v Gore*,[101] developed a distinction between '"high politics," which involves struggles over competing values and ideologies, and "low politics," which involves struggles over which group or party will hold power'.[102] The same distinction can be applied in the context of constitutional amendments. Low politics constitutional amendments have less to do with the deepest meanings of the Constitution than with pragmatic outcomes that favour those passing the amendments. They involve strategic decisions allowing political actors to avoid being held

[100] Roldán Xopa (n 98) (arguing that 'the mutual distrust among the main political actors incentivizes an "over-constitutionalization" of agreements to guarantee their stability and as a way to guarantee such agreements would not be subject to judicial review'.)

[101] *Bush v Gore* 531 US 98 (2000).

[102] Jack M Balkin and Sanford Levinson, 'Understanding the Constitutional Revolution' (2001) 87 Virgina Law Review 1061.

accountable for acts that could potentially be brought before courts or solving conflicts that would otherwise be politically very costly.[103]

Consider, for example, the amendments to the power to adjudicate inter-state border disputes and the amendment to conditionally accept the jurisdiction of the International Criminal Court (ICC). Although they were portrayed as a means to promote a core set of values or important causes, such values and causes were at least partly instrumentalized to achieve specific questionable purposes, as explained below.

Reforms to the power to adjudicate inter-state border disputes

In 2005, a constitutional amendment eliminated the Supreme Court's power to adjudicate inter-state border disputes and transferred it to the Senate.[104] Seven years later, in December 2012, the very same articles were amended to undo the amendment of 2005.[105] The arguments that were given to justify the urgency of the original amendment made just as little sense as the arguments given to justify the second. In 2005, Congress justified the court-curbing measure under two arguments: first, that the nature of inter-state border disputes was political because no statute set up the standards of adjudication for the Supreme Court to settle this kind of conflict; and, second, that the Senate, as representative of the States, should therefore settle the relevant disputes.[106] Then, in 2012, the reasons given to justify transferring the previously mentioned power back to the Supreme Court was that the amendment of 2005 had become 'dead letter' because Congress had not issued a statute to set up standards for the Senate to settle inter-state border disputes. Accordingly, the best way to proceed was to give the power back to the Supreme Court because, as it turned out, the standards of adjudication to settle these disputes already existed in the first place as the Court had the power to settle disputes over the powers of different states since 1995. Another reason given was that since the Senate was the body representing the States, it risked having conflicts of interest.

[103] For a detailed discussion on the concept of arbitrary constitutional amendments, see Mariana Velasco-Rivera, 'Reformas Constitucionales Arbitrarias' in José Ramón Cossío Díaz and Vicente Ugalde (eds), *El Estado de Derecho en el México Contemporáneo* (El Colegio de México 2023) 51–91.

[104] 'Decreto por el que se Reforman los Artículos 46, 73-IV, 76 y 105 de la Constitución Política de los Estados Unidos Mexicanos' Diario Oficial de la Federación (8 December 2005) <www.diputados.gob.mx/LeyesBiblio/ref/cpeum_crono.htm> accessed 11 October 2024.

[105] 'Decreto por el que se Reforman los Artículos 46, 76 y 105 de la Constitución Política de los Estados Unidos Mexicanos' Diario Oficial de la Federación (15 October 2012) <www.diputados.gob.mx/LeyesBiblio/ref/cpeum_crono.htm> accessed 11 October 2024.

[106] Cámara de Diputados, 'Diario de Debates' (8 December 2005) <www.diputados.gob.mx/LeyesBiblio/proceso/cpeum/CPEUM_163_DOF_08dic05.pdf> accessed 11 October 2024.

The reasons given to justify the amendments were not only contradictory but also far-fetched. First, on both occasions it was argued that the amendments were necessary because the body in charge of settling the disputes could not act due to the lack of a statute setting general adjudication standards. Paradoxically, instead of issuing the supposedly needed statute, the legislative body in charge of doing so justified its acts based on the non-existence of the statute. Second, on both occasions it was argued that the body to which the power was being transferred was ideal to settle inter-state border disputes for the same reasons given to take the power away from them in the first place. In 2005, the Senate was the best body to settle these disputes because it represented the States; in 2012, it was not for the same reason. As for the Supreme Court, in 2005 it could not settle these disputes due to the lack of a statute setting adjudication standards; in 2012, it could do so without the special statute.

As far-fetched as these justifications may sound, this kind of arguments are not uncommon to justify the adoption of constitutional amendments in Mexico. In this case, both amendments were adopted through a fast-track procedure in Congress and no state legislature opposed. The fact that the adoption of these amendments went widely unnoticed illustrates the context of little accountability in which constitutional change takes place in Mexico. Border disputes are a live issue in Mexico that involves questions regarding who is obliged to provide services or benefits of social programmes. As such, border disputes put the communities living in those areas in situations of legal uncertainty.[107] Even though the amendments were supposedly adopted due to the urgency of solving three pending cases, the reality is that the disputes have remained unresolved since 1997.[108] In fact, it is not clear if the conflicts are going to be settled at all because there is no record showing the return of the case files to the Supreme Court. As of 2024, the last record available in the Supreme Court case files database shows the files were dispatched to the Senate in 2005 in compliance with the third transitory provision of the reform decree of the same year.[109] Notably, the transitory provisions of the reform decree of 2012

[107] 'No Son De Aquí Ni Son De Allá: Ante la Falta de Apoyo de sus Autoridades de Calakmul, Campeche, Habitantes del Ejido Santa Rosa Piden Ayuda al Gobierno de Quintana Roo' Noticaribe (20 March 2018) <http://noticaribe.com.mx/2018/03/20/no-son-de-aqui-ni-son-de-alla-ante-la-falta-de-apoyo-de-sus-autoridades-de-calakmul-campeche-habitantes-del-ejido-santa-rosa-piden-ayuda-al-gobierno-de-quintana-roo> accessed 11 October 2024.

[108] SCJN, CC 9/1997 (*Quintana Roo v Campeche*) [pending]; SCJN, CC 13/1997 (*Quintana Roo v Yucatán*) [pending]; SCJN, CC 3/1998 (*Jalisco v Colima*) [pending].

[109] Suprema Corte de Justicia de la Nación, Búsqueda Temática <www2.scjn.gob.mx/ConsultasTematica> accesed 3 October 2024.

did not order the remittance of the files back to the Supreme Court.[110] To date, the cases are still pending adjudication.

Reform to conditionally accept the jurisdiction of the International Criminal Court

Given that the adoption of the Rome Statute implied accepting the jurisdiction of an international court (ie the ICC), a question regarding whether it amounted to the surrender of state sovereignty was very much present among the international community during and after its adoption process.[111] As a response to such concerns, some countries deemed it necessary to amend their constitutions to habilitate its adoption by their national governments.[112] In Mexico, President Zedillo signed the Rome Statute towards the end of his term in September 2000. But the treaty was only ratified by the Senate (where the PRI held the relative majority of seats, ie 59 out of 128) five years later on 21 June 2005,[113] a day after the enactment of an amendment to Article 21. Passed with the cooperation of mainly the PRI and PAN, the amendment in question conditionally accepts the jurisdiction of the ICC as follows: 'The Federal Executive may accept the jurisdiction of the International Criminal Court, provided that he has obtained the Senate's approval on a case-by-case basis.'[114]

Strictly speaking, introducing an amendment to accept the jurisdiction of the ICC was not necessary because the Constitution already provided a general framework for the adoption and ratification of international treaties (ie Articles 76-I and 89-X). However, the Fox administration (2000–06) seemed to have been of the opinion that said framework did not authorize the ratification

[110] 'Decreto por el que se reforman los artículos 46, 76 y 105 de la Constitución Política de los Estados Unidos Mexicanos' Diario Oficial de la Federación (15 October 2012) <www.diputados.gob.mx/LeyesBiblio/ref/cpeum_crono.htm> accessed 11 October 2024.

[111] Leila Nadya Sadat, *The International Criminal Court and the Transformation of International Law: Justice for the New Millennium* (Transnational Publishers 2002) xi; Robert Cryer, 'International Criminal Law vs State Sovereignty: Another Round?' (2005) 16 European Journal of International Law 979, 983–88.

[112] Such is the case in France, where the Constitution was modified to introduce a provision (Article 53-2) explicitly allowing for the recognition of the jurisdiction of the ICC: 'The Republic may recognize the jurisdiction of the International Criminal Court as provided for by the Treaty signed on 18 July 1998.' This modification took place after the Constitutional Council, exercising its Article 54 powers, examined the Rome Statute to determine whether there was an incompatibility between the French Constitution and the treaty. As the Constitutional Council determined the existence of an incompatibility, Article 53-2 was introduced to resolve it. See Conseil Constitutionnel, Decision No 98-408 (22 January 1999) <www.conseil-constitutionnel.fr/en/decision/1999/98408DC.htm> accessed 11 October 2024. I thank Marie Gren for her help on this point.

[113] The Rome Statute came into force on 1 January 2006. For more information about important dates on the adoption process of the statute, see Gabriel Mario Santo Villarreal, 'La Corte Penal Internacional' (Centro de Documentación, Información y Análisis de la Cámara de Diputados 2010) <www.diputados.gob.mx/sedia/sia/spe/SPE-ISS-10-10.pdf> accessed 11 October 2024.

[114] Constitution of 1917, Art 21, as amended, Diario Oficial de la Federación (20 June 2005).

of the Rome Statute. Roughly a year after the treaty was signed, President Fox submitted a constitutional amendment initiative that sought to ensure compliance with some international instruments and to habilitate the ratification of others, in this particular case the Rome Statute.[115] The text of the proposed amendment did not make explicit reference to the ICC. Instead, it included general provisions applicable to treaties of which Mexico was a state party. In particular, the proposed text covered three points: the recognition of the jurisdiction of international courts according to the relevant treaty; an obligation to recognize and comply with international criminal procedures and rulings according to the relevant treaties; and the obligation of authorities at all levels of government to guarantee the compliance of international court rulings.[116]

Two things stand out from the adoption of this amendment to Article 21: first, the text adopted was the opposite of what President Fox's proposal intended, which illustrates the power that legislative committees (and the parties in them) may have in formal constitutional change processes. Second, even though the passage of the amendment was no exception to the fast-track trend on the approval of amendments in each of the chambers of Congress and the lack of opposition by state legislatures identified in this chapter,[117] two years passed (including a mid-term election where the membership of the Chamber of Deputies was completely renewed)[118] before the relevant legislative committees in the Chamber of Deputies (as the reviewing chamber) submitted their report to the floor. This suggests the existence of potential disagreement as to the substance of the amendment as proposed by the Senate or the ratification of the Rome Statute altogether. Yet unearthing the nature and extent of the disagreement from official records proves difficult in that the minutes of legislative committee meetings, when available, are very limited in detail.[119] In the end, the text was approved in the exact terms of the Senate's proposal.

As adopted, the text narrowed the scope of the president's proposal by making reference only to the ICC and, most importantly, it conditioned the

[115] 'Iniciativa que Reforma el Articulo 21 Constitucional referente a la Corte Penal Internacional' Sistema de Informacion Legislativa (4 December 2001) <http://sil.gobernacion.gob.mx/Archivos/Documentos/2001/12/asun_1409_20011210_742531.pdf> accessed 11 October 2024.

[116] ibid.

[117] First, the Senate passed the amendment the day after the legislative committee presented its report (14 December 2002). Then, two years later, the Chamber of Deputies passed the amendment by 347 votes the same day the legislative committee presented its report (9 December 2004). Finally, it was approved by the vote of twenty state legislatures—without opposition—on 4 May 2005 and published by the executive on 20 June, the day before the Senate's ratification of the Rome Statute. See Cámara de Diputados, 'Proceso Legislativo Reforma Constitucional 20 de junio de 2005' <www.diputados.gob.mx/LeyesBiblio/proceso/cpeum/CPEUM_161_DOF_20jun05.pdf> accessed 11 October 2024.

[118] The mid-term election took place on 6 July 2003.

[119] In this case, the minutes of the Senate's legislative committees are available online only from 2003 onwards.

acceptance of the ICC's jurisdiction to the approval of the Senate on a case-by-case basis. As noted, it is perhaps impossible to know the real motives behind the text that was adopted. Its adoption, nonetheless, sheds light on the consequential role legislative committees may play in constitutional amendment processes. From public legislative records, one learns that the joint legislative committees in the Senate, where the text that was adopted was drafted, were dominated by the PRI, and that the PAN caucus (ie the party in government) did not oppose.[120] It is also telling that after the Senate's approval, the proposal was only passed once the membership of the Chamber of Deputies was renewed after the mid-term election. This suggests how much those who drafted the approved text cared about it. The fact that the Chamber of Deputies did not consider it until it did means that modifying the text (in which case it would have had to go back to the Senate for approval) was not an option. After the renewal of the Chamber of Deputies, the proposal was approved on the same day the legislative committee report was presented to the floor.

Regarding the potential disagreement around the adoption of the Rome Statute, debates at the Senate and Chamber of Deputies' floors show that the pending ratification raised national sovereignty concerns among some legislators. For example, Senator David Jiménez González (PRI) considered that 'submitting to a jurisdiction of this nature obliges us to surrender a very important part of our sovereignty and to substantially modify our judicial system'.[121] The congressional records of the debates on the floor also show explicit statements explaining how the wording of the amendment dealt with the national sovereignty concerns while internationally sending a clear message of Mexico's true commitment to human rights.[122] In this way, the constitutional amendment served to circumvent the diplomatic costs of not ratifying, while creating a constitutional vacuum as to the status of the Rome Statute.

The congressional records also show that there were concerns about the constitutional vacuum that the amendment would create. PRD senator Demetrio Sodi pointed out the practical implications that subjecting the acceptance of the ICC jurisdiction to Senate authorization on a case-by-case

[120] As per information available at Sistema de Información Legislativa <http://sil.gobernacion.gob.mx/portal> accessed 21 August 2024.

[121] 'Proceso legislativo reforma constitucional 20 de Junio de 2005', Cámara de Senadores 'Diario de Debates' (14 December 2002) <www.senado.gob.mx/66/diario_de_los_debates/documento/1404> accessed 13 October 2024.

[122] Such is the case, for example, with the statement by PAN senator César Jáuregui Robles: 'the formula that we have found, after multiple attempts at drafting, and after being criticised and rushed by non-governmental organisations, academics and legal professionals, is a compromise that allows Mexico to access a complementary international order, but, at the same time, provides greater security for our nationals'. See ibid.

basis would have in a scenario where that court decided to exercise its jurisdiction in Mexico:

> if the government in question does not want to prosecute such crimes [at the domestic level] but that same government has to accept and approve [the jurisdiction of the ICC] [. . .] if it does not want to prosecute it in Mexico, then it would also not want it to be prosecuted at the international level.[123]

The amendment raised questions regarding the validity of the ratification of the Rome Statute by Mexico. Article 120 of the Rome Statute explicitly prohibits reservations. That is to say, every State member recognizes the jurisdiction of the ICC because the very objective of the Statute is to guarantee the enforcement of international justice, thus the creation of the ICC.[124] Some argued that the amendment could amount to an (unlawful) reservation to the Rome Statute. Representing the PRD caucus, Senator Jesus Ortega pointed out that the proposed amendment was not accepting the jurisdiction of the ICC unconditionally, and proposed instead the adoption of a text closer to President Fox's intentions.[125] The proposal was rejected and thereafter the PRD caucus refused to be present during the vote passing the proposed amendment.[126] Similarly, in the Chamber of Deputies, Francisco Amadeo Espinosa Ramos, representing the PT caucus, considered that the text as proposed

> in and of itself constitutes a reservation to the Rome Statute in that the President, with the Senate's approval, will be able to accept the jurisdiction of the ICC. Which, in turn, means that it [the jurisdiction] is not being accepted unconditionally. Instead, the President and the Senate will determine [. . .] who to subject to the ICC. For these reasons, the PT caucus considers the proposal should not be passed. Additionally, accepting the jurisdiction of the ICC [. . .] implies surrendering [our] state sovereignty to an international body, consequently, our vote will be against [the proposal].[127]

[123] ibid.

[124] The preamble of the Rome Statute states: 'The States Parties to this Statute [. . .] Determined to these ends and for the sake of present and future generations, to establish an independent permanent International Criminal Court in relationship with the United Nations system, with jurisdiction over the most serious crimes of concern to the international community as a whole [. . .] Resolved to guarantee lasting respect for and the enforcement of international justice.' See Rome Statute of the International Criminal Court (17 July 1998) UNTS 2187.

[125] PRD's caucus proposal, presented by Senator Jesús Ortega Martínez, reads as follows: 'The Mexican State fully recognizes the complementary jurisdiction of the International Criminal Court under the terms and conditions established in the Rome Statute and its regulatory law.' See Cámara de Diputados (n 117).

[126] ibid.

[127] ibid (9 December 2002).

The political convenience of passing this constitutional amendment is clear: scoring diplomatic and political points by ratifying the Statute but, at the same time, creating a constitutional vacuum that allowed state sovereignty concerns to be addressed, while internationally sending a clear message about Mexico's commitment to human rights. Is the constitutional reform of Article 21 a stealth reservation to the Statute?[128] If the amendment was designed to prevent grave violations of human rights from being scrutinized, could it be considered an unconstitutional constitutional amendment? If the amendment amounts to a reservation, what are the implications for the ratification that took place after its adoption? Did Mexico actually ratify the treaty? At least in theory, such a constitutional vacuum could shield the Mexican government from the jurisdiction of the ICC.

In hindsight, both the amendment on the power to settle inter-state border disputes and the jurisdiction of the ICC served very specific functions that do not correspond to the reasons given to justify them. In the case of the power to settle inter-state border disputes, the justification was clearly not the social urgency of solving the pending cases or ensuring the separation of powers, as we can see from the fact that the relevant cases were not adjudicated. As for the amendment to Article 21, precisely at the time of its adoption drug violence in Mexico started to soar.[129] Only a year later, in his inauguration address, Felipe Calderón—accompanied by the military—would declare the war on drugs, which consisted in the militarization of the public security strategy. President Calderón appointed military members (licensed or retired) as heads of public security bodies and deployed thousands of military elements to carry out public security functions.[130] This public security strategy had terrible consequences, including disappearances: according to official figures, between 2006 and 2023, over 100,000 people disappeared.[131] Throughout the years, the Mexican State has accumulated observations and recommendations from international human rights bodies (eg the UN Committee on Enforced Disappearances and

[128] See Manuel Becerra Ramirez, 'México Ratifica El Estatuto de Roma Que Crea La Corte Penal Internacional, Después de Reformar La Constitución' (2006) 1 Anuario Mexicano de Derecho Internacional 951–54.

[129] Luis González Placencia, '10 Años de Guerra: Breve Recuento' (Animal Político, 29 November 2016) <www.animalpolitico.com/analisis/autores/phronesis/10-anos-guerra-breve-recuento> accessed 11 October 2024 (explaining how the Fox administration drug policy multiplied and diversified criminal groups and their business).

[130] Comisión Mexicana de Defensa y Protección de los Derechos Humanos, 10 Años de Guerra: Ni se Conmemoran ni se Olvidan (Animal Político, 29 November 2016) <https://animalpolitico.com/analisis/organizaciones/verdad-justicia-y-reparacion/10-anos-guerra-se-conmemoran-se-olvidan> accessed 11 October 2024.

[131] Colectivo EPU, *Informe Temático sobre la Situación de Personas Desaparecidas* (Colectivo EPUMX, Mexico 2023) 12 <https://centroprodh.org.mx/colectivo-epu-mx-2024/colectivo-epu-mx-informe-general/colectivo-epu-mx-informe-desaparicion-forzada> accessed 23 July 2024.

the Working Group on Enforced or Involuntary Disappearances) and international court rulings urging it to address the problem of forced disappearances. In 2016, the Interamerican Commission on Human Rights (IACHR) issued a report where it declared that 'the disappearance of persons in large swaths of Mexican territory has reached critical levels' and referred to 'the existence of a practice of forced disappearances at the hands of agents of the State or with their involvement, acquiescence, or tolerance'.[132] In 2022, the UN Committee on Enforced Disappearances reported that

> between 2006 and 2021, there was a steep rise in the number of disappearances in the country, with more than 98 per cent of them occurring during this period. These data show the close correlation between the increase in the number of disappearances and the so-called 'war on drug trafficking', which began during the six-year term of Felipe Calderón (2006–2012), when a policy characterized by the deployment of the armed forces to perform public security functions was implemented. This policy was maintained and has even been stepped up in subsequent six-year terms. Thus, while in the second half of the last century disappearances were mainly characterized as a means of political repression and committed by government agents and the armed forces, mostly against opposition social groups, from 2006 onwards, they have involved a wide range of perpetrators, modalities and victims.[133]

The official position of the government has shifted from a denial of the problem by the Calderón (2006–12) and Peña Nieto (2012–18) administrations (eg in 2015 the federal government rejected the IACHR report conclusions)[134] to a more ambivalent position for most of the López Obrador administration (2018–24) (ie early in his administration policy measures were taken, with reports showing meagre results in the implementation of and compliance with recommendations and rulings),[135] but the situation remains critical. Crucially, as President López Obrador's last act and in collaboration

[132] IACHR, 'Human Rights Situation in Mexico' (IACHR 2015) OEA/Ser.L/V/II Doc 44/15 63 <www.oas.org/en/iachr/reports/pdfs/Mexico2016-en.pdf> accessed 11 October 2024.

[133] Committee on Enforced Disappearances, 'Report of the Committee on Enforced Disappearances on Its Visit to Mexico under Article 33 of the Convention—Information on the Visit and Findings' (United Nations 2022) 3 <https://tbinternet.ohchr.org/_layouts/15/treatybodyexternal/Download.aspx?symbolno=CED%2FC%2FMEX%2FVR%2F1%20%28Findings%29&Lang=en> accessed 11 October 2024.

[134] See eg Alma E Muñoz, 'Grave Crisis de Derechos En México: CIDH; El Gobierno Refuta Conclusión' *La Jornada* (Mexico, 5 October 2015) <www.jornada.unam.mx/2015/10/03/politica/005n1pol> accessed 11 October 2024.

[135] Colectivo EPU (n 131) 28–29.

with the newly elected Congress and President-Elect Claudia Sheinbaum, a constitutional amendment that perpetuates the militarization of public safety and public life in Mexico was rammed through Congress in the last days of his term.[136] The violence associated with the militarization of public safety is an issue that could potentially fall under the jurisdiction of the ICC on crimes against humanity.[137] Yet, it is unclear what would be the effect of Article 21 of the Constitution should the ICC decide to open an investigation. In such a case, the government could potentially argue that Mexico did not ratify the Rome Statute and dodge the jurisdiction of the ICC. Nevertheless, the amendment was framed as a manifestation of the country's commitment to the protection of human rights.[138]

Human Rights Reform of 2011

In June 2011, eleven articles of the Constitution were amended to adopt what was featured as a progressive constitutional framework advancing the protection of human rights. The most featured modification of this amendment was the explicit inclusion of human rights treaties as part of the Constitution and the *pro homine* principle, whereby 'provisions relating to human rights shall be interpreted [. . .] working in favor of the broader protection of people at all times'.[139] Another, less featured aspect of this reform was the transfer of the Supreme Court's power to investigate serious human rights violations to the Ombudsman, Comisión Nacional de Derechos Humanos (CNDH). Although this reform seemed to be redefining fundamental premises on human rights protection in a very progressive way, both the inclusion of human rights treaties and the transfer of the investigation power to the CNDH arguably respond to

[136] Emiliano Rodríguez Mega, 'Mexican Senate Votes to Give Military Control of Civilian National Guard' *The New York Times* (26 September 2024) <www.nytimes.com/2024/09/25/world/americas/mexico-national-guard-military-control.html?smid=tw-share> accessed 3 October 2024; Catalina Pérez Correa, '¿Por Qué Negar Lo Que Todos Vemos?' *El Universal* (24 September 2024) <www.eluniversal.com.mx/opinion/catalina-perez-correa/por-que-negar-lo-que-todos-vemos> accessed 3 October 2024.

[137] Article 7 of the Rome Statute states: 'For the purpose of this Statute, "crime against humanity" means any of the following acts when committed as part of a widespread or systematic attack directed against any civilian population, with knowledge of the attack [. . .] (i) Enforced disappearance of persons.' See Rome Statute of the International Criminal Court, Art 7 (17 July 1998) UNTS 2187.

[138] Sistema de Información Legislativa, Legislatura LVIII, Cámara de Senadores, Dictámen de Comisiones Unidas (13 December 2002) 6–7.

[139] Constitution of 1917, Art 1, paras 1–2, Diario Oficial de la Federación (10 June 2011): 'In the United Mexican States, all individuals shall be entitled to the human rights granted by this Constitution and the international treaties signed by the Mexican State, as well as to the guarantees for the protection of these rights. Such human rights shall not be restricted or suspended, except for the cases and under the conditions established by this Constitution itself. The provisions relating to human rights shall be interpreted according to this Constitution and the international treaties on the subject, working in favor of the broader protection of people at all times.' (Translation by Constitute Project.)

aims that run counter to those publicly put forward to justify the amendments and show how the government and political parties in Congress resort to direct entrenchment in a way that allowed them to circumvent international human rights law and prevent the development of robust constitutional standards for the analysis of grave human rights violations.

First, the explicit inclusion of human rights treaties as part of the constitutional order establishes that

> all individuals shall be entitled to the human rights granted by this Constitution and the international treaties signed by the Mexican State, as well as to the guarantees for the protection of these rights. *Such human rights shall not be restricted or suspended, except for the cases and under the conditions established by this Constitution itself.*[140]

The commitment to the protection of human rights, however, comes as a very limited one. Similar to the amendment conditionally accepting the jurisdiction of the ICC, the practical implication of this reform is that it allows the circumvention of international human rights law obligations. The formulation of the clause opens the possibility of introducing rights restriction regimes through constitutional amendments. In fact, this formulation was hardly a coincidence. The pre-trial detention regime called *arraigo* (a regime of exception to due process protections in criminal cases) had been constitutionalized through the criminal justice system reform of 2008. This mechanism was introduced to ensure the success of criminal investigations by allowing prosecutors to detain suspects of organized crime up to eighty days before presenting them before a judge.[141] If the clause allowing for constitutional rights restrictions to prevail over international human rights law had not been adopted, the new text of Article 1 (under the *pro homine* principle) would have put the constitutional provision establishing the *arraigo* scheme at risk of being considered inconsistent with international human rights standards. In other words, the survival of a policy that was essential for the government's strategy on public safety

[140] Constitution of 1917, Art 1, sec 1, Diario Oficial de la Federación (10 June 2011) (emphasis added).

[141] Constitution of 1917, Art 16, sec 8, Diario Oficial de la Federación (18 June 2008): 'In the case of organized crime, and at the request of the Public Prosecution Service, judicial authority can order to put a person into hold restraint, complying with the terms of time and place established by law and without exceeding forty days, whenever necessary for the success of the investigation, the protection of people or legal goods, or when there is reason to believe that the accused could avoid the action of justice. The forty days term can be extended, provided that the Public Prosecution Service proves that the causes that originate hold restraint still remain. In any case, the hold restraint shall not last more than eighty days.' (Translation by Constitute Project.)

would have been under serious threat of being judicially challenged and struck down (for its inconsistency with international human rights standards) had the constitutional restrictions clause not been adopted. As will be discussed in more detail in Chapter 7, the possibility of introducing regimes of exception allowed both control over judicial interpretation and policies to be shielded from judicial scrutiny. As long as such restrictions are in the Constitution, there is no obstacle to implement policies that violate basic human rights as the case of *arraigo* in relation to criminal process rights illustrates. Indeed, the Supreme Court has already established that in human rights matters, rights restrictions introduced in the Constitution would prevail over international human rights law.[142]

Additionally, the Human Rights Reform of 2011 stripped the Supreme Court of its power to investigate serious human rights violations.[143] Before the amendment, under Article 97, paragraph 2, of the Constitution, the Supreme Court had the power to investigate and review *any kind of government act*[144] seriously violating rights. Its broad formulation gave the Court discretion to decide when to exercise it. The exercise of this power was mostly triggered by the Court or by a direct petition of the president after social and media pressure. The Supreme Court exercised it to investigate very serious cases such as extrajudicial killings,[145] police brutality at mass scale,[146] high-level government officers conspiring against and kidnapping a journalist,[147] and the death of forty-nine infants in a state-run daycare.[148] The ample margin of discretion given to the Court by the open-ended nature of the provision put the judges in a difficult position in that, from the point of view of those officers implicated, the exercise of this power was easy to disqualify as politically motivated.

[142] SCJN, 9 September 2013, Contradicción de Tesis [CT] 293/2011, SCJN, 9 September 2013, CT 21/2011, and José Ramón Cossío and others, *La Construcción de Las Restricciones Constitucionales A Los Derechos Humanos* (Porrúa 2013).

[143] Before its elimination, the text of the provision established: 'The Nation's Supreme Court of Justice may appoint any or several of its members, or any District Judge or Circuit Magistrate, or may appoint one or several Special Commissioners, when it deems convenient or whenever the President of the Republic or any of the house of the Congress of the Union, or the Governor of a State should request it, only for the purpose of investigating a fact or facts constituting a serious violation to any constitutional right.' Mexican Constitution, Art 97(2), English version, SCJN, 2010 <www.wipo.int/wipolex/en/text.jsp?file_id=329447> accessed 11 October 2024.

[144] Elsewhere I argue that this constitutional device was intended for the Supreme Court to structurally evaluate the design and implementation of public policies that may lead to human rights violations, as opposed to the limited analysis and effects when a case is analysed under *amparo*. See Mariana Velasco-Rivera, *La Facultad de Averiguación: Lo que Perdió la Suprema Corte de Justicia de la Nación para el Análisis Estructural de Políticas Públicas* (Tirant lo Blanch 2014).

[145] SCJN, 5 March 1996, Facultad de Investigación [FI] 3/96.

[146] SCJN, 6 February 2007, FI 3/2006.

[147] SCJN, 30 November 2007, FI 2/2006.

[148] SCJN, 16 June 2010, FI 1/2009 .

Judicial scrutiny of this type of government action meant a direct confrontation with the other branches and levels of government. I have argued elsewhere that the ample discretion the Court had in this type of case could have been used to establish clear acting guidelines for government officials in the implementation of public policies in line with constitutional and human rights law.[149] However, the Court never established a clear doctrine to determine what 'serious human rights violations' meant and what, in fact, was the purpose of such constitutional provision. Each time the power was exercised, the reasoning to determine the existence of the violations was different, unclear, and the judges always failed to find the officials at fault.[150] Unsurprisingly, in those cases where the Supreme Court declared the existence of serious violation of rights, social turmoil was not assuaged. In fact, after such declarations, the public discontent would often grow with impressions of impunity tolerated and even covered up by the Supreme Court[151]—which at the same time put its legitimacy into question.[152]

The political inconvenience of the investigation power was the elephant in the room. Although no one really explicitly addressed it as such, the political discomfort caused by it is clear from the timing at which some of the initiatives

[149] Velasco-Rivera (n 144).

[150] The standard to determine the existence of 'serious human rights violations' was the 'state of affairs of generalized disorder' (*estado de desorden generalizado*). The standard, however, remained very broad and unclear, making it very hard to determine when exactly the 'disorder' was generalized to turn human rights violations into 'serious' ones. Even on those occasions when the Supreme Court found serious human rights violations had taken place, it never named the authorities at fault (SCJN, 16 June 2010, FI 1/2009.

[151] See eg Ricardo Rocha, 'Atenco y la Infamia' (Sin Permiso, 15 February 2009) <www.sinpermiso.info/textos/atenco-y-la-infamia> accessed 11 October 2024; Reforma, 'La Libra Mario Marín' Reforma (Mexico, 7 January 2008); Roberto Zamarripa, 'Los Acuerdos se Complican: Política Bajo Presión' Reforma (Mexico, 6 January 2008); Denise Dresser, 'Saldo del 2007' Reforma (Mexico, 31 December 2007); Rolando Herrera, 'Me da Vergüenza el Fallo de la Corte' Reforma (Mexico, 15 December 2007); Lorenzo Meyer, 'Cambiamos para Seguir Iguales' Reforma (Mexico, 13 December 2007); René Delgado, 'Impunidad Garantizada' Reforma (Mexico, 1 December 2007).

[152] In this respect, PRI senator Pedro Joaquín Coldwell argued, 'we are stripping the Court's jurisdiction to investigate serious human rights violations because [...] in practice it is not binding and because it has only contributed to question [the legitimacy] of the Court'. See Senado de la República, 'Sesión Ordinaria de Fecha 8 de marzo de 2011' <www.senado.gob.mx/66/diario_de_los_debates/documento/2058> accessed 13 October 2024. See also J Francisco Castellanos Madrazo, 'Apuntes sobre la Facultad de Investigación de la Suprema Corte de Justicia' (2008) 25 Revista del Instituto de la Judicatura Federal 30; Francisco Rivas, 'Desafían en Puebla Resolución de Ministros' Reforma (Mexico, 27 November 2007); 'Proponen Quitar Facultad Investigadora a la Corte' *El Universal* (Mexico, 27 July 2010) <www.eluniversal.com.mx/notas/697921.html> accessed 27 May 2017; Ricardo Alemán, 'Atenco: ¿Quién hará justicia?' *El Universal* (13 February 2009) <www.eluniversal.com.mx/columnas/76830.html> accessed 27 May 2017; Carmen F Aristegui, 'Las Costumbres del Poder' Reforma (Mexico, 27 March 2009); Sergio Sarmiento, 'Fallos de la Corte' Reforma (Mexico, 4 December 2007); Denise Dresser, 'Autogolpe' Reforma (Mexico, 3 December 2007); Jesús Silva-Herzog Márquez, 'Los Festejos de la Impunidad' Reforma (Mexico, 3 December 2007); Juan E Pardinas, 'Seis a Cuatro' Reforma (Mexico, 2 December 2007).

to strip the Supreme Court from its jurisdiction were presented and its sponsors. In total, five initiatives were presented—three of which were sponsored by the PRI, one by the PVEM, and one by the Congress of Jalisco.[153] The first initiative, sponsored by the Congress of Jalisco, was presented in July 2006, a month and a half after the Supreme Court exercised the power in Lydia Cacho's case.[154] In this case, the governor of Puebla conspired against and illegally imprisoned a journalist as retaliation for a book she wrote[155] denouncing a criminal network of child pornography and prostitution that involved a friend of the governor. The second initiative, sponsored by PRI senator Renán C. Zoreda, was presented in July 2007, six months after the power was exercised in a case of police brutality in Atenco, a municipality in the State of Mexico where Enrique Peña Nieto (PRI) was governor at the time.[156] As mentioned earlier, the political elite never explicitly recognized its discomfort with the investigation power over serious human rights violations; instead, far-fetched arguments were brought forward to justify taking it away from the Supreme Court, but no one seemed to disagree[157]—not even the opposition, who could have denounced such a manoeuvre to score political points against the PRI. Four out of the total six cases reviewed under the investigation power involved PRI state governors, including incumbent president Enrique Peña Nieto. Even the Supreme Court actively advocated for its elimination. In December 2010, Chief Justice Guillermo Ortíz Mayagoita revealed that the majority of Justices explicitly asked the members of Congress to eliminate the power to investigate serious violations of human rights.[158]

The arguments put forward to justify the elimination of the investigation power were unpersuasive at best. First, it was argued that it did not have a judicial nature and therefore was keeping the Court from becoming a 'true' constitutional tribunal; second, that the opinions issued under this power were not binding; and, third, akin to the inter-state border dispute amendment, that a statute establishing procedures and guidelines for its exercise did not exist. Perhaps, strictly speaking, it is true that the investigation power did not necessarily have a judicial nature, but even in such a case it is hard to assert the need to strip it away from the Supreme Court. A purist separation-of-powers

[153] Velasco-Rivera (n 144) 11.
[154] ibid.
[155] Lydia Cacho, *Los Demonios del Edén: El Poder que Protege a la Pornografía Infantil* (Penguin Random House Grupo Editorial México 2012).
[156] Velasco-Rivera (n 144) 11.
[157] ibid 12–20.
[158] Víctor Fuentes, '. . . Y la Corte aplaude la decisión' Reforma (Mexico, 17 December 2010).

argument, if stretched, could also justify eliminating the impeachment mechanism for not having, strictly speaking, a legislative nature or the presidential veto for not having an executive nature. As for the other two arguments—especially the argument on the absence of regulation—it is paradoxical that the legislative body had to justify the elimination of the power (through a constitutional amendment) based on the absence of something that was precisely its job to create (through ordinary legislation).

As far-fetched as the arguments given to justify the elimination of the investigation power were, it is perhaps unsurprising that no one questioned them. It would in fact have been harder to imagine the legislative body and all members of the political elite pushing for a piece of legislation to make the opinions issued under the investigation power binding and issuing a statute regulating its exercise. Such a measure would have strengthened the system of judicial oversight, yet the parties that had the power to adopt it (ie PRI and PAN) had little incentive to proceed in that way. In the end, those parties were the ones who had been put in the spotlight by the investigation power. The Supreme Court's advocacy in favour of stripping away its own jurisdiction is also understandable. The political costs of its exercise and of developing a robust constitutional doctrine for the analysis of public policies from a constitutional rights perspective were potentially very high. And any rulings could be overridden at any time through a constitutional amendment. In a context where the amendment mechanism is available for direct entrenchment, there are few incentives for judges to engage in robust interpretative exercises. The less the judge says, the fewer the opportunities for political confrontation and the fewer legitimacy costs to pay. In short, the elimination of the investigation power was an effective way to both get rid of a mechanism that was putting the spotlight on authoritarian practices and abuses of power (in particular by the PRI) far too often and for the Supreme Court to dodge the political costs of engaging in robust constitutional interpretation.

IV. Conclusion

In hindsight, the three examples above (the amendment to conditionally accept the jurisdiction of the ICC, the power to settle inter-state border disputes, and the Supreme Court's investigation power stripping) show how constitutional amendments serve very specific functions that are not necessarily in line with the reasons given to justify them. It should be noted that the potential and seriously problematic consequences of the amendments analysed here are not necessarily created by the fact that the Constitution is frequently amended. Rather, as will be discussed in Chapter 7, the real danger is the possibility of exercising unchecked power.

The consequences of being able to get away with political artifices such as the ones described here vary in their gravity. For instance, in the case of the jurisdiction of the ICC, the avoidance of accountability could entail dodging an international trial for crimes against humanity. In the case of the power to settle inter-state border disputes, it was clearly not the social urgency of solving the pending cases or the need to protect the separation of powers that drove the amendments, as we can see from the fact that the cases at issue were not solved. Although in this case the consequence is not as serious (criminally speaking), it still leaves entire communities in a situation of uncertainty regarding, for example, the provision of basic services and social programmes. Similarly, the human rights reform got rid of a mechanism that was putting the spotlight on the authoritarian practices and power abuses of the PRI far too often.[159] Although these amendments seem to have been about limiting available human rights protections, not all have run in that direction. In the last two decades, what can be understood as a proliferation of socioeconomic rights in the Constitution has taken place. Article 4 has been amended on different occasions to include the previously mentioned 'right to sports' and 'right to nutritious, quality and sufficient food', as well as the 'right to a healthy environment for his/her own development and well-being', 'right of access, provision and drainage of water for personal and domestic consumption in a sufficient, healthy, acceptable and affordable manner', and 'right of access to culture'. Yet, in the absence of political will to implement these kinds of provisions, the judiciary becomes the most relevant actor to develop them into more than just aspirational declarations.[160] That is, the development of socioeconomic rights doctrines largely depends on a strong independent judiciary. Yet, as I have already suggested and will explain in more detail in Chapter 7, given the constellation of how constitutional change works in the Mexican context and due to the budgetary impact the adjudication of socioeconomic rights entails, there are not many chances of seeing an activist judiciary in this regard—judges will always be able to say that socioeconomic rights are subject

[159] To be sure, even when some of these reforms, specifically the human rights reform, were in fact to produce positive effects in the protection of rights, this would be more the result of the 'civilizing force of hypocrisy' than of the true commitment of political parties to human rights protection or democracy. Elster (n 8) 1783.

[160] Raúl Mejía Garza, 'Estado Social y Derecho Social' in Luis F Aguilar and Jorge A Alatorre (eds), *El Futuro del Estado Social* (Miguel Angel Porrúa 2014) 228.

to legislative discretion because of their budgetary impact. It is difficult to believe these reforms aim at anything else than showing commitment to certain social causes without necessarily having the intention of translating them into public policies.

* * *

It is clear that after 1988, Mexican politics were restructured in such a way that constitutional amendment remained available for political entrenchment. Unlike what was predicted by Weldon and others, when it comes to formal constitutional change, political pluralization did not entail the disappearance of the PRI as a relevant political force. As noted from the outset, the findings in this chapter suggest Mexico's party system is characterized by three features: strong party discipline, the possibility of cross-party cooperation, and the centralization of constitutional decision-making. Chapters 5 and 6 explore the conditions that contribute to explaining said features. In particular, they explore how the unravelling of the hegemonic party rule did not entail the elimination of the conventions and practices that became part of the Mexican constitutional culture throughout the hegemonic years and beyond, nor did it prevent the formation of new political unwritten norms to allow access to direct political entrenchment.

5

Constitutional Change and Constitutional Culture in Mexico

I. Introduction

This chapter provides an account of constitutional culture in Mexico as one of the key elements of that country's economy of constitutional change. Constitutional culture features many different subcultures (eg legal professionals, the political elite, and social movements), some of which may be more influential than others in effecting constitutional change.[1] In Mexico, the governing elite subculture is particularly important to understanding the trends in formal constitutional change identified in Chapter 4. Since the late nineteenth century, the governing elite has had disproportionate power to access the amendment mechanism to respond to different political needs which, at the same time, shaped understandings, attitudes, and beliefs regarding the function of constitutional amendment as a political entrenchment mechanism in that country. To shed light on those long-standing understandings, Section II examines how, over the course of a century, different presidents resorted to constitutional amendment mechanisms to fulfil political needs or to advance their interests and agendas. Both Benito Juárez and Lázaro Cárdenas, who enjoyed wide levels of popular support, as well as presidents with less democratic credentials, like Porfirio Díaz, Plutarco Elías Calles, José López Portillo, and Miguel de la Madrid, used constitutional amendments in this way. In so doing, they sought to fulfil political needs that include, but are not limited to, facilitating their remaining in power by lifting presidential term limits, gaining control over judicial appointments, securing a judiciary friendly to specific

[1] Jack M Balkin, *Constitutional Redemption: Political Faith in an Unjust World* (Harvard UP 2011) 178, 182–83 (arguing, 'equally important are what we might call nodes of power and influence in legal culture. The characterization of positions along the spectrum of plausibility is affected by the beliefs and actions of importantly placed individuals and groups. It is affected by political activism and by the willingness of certain members of the bar, or certain important political figures, to support a particular position and put their credibility or authority behind it. [. . .] These nodal points of authority and influence are architectural features of a legal culture [. . .]. The network of nodal figures and institutions helps determine which ideas and positions ascend into plausibility and dominance and which are cast into the dustbin of history').

The Politics of Constitutional Rigidity. Mariana Velasco-Rivera, Oxford University Press.
 DOI: 10.1093/9780191981876.003.0005

political agendas, dealing with a rising political opposition, and resetting the national narrative to cope with serious legitimacy crises. These episodes of constitutional change shaped Mexico's constitutional culture in important ways.

In Section III, I turn to discuss the unwritten rules that allowed presidents to exercise unchecked power which, at the same time, eased access to the amendment mechanism in the late nineteenth century and most of the twentieth century, namely party discipline and what was understood as the 'metaconstitutional' powers of the president.[2] The expectation was that with democratization, the unwritten rules that had formed throughout a century would disappear and the constitutional system of separation of powers and checks and balances would begin to effectively constrain power. As a result, amending the Constitution would cease to be easily achieved. In Section IV I argue that even though the informal institutions that allowed the president to exercise unchecked political power mostly disappeared as the PRI hegemonic rule unravelled,[3] the patterns of amendment in the decades that followed suggest that new unwritten rules, inevitably influenced by old ones, emerged and gave way to the formation of a regime where cross-party entrenchment enables continued access to the constitutional amendment mechanism.

As a conclusion, I identify certain uses of and practices around constitutional amendment that can still be found today.

II. Political Entrenchment throughout Mexico's Constitutional History (1856–1988)

Throughout Mexican constitutional history, the Constitution has played a central role in political entrenchment. Ever since the fall of the Second Mexican Empire, the Constitution and the law have had a prominent role in the political discourse justifying regimes and state action with all sorts of purposes, including undemocratic ones. As early as 1867, Benito Juárez tested the limits of the constitutional order by trying to amend the Constitution by referendum—a mechanism that was not included in the amendment rule of the Constitution of 1857. For Porfirio Díaz, the Constitution, specifically the constitutional amendment mechanism, played an essential role in maintaining his thirty-year

[2] Jeffrey Weldon, 'Political Sources of Presidencialismo in Mexico' in Scott Mainwaring and Matthew Soberg Shugart (eds), *Presidentialism and Democracy in Latin America* (CUP 1997) 253–54.

[3] Gretchen Helmke and Steven Levitsky, 'Informal Institutions and Comparative Politics: A Research Agenda' in Thomas Christiansen and Christine Neuhold (eds), *International Handbook on Informal Governance* (Edward Elgar 2013) 92.

dictatorship. Moreover, the revolutionary movement against Díaz in 1910 was justified as a movement to re-establish the constitutional order of 1857. Finally, for the PRI regime, the discourse surrounding the Constitution and, in particular, the amendment mechanism was central both for justifying and maintaining the regime over time.

Benito Juárez and the limits of institutions

The years immediately after the fall of the Second Mexican Empire (1863–67) seem to have been crucial for the formation of attitudes and understandings regarding the function of the Constitution and the amendment mechanism in Mexico's constitutional culture. As part of the resistance to the Second Empire, Benito Juárez established the 'Itinerant government'—which consisted of maintaining to the extent possible a parallel government challenging the monarchy. Once the Empire fell in 1867, the legitimacy of the Constitution of 1857 was not in question. Now the only remaining issue seemed to be the transfer of power. In August 1867, Juárez issued a *convocatoria a elecciones* (call for elections)[4] of 'higher authorities' (ie president, chief justice of the Supreme Court, and congressmen). Notably, the *convocatoria* included an order to have a referendum on a series of constitutional amendments aimed at strengthening the executive power vis-à-vis the legislative power.

The referendum proposal unleashed a heated debate on whether it was legitimate to call for such a referendum while ignoring the amendment rules provided in the Constitution.[5] The government defended the measure as a legitimate direct appeal to the people on whether to amend the Constitution,[6] but opposition to the proposal was vast. Journalists questioned it as a plot against the sovereignty of the nation (as reflected in the existing constitutional framework) and an artful conspiracy against institutions.[7] Moreover, a few governors refused to publish the section containing the amendment

[4] The text of the *convocatoria* (14 August 1867) can be found in Manuel Dublán and José María Lozano, *Legislación mexicana ó colección completa de las disposiciones legislativas expendidas desde la Independencia de la República*, Tomo X 1876–1912, no 6072 (Imprenta del Comercio, o Cargó de Dublán y Lozano, hijos 1878) 44–49 <http://cdigital.dgb.uanl.mx/la//1080042593_C/1080043442_T10/1080043442_T10.html> accessed 16 August 2024.

[5] Charles A Hale, *The Transformation of Liberalism in Late Nineteenth-Century Mexico* (Princeton UP 2014) 70–71 (arguing, 'approval would mean dispensing with the normal procedure for amending the constitution [. . .] and would allow instead for the reforms to be decided by majority vote in the Chamber of Deputies').

[6] Dublán and Lozano (n 4) 49–56.

[7] Hale (n 5) 71.

proposals to prevent people from voting in the referendum.[8] Eventually, Juárez capitulated to the opposition and decided to leave the matter to the 'wisdom of Congress' and submit the changes through the amendment process provided by the Constitution.[9] A few years later (1873), during Sebastián Lerdo de Tejada's presidency, the amendments in question were enacted.

This is an important episode where a political figure of high standing attempted to effect constitutional change outside the institutional means available. Notably, the subject matter of the amendments (ie strengthening the executive), however, went generally unchallenged.[10] Those who resisted the amendments did not necessarily oppose their substance but instead the attempt at circumventing the procedure established by the Constitution. The official position portraying the referendum as a legitimate direct exercise of popular sovereignty was rejected. In this way, the opposition to the referendum and Juárez's capitulation arguably constitutes a precedent whereby constitutional change through non-institutional means ought to be rejected.

Porfirio Díaz and presidential re-election

The issue of presidential re-election was part of the constitutional debate for several years and was politically capitalized by General Porfirio Díaz to bring forward his political agenda. Initially, Díaz gained political saliency for his strong views against re-election and the revolts he attempted first against Juárez's re-election in 1871[11] and then against Lerdo de Tejada's in 1876.[12] Once in power, Díaz changed his views on the issue and made sure to change the constitutional text accordingly.[13]

The original text of Article 78 of the Constitution of 1857 was silent on the issue of re-election; it only stated the inauguration date and the duration of the presidential term (ie four years).[14] In 1878, during Díaz's first presidency,

[8] José Fuentes Mares, 'La Convocatoria de 1867' (1965) 14 Historia Mexicana 423, 436.

[9] Hale (n 5) 74.

[10] See Hale (n 5) 71 (arguing, '[a] few journalists like Manuel María de Zamacona, editor of *El Globo*, opposed the reforms themselves, while most, like Pantaleón Tovar of *El Siglo XIX*, objected more to the way in which they were presented to the people').

[11] Plan de la Noria (8 November 1871).

[12] Plan de Tuxtepec (10 January 1876). See also Imer Flores, 'La Constitución de 1857 y sus Reformas' in Diego Valadés and Miguel Carbonell (eds), *El Proceso Constituyente Mexicano: A 150 Años de la Constitución de 1857 y 90 de la Constitución de 1917* (UNAM 2007) 299–301.

[13] It is important to note that, like the referendum debate, these debates are forerunners to many of the constitutional questions during the twentieth and twenty-first century in Latin America (eg Bolivia, Colombia, and Venezuela).

[14] Constitution of 1857, Art 78, Diario Oficial de la Federación (5 February 1857) ('The President shall assume office on December 1st and shall remain in office for four years').

Article 78 was amended to prohibit consecutive re-election.[15] This move allowed him both to be consistent with his previous position against Juárez's and Lerdo's consecutive re-election and to run for office for a second time in 1884. Towards the end of Díaz's second presidency, in 1887, Article 78 was amended again to allow consecutive re-election, securing his ability to run for office for a third time.[16] Moreover, in 1890, Article 78 of the Constitution was amended once again to return to the original text.[17] As the original text was silent on the issue of re-election, returning to it meant removing all limitations on presidential re-election. Such an amendment allowed Díaz to run for re-election indefinitely through the first decade of the twentieth century (seven times in total), until he was forced to resign in 1911 in the wake of the Mexican Revolution.

The changes to Article 78 illustrate how Porfirio Díaz used the constitutional amendment mechanism for direct political entrenchment; more specifically, to perpetuate himself in power. In such an early stage in the history of liberal constitutionalism in Mexico, in addition to Juárez's amendment by referendum attempt, the fact that Díaz chose to use the constitutional means available to entrench himself and his political project is not of minor significance. It established a threshold on the acceptable measures to bring forward a political agenda and what the Constitution (specifically, constitutional amendment) could be used for. In Jack Balkin's terms, these kinds of measures were now on-the-wall possibilities.[18] The political conditions allowed Díaz to choose certain institutional means (ie the amendment mechanism) over others.[19] As will be seen, his strategy as president consisted of forming a *partido de gobierno*

[15] Constitution of 1857, Art 78, as amended, Diario Oficial de la Federación (5 May 1878) ('The President shall enter into office on 1 December, and shall hold office for four years, he shall not be eligible for re-election for the following term, nor shall he hold the office of President for any reason until four years have elapsed since he ceased to hold office'). For a detailed discussion on these amendments see Flores (n 12) 301-304.

[16] Constitution of 1857, Art 78, as amended, Diario Oficial de la Federación (21 October 1887) ('The President shall enter into office on 1 December, and shall hold office for four years, and shall be elegible to be reelected for a consecutive term; thereafter he shall be unable to hold the office of President unless four years have elapsed from the day he ceased to hold office'.).

[17] Constitution of 1857, as amended, Art 78, Diario Oficial de la Federación (8 December 1890) ('The President shall assume office on December 1st and shall remain in office for four years').

[18] In his work, Balkin develops the idea of on-the-wall and off-the-wall in constitutional interpretation. This idea refers to what are acceptable and unacceptable interpretations of the Constitution in a given society in a particular historical moment. As seen in Chapter 3, the concept of on-the-wall and off-the-wall, in my view, also applies for what is an acceptable use of the different mechanisms of entrenchment in a given constitutional order. See Jack M Balkin, *Constitutional Redemption: Political Faith in an Unjust World* (Harvard University Press 2011) 179–83.

[19] For an in depth discussion on the Díaz regime, see Lorenzo Meyer, 'México en el Siglo XX: La Concentración del Poder Político' in Marco Palacios (ed), *La Unidad Nacional en América Latina: Del Regionalismo a la Nacionalidad* (1983) 131–48.

(party of government) through co-optation and negotiation.[20] In doing so, Díaz secured a subservient legislative branch and prevented the rise of potential candidates wanting to run for the presidency.[21]

Díaz had strong intellectual support from a group of intellectuals and politicians that came to be known as the *Científicos*. The *Científicos* overtly supported his authoritarian government. Their intellectual force helped frame the Díaz regime within a liberal constitutional discourse. Since the Díaz regime was characterized by significant material progress and stability, the *Científicos* justified his permanence in power and indefinite re-election as a necessary step towards the realization of liberal ideals.[22] Economic progress had to come before any democratic idea. Díaz was portrayed as the only one who had been capable of securing peace and progress and, therefore, the only one able to consolidate the Republic. Regardless of the accuracy of such an assessment, it played an important role in justifying the permanence of Díaz in power as part of a larger liberal project.[23] The *Científicos* championed *historical constitutionalism*. In their view, the constitutional text should reflect social and historical reality, and the amendment mechanism was the ideal means for this task.[24] A less influential legal movement known as *doctrinaire constitutionalism* would resist the *Científicos* tendency to 'reformism'. This movement defended a

[20] Hale (n 5) 137; Meyer (n 19) 140.

[21] He had also reduced the military to prevent other ambitious individuals from trying to take power as he had attempted to do. See Meyer (n 19) 139.

[22] In the National Convention of the Partido Liberal in April 1892, the party justified its decision to nominate Porfirio Díaz to run for re-election for a third time as a necessary evil without which progress and peace could not be realized: 'it is a question of bringing an extremely complex work to the end of its most delicate period where the question of our credit, factor of our prosperity; our fiscal organization [. . .] our progress, source of public wealth, and our financial power; and above all, the advancement of peace, which is the basis of the solution to any of these problems [. . .] are at stake. [. . .] In countries born to liberty by their origin and by their history, and nurtured in liberty, like the country of Washington, a repeated reelection would be an impossible case. However, in nations with political conditions like ours, [re-election] may be, it is, necessary due to extraordinary reasons. Mexican democracy is not abdicating, it obliges. We have no doubt that our nominee will understand the high importance of the duty imposed on him and will show himself worthy of it. The children of the generation that created [Mexico's] constitutional law and emancipated [our] spirits with *la Reforma*, as the citizens who represent the majority of the Partido Liberal, we rise before the Nation inviting it not to fight in the elections [. . .] but to demonstrate its will and its power'. See Román Iglesias González (ed), *Planes políticos, proclamas, manifiestos y otros documentos de la Independencia al México moderno, 1812–1940* (IIJ-UNAM 1998) 495, 498–500 <https://biblio.juridicas.unam.mx/bjv/id/121> accessed 17 August 2024. See, more generally, Emilio Rabasa, *La Constitución y la Dictadura: Estudio sobre la Organización Política de México* (Porrúa 1956).

[23] It was a powerful rhetorical tool to resort to because the Porfirian regime did provide 'a generation of unprecedented peace and stability' in comparison to the convoluted fifty years after independence. Here peace and stability should be understood as the absence of civil war. Peace and stability were ensured through recurrent repression. See Alan Knight, *The Mexican Revolution: Porfirians, Liberal and Peasants*, vol 1 (University of Nebraska Press 1990) 15.

[24] See Charles A Hale, 'The Civil Law Tradition and Constitutionalism in Twentieth-Century Mexico: The Legacy of Emilio Rabasa' (2000) 18 Law and History Review 257, 259.

strict adherence to the written Constitution and the need for social change for the realization of the ideal of constitutionalism.[25]

Part of the legacy of the Díaz regime for Mexican constitutional culture is the embracement of historical constitutionalism and the normalization of the use of the amendment mechanism for the advancement of political projects and agendas. Importantly, the amendment mechanism was not only used as a means to legitimize Díaz's permanence in power; it was also central for bringing his policy agenda forward (eg the tax system, bank system, and internal commerce were some of the issues that were regulated by constitutional amendments).[26] Díaz was not an outright dictator; he did not just stay in power or implement his agenda without recourse to the legal system. Instead, like today's legal autocrats, he used the constitutional means available to remain in power and entrench his political project.

The legal foundations of the Mexican Revolution

Unlike other revolutionary movements (such as the Mexican War of Independence of 1810 that repudiated the rule of Spain), the revolution of 1910 was not to abolish the constitutional order but to restore it.[27] In fact, the constitutional project of 1917 was presented as a set of amendments to the Constitution of 1857, not as a brand-new Constitution.[28]

In the beginning, the revolutionary movement was fuelled by an outcry for electoral democracy. *Sufragio efectivo, no reelección* ('Effective suffrage, no

[25] ibid 259.

[26] See the amendments adopted by the Díaz government in Gobierno de Porfirio Díaz (28 May 2015) <https://constitucion1917.gob.mx/es/Constitucion1917/Gobierno_de_Porfirio_Diaz_02> accessed 16 August 2024.

[27] This idea is in line with what Hannah Arendt describes as the original meaning of 'revolution', which in her view meant the restoration of a previous order. In her words, 'the word was first used not when what we call a revolution broke out in England and Cromwell rose to the first revolutionary dictatorship, but on the contrary, in 1660, after the overthrow of the Rump Parliament and at the occasion of the restoration of the monarchy. In precisely the same sense, the word was used in 1688, when the Stuarts were expelled and the kingly power was transferred to William and Mary. The "Glorious Revolution", the event through which very paradoxically the term found its definite place in political and historical language, was not thought of as a revolution at all, but as a restoration of the monarchical power to its former righteousness and glory'. See Hannah Arendt, *On Revolution* (Penguin Books 1990) 42–43.

[28] See Diario de Debates del Congreso Constituyente, Periodo Único, Tomo I, no 12, 260–70 (1916) (Speech of Venustiano Carranza): 'One of the greatest satisfactions I have had so far [. . .] is what I am experiencing right now. Fulfilling one of the promises that I made in the name of the revolution, I come to put in your hands: [. . .] the draft of the reformed Constitution. This project includes all political reforms that experience and careful observation over the years have been suggested to me as indispensable for cementing [. . .] the institutions, [to channel] the nation['s] march towards progress along the path of freedom and law.'

re-election') was the rallying cry of Francisco I Madero against Porfirio Díaz, who had been re-elected for the seventh time in a sham electoral process in July 1910. After Díaz's exile and Madero's (extra-constitutional) election as president in 1911, Article 78 of the Constitution of 1857 was amended once again—this time to ban re-election in absolute terms.[29] Had it not been for Victoriano Huerta's coup against President Madero in 1913,[30] the revolution would have ended with the last amendment to Article 78 banning presidential re-election. Huerta's coup unleashed the continuation of the armed movement led by Venustiano Carranza—governor of the northern state of Coahuila—whose rallying cry was for restoring the constitutional order of 1857 against Huerta's illegal government.[31] Notably, neither Madero's nor Carranza's movements repudiated the Constitution of 1857. Madero was challenging a too-powerful president who had entrenched himself in power for three decades and calling for an amendment to the Constitution (banning presidential re-election) to avoid such a situation recurring. Carranza, on the other hand, repudiated the government of Victoriano Huerta, not the Constitution of 1857.

The revolutionary movement had a common cause while Huerta was in power, but once he resigned on 15 July 1914, the conflicts among Carranza, Emiliano Zapata, and Francisco Villa, *los jefes militares* (the military chiefs),

[29] Constitution of 1857, as amended, Art 78, Diario Oficial de la Federación, Decree No 34 (1911): 'The President and the Vice-President shall enter into office on 1 December, they shall hold office for six years and shall never be eligible for re-election. The President may never be elected Vice-President. The Vice-President may not be elected President for the immediate following period. [...].' In the *Plan of San Luis Potosí*, besides the outcry against re-election, Madero had demanded, among other things, the restitution of land to unjustly divested owners under Díaz's regime. Once in power, he seemed to have lost any intention of making any significant change to Díaz's regime. In reaction, with the purpose of vindicating the revolutionary movement, Emiliano Zapata published the *Plan of Ayala* (28 November 1911) in which he repudiated Madero's government and called for the land restitution Madero himself had promised. Uprisings against Madero sprang up all over the country, but he managed to stay in power until a coup d'état led by Victoriano Huerta in February 1913, in which President Madero and Vice-President Pino Suárez were forced to resign, were imprisoned, and shortly after were assassinated (this episode is commonly known as *La Decena Trágica*). See also Flores (n 12) 301.

[30] 6 November 1911.

[31] Upon the president and vice-president's resignation, Pedro Lascuráin—who was president for forty-five minutes—took power to name Victoriano Huerta head of the Ministry of Interior, only to immediately resign thereafter and pave the way for Huerta to become the new president. The Chamber of Deputies ratified Madero's and Pino Suárez's resignations and, according to the Ciudadela Agreement—also known as the US Embassy Agreement—Victoriano Huerta became the interim president. As soon as the state governors were notified of the situation, Venustiano Carranza repudiated Huerta as the new president and called upon all governors to join forces to re-establish the Constitution of 1857. On 26 March 1913, Carranza formalized his movement with the Plan of Guadalupe, through which all branches of the federal or local governments would become the target of a coup should they continue to support Huerta after thirty days. The document named Carranza commander in chief of the Ejército Constitucionalista (Constitutionalist Army) and interim president until the peace was re-established. Carranza found allies in several States and regions of the country—for example, Emiliano Zapata (leader of the peasant armed movement) and Francisco Villa (general in the military), who held more radical social beliefs, and Álvaro Obregón (general in the military)—allowing the movement to become militarily powerful.

surfaced.[32] Things eventually evolved into civil war. Interestingly, for the revolutionary groups, the Constitution and the law played a central role in their struggle. This is exemplified by political manifestos explicitly seeking to use institutional mechanisms to entrench revolutionary interests—namely, the *Plan de San Luis Potosí*, the *Plan de Guadalupe and Adiciones al Plan de Guadalupe*, and the *Plan de Ayala.*

The *Plan de San Luis Potosí* is the political manifesto that sparked the Mexican Revolution. In it, Madero denounced Díaz's seventh re-election and called for the restitution of land and for a constitutional amendment prohibiting re-election.[33] Although in this plan Madero repudiated Díaz's government, he questioned neither the Constitution nor the constitutional changes adopted during the dictatorship. The plan explicitly declared that all existing laws shall remain valid and those that were inconsistent with the principles inherent to the plan were to be reformed.[34] The *Plan de Guadalupe* was a political manifesto issued by Carranza in March 1913 that challenged Huerta's government. It created the 'Constitutionalist' army and outlined the action plan to re-establish constitutional government after deposing Huerta. After Huerta was deposed, and the conflicts among the revolutionary groups surfaced (revolutionary groups were demanding Carranza's resignation as commander in chief), the *Plan de Guadalupe* was amended in December 1914 to explicitly include the agrarian and labour demands of the revolution. In this amendment, Carranza, as commander in chief, explicitly committed to 'issue the necessary laws, provisions and measures to satisfy the economic, social and political needs of the country [and] bring the reforms that the public opinion demand as essential to establish a regime that guarantees equality for all Mexicans'.[35] The *Plan de Ayala*, the political manifesto issued by Zapata in November 1911, essentially adopted Madero's *Plan de San Luis Potosí.* Its initial slogan was *Reforma, libertad, justicia y ley* ('Reform, liberty, justice, and

[32] See Luis Javier Garrido, *El Partido de la Revolución Institucionalizada. Medio Siglo de Poder Político en México: La Formación del Nuevo Estado (1928–1945)* (Siglo XXI 1991) 34 (arguing, '"[t]he Revolution" [. . .] was then divided by the conflicts between *caudillos.* On the one hand, the *Zapatistas* who, in the south, claimed for the realization of a sweeping agrarian reform; and, on the other, the *Villistas* from the north, whose imprecise program referred to a series of popular reforms, manifested their opposition against Carranza's intention to impose his ideology. [. . .] In the summer of 1915, while Carranza was trying to impose and consolidate an incipient state apparatus, agrarian vindications multiplied nationwide').

[33] Plan de San Luis Potosí, Arts 1, 3, and 4 (5 October 1910).

[34] Plan de San Luis Potosí, Art 3 (5 October 1910).

[35] Adiciones al Plan de Guadalupe y Decretos Dictados Conforme a las Mismas: Plan de Guadalupe, Latin American Pamphlet Digital Collection—Curiosity Digital Collections <https://curiosity.lib.harvard.edu/latin-american-pamphlet-digital-collection/catalog/43-990053677480203941> accessed 15 August 2024. See also chapter 2 of Eber Betanzos Torres and Jaime Chávez Alor, *Los Constituyentes de 1917* (Fondo de Cultura Económica 2017).

law')[36] and called for the restitution of land to their legitimate proprietors and the establishment of special tribunals to adjudicate land ownership conflicts after the revolution.[37]

Importantly, the three plans (*San Luis Potosí*, *Ayala*, and *Guadalupe*) recognized the legitimacy of the Constitution of 1857 and their ultimate goal was to use the institutional means provided by it (ie the constitutional amendment mechanism and the legislative initiative) to bring about the needed changes to guarantee the realization of the revolutionary ideals (prominently, the restitution of land and the protection of labour rights). In fact, in the years of civil war (those between Huerta's fall and the enactment of the Constitution of 1917), both Carranza and Zapata issued pieces of legislation to implement their plans.[38] Moreover, all three plans included provisions that would guarantee the orderly transition of power after the revolution—for example, calls for elections. These plans, in my view, reveal the extent to which the different revolutionary groups had a common understanding of the function of the constitutional order—namely, political entrenchment.

Eventually, the social and economic rights demands included in the three plans ended up being reflected in the constitutional text of 1917 (ie Articles 3, 27, and 123)—which made Mexico the first country in the world to include this kind of provisions in a constitution. Despite their innovative character, these articles were adopted by the constituent assembly without discussion.[39]

Political entrenchment between 1928 and 1945

Even though the revolution formally ended with the enactment of the Constitution of 1917, the conflict between the revolutionary *caudillos* continued until the founding of the Partido Nacional Revolucionario (National Revolutionary Party) (PNR) in 1929, which would become the PRI in 1946.[40] The founding of the party brought political stability. However, power

[36] Berta Ulloa, 'Cartas de Amor al Pueblo' in Daniel Cosío Villegas and others (eds), *Historia general de México: Versión 2000* (Colegio de México 2004) 774.

[37] Plan de Ayala, Art 6 <http://academic.brooklyn.cuny.edu/history/johnson/ayala.htm> accessed 15 August 2024.

[38] Carranza issued, among other pieces of legislation, the Ley del Municipio Libre (1914), Ley de Divorcio (1915), Ley Agraria (1915), and Ley sobre el Petróleo (1915). See Adiciones al Plan de Guadalupe (n 35). Zapata issued the 'Programa de Reformas Políticas y Sociales reglamentó los principios del Plan de Ayala' (1916). See Ulloa (n 36) 801.

[39] See Ignacio Marván, *Nueva Edición del Diario de Debates del Congreso Constituyente de 1916–1917* (SCJN 2013) Arts 3, 27, and 123.

[40] Lorenzo Meyer argues that the most important thing Plutarco Elías Calles did was creating the PNR by the end of his official presidential term. In the middle of the political crisis that the murder of

would remain consolidated not in one person but in a political organization that remained in government for over seventy years. As previously seen, the Constitution had become a means for political entrenchment since the fall of the Second Mexican Empire. This did not change with the founding of the PNR. On the contrary, the Constitution had a central role in legitimizing the single-party regime: 'Legal forms and constitutional discourse were key components in the construction of the post-revolutionary regime.'[41] As Pilar Domingo put it,

> constitutionalism was an essential component of the Mexican political system, and central to its legitimation. Constitutional forms have been unswervingly maintained, electoral calendars consistently respected and upheld, albeit through highly fraudulent and often violent practices, and the separation of powers, although essentially limited, have formed the institutional bulwark of the regime.[42]

The political conditions of the PRI regime allowed for continued access to the amendment mechanism for political entrenchment between 1929 and 1988. Presidents Calles, Cárdenas, López Portillo, and De la Madrid are prominent examples. Under President Plutarco Elías Calles (1924–28), the Constitution (both rhetorically and institutionally) clearly served as a means to entrench key political interests. In 1926, giving up on the political principle that fuelled the Mexican Revolution (ie no re-election), Article 83 of the Constitution was amended to allow non-consecutive re-election and pave the way for Álvaro Obregón's re-election in 1928 (Obregón had been president from 1920 to

President Obregón caused among the *obregonistas*, Calles managed to avoid another violent transition by convincing the most important military commanders to agree in naming a civilian—Emilio Portes Gil—to become the interim president; and then created the PNR. In his last state of the union address he referred to the 'need of ending the *caudillo* phase and beginning the construction of a mechanism that allowed peacefully solving the power transitions [. . .] [a] great revolutionary party would be the first step'. The political party that started as a coalition of the revolutionary forces would soon become the sponsor of an improved version of an authoritarian regime: 'The PNR surged from all auto-defined revolutionary forces; formally its goal was to make the 1917 Constitution's provisions real. In practice, the new party was rather a confederation of the main leaders and organizations that acquiesced with Calles' headship. The main concern of [. . .] the PNR was to shape and maintain real consensus between factions through the negotiation of demands and aspirations, thus solving the elite internal conflicts and so getting rid of the violence. In this first stage, the organization and incorporation of workers and peasants to the party and the political process [. . .] had a very much secondary importance.' See Lorenzo Meyer, 'La institucionalización del Nuevo Régimen' in Daniel Cosío Villegas and others (eds), *Historia general de México: Versión 2000* (Colegio de México 2004) 831–34.

[41] Pilar Domingo, 'Judicial Independence: The Politics of the Supreme Court in Mexico' (2000) 32 Journal of Latin American Studies 705, 710.

[42] ibid 709.

1924). Then, in 1927, the presidential term was extended from four to six years. Crucially, since the times of Calles, the judiciary had an important place in the presidents' minds. As noted by Pilar Domingo, recently after the adoption of the 1917 Constitution, the Supreme Court adopted an independent role vis-à-vis the executive, at times ruling against the government interests (in particular regarding the interpretation of the socioeconomic rights provisions of the Constitution).[43] Accordingly, constitutional amendments in the 1920s and 1930s 'aimed directly at curbing the judiciary's scope for independent action effectively harnessed the judges to the revolutionary project'.[44] Constitutional reforms of the judiciary have since become common practice.[45]

The Constitution of 1917 established a judicial appointment and a tenure system that, on the surface, seemed to guarantee judicial independence from the executive but not so from local *caudillos* that had control over who was to be nominated.[46] It consisted of both chambers of Congress jointly appointing the eleven members of the Supreme Court by absolute majority through secret ballot from a list of candidates proposed by the state legislatures. Once appointed, justices had life tenure and could only be removed for misconduct through a disciplinary trial. Lower court judges were appointed by the Supreme Court and would remain so until the judicial reform of 1994 through which the Consejo de la Judicatura Federal (Federal Judicial Council) was created.[47]

In August 1928, the judicial appointment and tenure system was overhauled allegedly as a measure to guarantee judicial independence; in particular, to eliminate the eminently political interests at stake in the appointment process[48] and to tackle docket backlog.[49] The amendment took the exclusive power of Supreme Court appointments away from Congress and gave the president a key role. The appointment procedure was replaced by a presidential nomination system that required the Senate's ratification.[50] Moreover, Article 94 of the Constitution was reformed to increase the number of members from

[43] ibid 711.
[44] ibid.
[45] As noted by Pilar Domingo and documented by Fix-Zamudio and Cossío Díaz, constitutional amendments affecting the Supreme Court were adopted in 1946, 1951, 1962, 1967, 1974, 1975, 1977, 1979, 1982, and 1987. See ibid 721 and Héctor Fix-Zamudio and José Ramón Cossío Díaz, *El Poder Judicial en el Ordenamiento Mexicano* (Fondo de Cultura Económica 1996) 155–60.
[46] Domingo (n 41) 712.
[47] ibid.
[48] José Ramón Cossío Díaz, *La Teoría Constitucional de La Suprema Corte de Justicia* (Fontamara 2008) 35.
[49] This same argument has been used to justify reforms to the judiciary in recent Mexican constitutional history. Examples of this are the judicial reform of 1994 and 1996, the constitutional amendment on the criminal justice system in 2008, and the constitutional amendment on human rights and the *amparo* suit in 2010.
[50] Constitution of 1917, as amended, Art 96, Diario Oficial de la Federación (20 August 1928). See also Cossío Díaz (n 48) 33.

eleven to sixteen, to establish that the Supreme Court would act *en banc* and in three chambers, and to impose a prohibition of salary reduction while in office. Article 111 was reformed to establish the possibility for the president to remove judges of all ranks—with majority approval in Congress—for misconduct.[51] Although some of the measures adopted may be understood as clear attempts to deal with the problem of docket backlog (ie, increasing the membership of the Supreme Court and creation of three chambers), the modification of the judicial appointment system and the power to remove judges cannot. Instead, the latter are measures that undermined judicial independence by expanding the power of the president over the appointment and removal of judges.[52] One of the most notable elements of the reform was not in the main body of the amendment (ie the constitutional text) but in the transitory provisions (a practice that continues today).[53] Besides modifying the appointment system, one of the transitory provisions ordered the replacement of all sitting justices, giving President Calles the power to fill all sixteen new vacancies.[54] According to Pilar Domingo, this amendment marked the beginning of the subordination process of the Supreme Court to the executive:

> The 1928 reform was welcomed by the more progressive elements of the revolution as a way of controlling what at the time was seen as a reactionary judiciary, that served the interests of the regional caudillos and landlords, to the detriment of the revolutionary reforms.[55]

The use of constitutional means for political entrenchment that characterized the Calles administration was also a feature of Lázaro Cárdenas' presidency (1934–40). Cárdenas resorted to direct and indirect means of entrenchement (ie constitutional amendments and ordinary legal means) to ensure support from the social sectors (ie confederations of workers, peasants, bureaucracy, and the military) which would later be affiliated with the PRI and to consolidate the corporatist character of the regime. Five measures stand out: a

[51] Constitution of 1917, as amended, Art 111, Diario Oficial de la Federación (20 August 1928).
[52] See eg Michael C Taylor, 'Why No Rule of Law in Mexico: Explaining the Weaknesses of Mexico's Judicial Branch' (1997) 27 New Mexico Law Review 141, 146–47; Cossío Díaz (n 48) 37; Domingo (n 41) 712.
[53] For a discussion of the contemporary (abusive) use of transitory provisions, see Mariana Velasco-Rivera, 'Reformas Constitucionales Arbitrarias' in José Ramón Cossío Díaz and Vicente Ugalde (eds), *El Estado de Derecho en el México Contemporáneo* (El Colegio de México 2023) 51–91; Estefanía Vela Barba, 'Los (malditos) artículos transitorios de la reforma constitucional de la Guardia Nacional' (2023) <https://eljuegodelacorte.nexos.com.mx/los-malditos-articulos-transitorios-de-la-reforma-constitucional-de-la-guardia-nacional> accessed 15 August 2024.
[54] Taylor (n 52) 146–47.
[55] Domingo (n 41) 712.

judicial overhaul; land restitution; the creation of workers' confederations; expropriating the oil industry; and reforming the party. The first measure was a judicial overhaul to ensure his policy agenda survived judicial review. On 15 December 1934, two weeks after taking office, an amendment to Article 94 of the Constitution of 1917 increased the membership of the Supreme Court from sixteen to twenty-one and added a fourth chamber specializing in labour law matters. Additionally, life tenure was replaced by fixed terms of six years—which coincided with the presidential term.[56] Most notably, and going beyond what Calles had done, the second transitory provision of the reform provided that not only all active members of the Court *but all* sitting judges (district and circuit courts) would cease in their functions as of 31 December of that same year;[57] that is, two weeks after the reform was enacted.

Like Calles' and all other reforms to the judiciary during this period, this was justified as a measure to tackle the docket backlog—which, to be fair, was indeed a real problem.[58] But Lázaro Cárdenas showed little hesitation in revealing what he was looking for with this reform: to 'give special treatment to labour law matters through the creation of a chamber specializing in labour law and *integrat[ting] [the judiciary] with members with firm revolutionary convictions*'.[59] Cárdenas stressed that the reform was not aiming at weakening the Supreme Court but only at ensuring its 'correct' integration to enable collaboration between powers.[60] Additionally, he strongly argued against the life tenure system because of its 'anti-revolutionary nature'. In his view, the application and interpretation of 'revolutionary' law needed to be constantly looking towards what he saw as social improvement which required flexibility and spontaneity[61]—judicial life tenure represented the opposite. In the speech he delivered after being designated presidential candidate on 6 December 1933, he affirmed: 'the integral realization of the social provisions of the [. . .] Constitution [. . .] essentially needs a revolutionary interpretation of the law by men who sincerely feel the revolution'.[62]

Representatives in Congress adopted an acritical approach to their constitutional role as members of the body designated to process constitutional

[56] Domingo (n 41) 712.
[57] Constitution of 1917, as amended, Art 111, Diario Oficial de la Federación (15 December 1934). See also Cossío Díaz (n 48) 39, 42.
[58] Emilio Rabasa, 'Organización de la Suprema Corte de Justicia y del juicio de amparo' in Imer Flores (eds), *Doctrina Constitucional Mexicana* (INEHRM 1987) 225–38; Lucio Cabrera Acevedo, *La Suprema Corte de Justicia durante el Gobierno del Presidente Plutarco Elías Calles (1924–1928)* (Suprema Corte de la Nación 1998) <http://ru.juridicas.unam.mx/xmlui/handle/123456789/10119> accessed 15 August 2024.
[59] Cossío Díaz (n 48) 40 (emphasis added).
[60] ibid.
[61] ibid 41.
[62] ibid 45.

amendments (an approach that, as shown in Chapter 4, remains today). It was determined that the reform should be approved because the moral standing and personal background of the newly elected President Cárdenas were a guarantee of success.[63] And so the reform was passed without much deliberation. The reform was an essential element to bringing forward and legitimating Cárdenas' policy agenda. In this regard, José Ramón Cossío argues that the Supreme Court was not understood as a mechanism to preserve the status quo but as a device that could be used to *juridificar* (juridify) the revolutionary conquests: 'the Court had to be on the side of the revolutionaries, juridify their positions and impact [. . .] the very understanding of the Constitution'.[64] What Cossío calls juridifying is what I understand as indirect political entrenchment of the revolutionary and the PNR agenda. President Calles' and President Cárdenas' examples illustrate that the Supreme Court and the judiciary were understood as tools to preserve interests and agendas. Hence early on after the adoption of the Constitution of 1917, the judiciary was targeted to ensure the survival of policy choices. The constitutional amendment mechanism was instrumental to achieve that goal. As Pilar Domingo put it, referring to the amendments under Calles and Cárdenas,

> [t]he judicial reform of 1934 was clearly designed to further subjugate the judiciary, with the purpose of ensuring minimum judicial interference in a highly complex political moment. Again, as with the reform of 1928, taking steps to subordinate what was seen as a conservative and reactionary institution was hailed as a progressive and desirable measure at the time, and one which would protect social reforms.[65]

Even after life tenure was reinstated under President Ávila Camacho in 1944, presidents continued to have substantial power through judicial appointments: Between 1945 and 1988, the majority of presidents appointed more than 50 per cent of justices during their terms.[66] Unsurprisingly, the Supreme Court remained largely harmless throughout the hegemonic party regime.

[63] ibid 41.
[64] ibid 46.
[65] Domingo (n 41) 713.
[66] Presidents were able to make several appointments because justices would not stay long in office. Sitting as a judge was considered a transitional post for party members with political ambitions. See ibid 725; Beatriz Magaloni, 'Authoritarianism, Democracy and the Supreme Court: Horizontal Exchange and the Rule of Law in Mexico' in Christopher Welna and Scott Mainwaring (eds), *Democratic Accountability in Latin America* (OUP 2005) 289. In 1994, on the occasion of the judicial reform, all members of the Supreme Court were replaced at once. Since then, the staggered system established to replace them was strictly observed except for the justices that passed away before finishing their term (ie Justice José de Jesús Gudiño Pelayo and Sergio Valls in 2010 and 2014, respectively). After 1994,

The second measure consisted of an extensive land restitution plan nationwide.[67] As a result, Cárdenas became the 'redeemer of the revolution' for the peasant sector—which, at the same time, secured popular support.[68] The worker sector also benefited from a judiciary that, unsurprisingly, picked up on Cárdenas' ideology and became more protective of workers' interests and extensively allowed strikes—only 10 per cent of strikes would be declared illegal[69] in a context in which the mechanism was intensively used (in 1935 there were 642 strikes around the country).[70] The judiciary also validated collective labour agreement clauses making union membership obligatory.[71] In practice, this transformed union leaders into powerful political actors who, along with widespread corruption, ensured the alignment of the complete sector with the regime.

The third measure was the creation of workers' confederations. Building on the ties Cárdenas already had with the peasant and labour sectors, confederations were created to firmly settle the organizations of already friendly groups.[72] These organizations did not emerge from bottom-up movements joining forces to become a counter force to the State and corporate private

serving as a Supreme Court justice stopped being understood as a transitional post for individuals with political ambitions and instead was seen as a position of high honor and responsibility. However, during the presidential term of Andrés Manuel López Obrador (2018-24) this arguably started to change. In 2019 Justice Eduardo Medina Mora surprisingly resigned without stating any cause in his resignation letter as required by the Constitution. To this day, it is unclear why and whether he was pressured to resign. A more clear cut case is that of Justice Arturo Zaldívar, who in 2023 broke with the norm and resigned from office one year short of the end of his fifteen-year term to join the presidential campaign of MORENA's candidate Claudia Sheinbaum. See Jorge Monroy, 'Abogado Lleva a La CIDH El Caso de Medina Mora Para Conocer Las Causas de Su Renuncia' *El Economista* (28 March 2022) <https://www.eleconomista.com.mx/politica/Abogado-lleva-a-la-CIDH-el-caso-de-Medina-Mora-para-conocer-las-causas-de-su-renuncia-20220328-0066.html> accessed 29 March 2025. For a discussion on Zaldívar's questionable behaviour before resigning to join Sheinbaum's presidential campaign, see eg Mariana Velasco-Rivera, 'When Judges Threaten Constitutional Governance: Evidence from Mexico' (*I·CONnect*, 16 June 2022) <www.iconnectblog.com/when-judges-threaten-constitutional-governance-evidence-from-mexico> accessed 7 July 2023; Mariana Velasco-Rivera, 'La (no) extensión de la presidencia de Zaldívar: lo bueno, lo malo y lo feo' (*El Juego de la Suprema Corte*, 18 November 2021) <https://eljuegodelacorte.nexos.com.mx/la-no-extension-de-la-presidencia-de-zaldivar-lo-bueno-lo-malo-y-lo-feo> accessed 2 December 2021; Mariana Velasco-Rivera, 'La consulta extraordinaria sobre la extensión de la presidencia de Zaldívar: ¿Es la vía idónea?' (*El Juego de la Suprema Corte*, 11 June 2021) <https://eljuegodelacorte.nexos.com.mx/la-consulta-extraordinaria-sobre-la-extension-de-la-presidencia-de-zaldivar-es-la-via-idonea> accessed 17 June 2021; Mariana Velasco-Rivera, '¿Qué Pasó Con El Transitorio Que Busca Extender La Presidencia de Zaldívar?' (*El Juego de la Suprema Corte*, 1 June 2021) <https://eljuegodelacorte.nexos.com.mx/que-paso-con-el-transitorio-que-busca-extender-la-presidencia-de-zaldivar> accessed 12 January 2024.

[67] Kenneth L Karst, 'Latin-American Land Reform: The Uses of Confiscation' (1964) 63 Michigan Law Review 327.

[68] *Lázaro Cárdenas II: Entre El Pueblo y El Poder* (directed by Clío, 1998) <https://sibi.upn.mx/cgi-bin/koha/opac-detail.pl?biblionumber=105060> accessed 25 October 2024.

[69] Cossío Díaz (n 48) 46.

[70] Meyer (n 40) 867.

[71] Cossío Díaz (n 48) 46.

[72] See Meyer (n 40) 864, 867–72 (regarding the Confederación de Trabajadores Mexicanos of 9 July 1935).

structures, but exactly the opposite: they were created as policing mechanisms of and for the government.[73] These confederations—along with forced unionization clauses—served as vote insurers and corruption hubs.[74] As previously mentioned, workers were forced to become members of unions—and pay their respective fees. The logic was simple: if an individual wanted to get and keep their job, they would have to (politically) stay in line with the regime. The costs of social or political dissent—let alone mobilization—were very high.

The fourth measure was the nationalization of the oil industry. On 18 May 1938, the oil industry was nationalized as a result of a conflict between foreign oil companies and the union. The latter—according to the labour rights provisions of the Constitution—was demanding a collective labour contract, arguing for unpaid salaries to be paid, profit sharing, and, in general, better working conditions. The conflict became of national interest when the union went on strike and gasoline became scarce. After a number of failed attempts by President Cárdenas and his cabinet to reach an agreement to settle the conflict, the workers brought the issue before the labour courts, which adjudicated the case in their favour. Among other things, the labour courts determined that oil companies could bear an annual wage increase of $26,000,000 MXN (approximately 7 million USD at that time) and ordered back payments corresponding to the period of the strike within seven days.[75] The oil companies challenged the decision via an *amparo* suit that reached the Supreme Court, which upheld the labour court's decision. The oil companies refused to comply with the ruling and, after failing to reach an agreement with President Lázaro Cárdenas, the decision was made to expropriate.[76] Just like the restitution of land, the political profit of the oil expropriation was immense. President Lázaro Cárdenas, rightly or wrongly, became a revolutionary saviour. This political move not only secured the support of the labour sector but also became an important part of the Mexican constitutional identity, as it meant seizing natural resources that rightfully belonged to the people from oppressors and foreigners.

The fifth and last move consolidating the regime was the reform of the party statutes to allow the affiliation of the previously mentioned confederations.

[73] See eg Michel Crozier, 'Sociología del Sindicalismo' in George Firedmann and Pierre Naville (eds), *Tratado de Sociología del Trabajo* (Fondo de Cultura Económica 1963) 172–94 (arguing that the primary social and autonomous role of unions in Mexico was limited by a context where institutions were controlled by the government oligarchy).

[74] See eg María S Xelhuantzi-López, *Democracy on Hold: The Freedom of Union Association and Protection Contracts in Mexico* (Communications Workers of America 2002).

[75] Lourdes Celis Salgado, 'Lázaro Cárdenas, La Formación Del Sindicato Petrolero y La Expropiación Petrolera (1935–1938)' in *Lázaro Cárdenas: Modelo y legado*, vol II (INHERM 2020) 177–83.

[76] ibid 170–76.

This measure made virtually all of the social sectors part of the same corporation, now to be named the Party of the Mexican Revolution (PRM). The institutional scheme was profoundly undemocratic. Being against the party became synonymous with being anti-patriotic, anti-revolutionary, and reactionary.[77] In other words, the political environment was not conducive to the formation of a strong democratic tradition and practices (eg political opposition, deliberation, etc).

Political entrenchment under the hegemonic PRI

The PRM became the PRI in 1946 and remained in power until the end of the twentieth century after a period of economic, social, and political crisis. Direct political entrenchment in that period also served as an effective tool to, among other things, cope with the rising opposition that could become a threat to the stability and continued existence of the regime.[78] Constitutional amendments, in this sense, functioned as a buffer of political pressure to avoid or temper crises that could produce political instability and threaten the survival of the regime. In other words, amending the Constitution served to neutralize the opposition. The *Reforma Política* (Political Reform) of 1977 is a prime example.[79] The PRI, still able to amend the Constitution on its own, conceded to some of the demands of the still small opposition party Partido Acción Nacional (PAN), chief among which was the adoption of the first iteration of the system of proportional representation. In so doing, the PRI integrated the PAN into the system and, in that way, ensured the latter did not challenge the legitimacy of the regime and opt for other means that could entail the formation

[77] In 1945, increasing political violence posed a serious challenge to the legitimacy of the PRM (specially the León massacre) that eventually led to the change of name to Partido Revolucionario Institucional (PRI) in 1946. See Stephen R Niblo, *Mexico in the 1940s: Modernity, Politics, and Corruption* (Rowman & Littlefield 1999) 152, 157. See also Pablo González Casanova, *El Estado y los Partidos Políticos en México* (Ediciones Era 1986); Jean-François Prud'homme, *Coyunturas y Cambio Político* (El Colegio de México 2015) 92.

[78] In this regard, Alonso Lujambio argued the excluded opposition forces would either be coopted, neutralized, repressed, or integrated (as a last resort) to the electoral competition by offering credible elections. Similarly, according to Soledad Loaeza 'it is a model in which political stability and economic growth has been obtained without opting for [. . .] dictatorship or western democracy [. . .]. [O]rganizing the minorities into the structures of the system [. . .] was a way of channeling potential conflict in that it neutralizes the threatening aspect that the exclusion from participation may cause'). Alonso Lujambio, *El Poder Compartido: Un Ensayo sobre la Democratización Mexicana* (Océano 2000) 22; and Loaeza (n 78) 353, 358.

[79] Ricardo Becerra, Pedro Salazar, and José Woldenberg, *La Mecánica Del Cambio Político En México: Elecciones, Partidos y Reformas* (Cal y Arena 2000) 75–148.

of a movement that could threaten its stability or survival.[80] The amendment can also be read as the government's response to the elections of 1976, where López Portillo ran unopposed for the presidency. That election was a tipping point as the credibility of the regime sank deep. During the hearings organized by the government prior to the adoption of the amendment, the secretary of the interior, on behalf of the federal government, was clear about what the government aimed for: '[the Political Reform] would contribute to make our society to be more about consensus and less about conflict'.[81] As will be seen in Chapter 6, the idea of consensus and cross-party cooperation played a central role in the formation of the new norms of political interaction at the critical juncture when the PRI regime was unravelling.

Direct political entrenchment also served to surmount economic emergencies and overcome political turmoil. This is the case, for example, of the constitutional amendment to Article 28 to exempt the bank industry from the constitutional ban on economic monopolies. This amendment was adopted after lame-duck president López Portillo issued an executive order expropriating banks in 1982. Without the former, the executive order would not have survived in courts. The executive order and the constitutional amendment that followed were the choices to respond to a debt crisis that brought the country close to economic collapse (the worst economic crisis in six decades).[82] In this case, amending the Constitution served a pre-emptive function in that it was necessary to ensure the measure survived judicial review.[83] Otherwise, chances were that the executive order would have been struck down. Although the judiciary was not considered to be fully independent, it would have been hard to get around the text of Article 28, which stated that in Mexico 'there shall be no monopolies [. . .] of any type'.[84] In this context, changing the textual basis for constitutional interpretation was perhaps the only way to secure the

[80] Soledad Loaeza, 'El Partido Acción Nacional: La Oposición Leal en México' (1974) 14 Foro Internacional 357 (arguing, 'the [PAN] originated in 1939 as a response to the social policies on education, family, the church, and the economy in general of the *Cardenismo*. In its origins we can notice that those who felt excluded from the revolution wished to achieve political participation'). See also Daniel Cosío Villegas, *El Sistema Político Mexicano: Las Posibilidades de Cambio* (Editorial J Mortiz 1972).

[81] Paulina Fernández Christlieb, 'El Partido Político en las Reformas Electorales: Concepto Oficial, México 1977–1982' (2006) 8 Estudios Políticos 111, 116.

[82] See Jonathan Kandell, 'José López Portillo, President When Mexico's Default Set Off Debt Crisis, Dies at 83' *The New York Times* (18 February 2004) <www.nytimes.com/2004/02/18/business/jose-lopez-portillo-president-when-mexico-s-default-set-off-debt-crisis-dies-83.html> accessed 15 August 2024 (arguing, 'the crisis pushed the Mexican state toward a program of budget cuts, privatizations of state firms, and credit restrictions that limited the state's ability to continue subsidizing domestic industrialization').

[83] See Magaloni (n 66) 283.

[84] Constitution of 1917, Art 28, 5 February 1917 ('En los Estados Unidos Mexicanos no habrá monopolios [. . .] de ningún tipo').

implementation of the government's decision. As will be explained in more detail in Chapter 7, the executive order was eventually held constitutional by the Supreme Court.[85]

When Miguel de la Madrid (1982–88) took office, the regime was clearly in the midst of a serious legitimacy crisis. Months before his inauguration, President López Portillo had nationalized banks to avoid economic catastrophe. People across all social sectors were upset, public criticism of the government was unprecedented, and there were also rumours of calls for violent uprisings.[86] The constitutional amendments introduced by President Miguel de la Madrid in December 1982, days after his inauguration, appear in sharp contrast to López Portillo's. Against the backdrop of the political turmoil created by the squandering and corruption of the latter, coupled with one of the most serious financial crises in Mexico's modern history,[87] De la Madrid's government agenda consisted of a number of measures that, in general terms, aimed at restructuring the economy and changing the narrative of the regime. Among these measures, De la Madrid included the *Renovación Moral* (moral renovation) to combat corruption and squandering.[88] To materialize it, he presented a bill to amend Title IV of the Constitution on public servants' accountability. The bill included, among other things, new constitutional principles (eg efficiency and honesty) to rule public service and the replacement of the term *funcionario público* (public officer) with *servidor público* (public servant). These changes were presented as a way of renovating public service: the introduction of new principles and the change of terms were intended to make public officials truly serve public interests instead of individual ones.[89] This amendment was largely symbolic, much like a billboard advertising the government's commitment to the rule of law and combating corruption. Clearly, a simple terminological change was not going to end the pervasive corruption that had been fuelled

[85] In a 15:2 decision, the executive order was held constitutional by the Supreme Court on 22 November 1983. For a thorough analysis of this case, see Ramón Sánchez Medal, *El Fraude a la Constitución y el Único Amparo en México contra una Reforma Demolitoria de la Constitución* (Editorial Porrúa 1988).

[86] Enrique Mueller, 'La crisis económica que atraviesa México causa una grave crispación en la actividad política' *El País* (1 September 1982) <https://elpais.com/diario/1982/09/01/internacional/399679211_850215.html> accessed 15 August 2024.

[87] See eg Juan Carlos Moreno-Brid and Jaime Ros, *Development and Growth in the Mexican Economy: A Historical Perspective* (OUP 2009) 124–76; Nora Claudia Lustig, *Mexico: The Remaking of an Economy* (Brookings Institution Press 2000).

[88] Miguel de la Madrid Hurtado, *El Ejercicio de las Facultades Presidenciales* (UNAM 1998) 49.

[89] Iniciativa del Ejecutivo, Exposición de Motivos (3 December 1982) <http://legislacion.scjn.gob.mx/Buscador/Paginas/wfProcesoLegislativoCompleto.aspx?q=b/EcoMjefuFeB6DOaNOimNPZPsNLFqe0s7fey1FqricnNbiZodZlaGwZxDFFrD0chXE4NlnikOFuFNwSQCTBuw==> accessed 15 August 2024.

for decades by the PRI. Policy measures to tackle corruption could have been implemented by ordinary legislation, but amending the Constitution, perhaps, added symbolic significance and raised the profile of the measure. To be sure, this is not to say that direct political entrenchment was only symbolic during the De la Madrid administration. To cope with the electoral strength that the opposition (ie the PAN) had gained, particularly in the north of the country, the Constitution was amended again to, among other things, increase proportional representation seats in the Chamber of Deputies from 100 to 200 and adopt the *claúsula de gobernabilidad* (governability clause) in 1986.[90] Amid the fear of losing control of the Chamber of Deputies, in the event that no party obtained 51 per cent of the national vote and no party obtained the absolute majority of seats, the governability clause ensured an absolute majority through the allocation of proportional representation seats to the party with the highest votes (ie most likely the PRI).[91]

Notably, while López Portillo's executive order most likely would not have survived without the amendment to Article 28, De la Madrid's amendments to tackle corruption could have been implemented by ordinary legislation. The regime, however, needed to change its narrative. The revolutionary narrative that for decades legitimized the PRI hegemonic regime was falling apart. Corruption, economic instability, and a general distrust in the government made it difficult to keep sustaining the idea that the PRI was the only legitimate path for the realization of the revolutionary ideals. The discourse surrounding the amendments to Title IV and the rest of the amendments adopted in De la Madrid's administration marked the change from the official revolutionary discourse to a discourse of *Estado de Derecho* (rule of law).[92] Amending the Constitution was De la Madrid's political choice to advertise such change. In a context of economic uncertainty created by the debt crisis, the discourse of the rule of law paired with a neoliberal economic policy seemed to be crucial to reassuring international creditors.[93]

[90] José Antonio Crespo, 'The Party System and Democratic Governance in Mexico' (CSIS 2004) volume XV, Study 2 (March 2004) <https://csis-website-prod.s3.amazonaws.com/s3fs-public/legacy_files/files/media/csis/pubs/ppcrespo%5B1%5D.pdf> accessed 15 August 2024.

[91] Juan Molinar Horcasitas and Jeffrey A Weldon, 'Reforming Electoral Systems in Mexico' in Matthew Soberg Shugart and Martin P Wattenberg (eds), *Mixed-Member Electoral Systems: The Best of Both Worlds?* (OUP 2003) 214–15.

[92] The change of narrative is clear from the political platform and speeches of President Miguel de la Madrid (1982–88). See eg Miguel de la Madrid Hurtado, *Los Grandes Problemas Nacionales de Hoy: El Reto Del Futuro* (Editorial Diana 1982).

[93] Miguel Basáñez, *El Pulso de los Sexenios: 20 Años de Crisis en México* (Siglo XXI 1990) 69–93; César Cansino, 'La "Transición Política" en México: Dinámica y Perspectiva' (1991) 8 Estudios Políticos 6.

III. Constitutional Rigidity Pre-1988

Elkins, Ginsburg, and Melton explain the endurance and de facto flexibility of the Mexican Constitution during the PRI hegemonic rule through the notion that constitutional amendments served as a tool that provided political goods allowing for the co-optation of interest groups and the creation of the necessary loyalty to make bargaining possible.[94] Like Elkins, Ginsburg, and Melton's, most explanations of the dysfunction of the presidential system, separation of powers, and the system of checks and balances (including the de facto flexibility) of the Mexican Constitution during that time hinge on the presence of political conditions, behaviours, and practices that gave way to unwritten rules[95] that enabled the president to exercise virtually unchecked power—namely, the *facultades metaconstitucionales* (metaconstitutional powers) which, rather than being defined by the master-text Constitution, emerged from the hegemonic nature of the party system of the time.[96] The metaconstitutional powers allowed the president to, among other things, easily access the constitutional amendment mechanism, unilaterally choose their successor (ie known as the *dedazo*[97]), and designate and remove governors and judges. According to Jeffrey Weldon, the metaconstitutional powers of the president depended on three factors: a unified government, high party discipline within the ruling party, and the president as the head of the ruling party.[98] Together, these factors resulted in a high centralization of decision-making in the hands of the president who, at the same time, was also the head of the party.

[94] Zachary Elkins, Tom Ginsburg, and James Melton, *The Endurance of National Constitutions* (CUP 2009) 197 ('[C]onstitutional amendment during the PRI regime was frequent, and amendments provided political goods. The PRI used the Constitution to incorporate social insurgencies and political dissidents while limiting their effective power').

[95] The notion of unwritten rules may include political norms, constitutional conventions, and more generally, in Helmke and Levitsky's terms, 'socially shared rules, usually unwritten, that are created, communicated, and enforced outside officially sanctioned channels'. Here, the notion of unwritten rules is understood in the latter sense. I use the terms 'unwritten rules' 'informal institutions', and 'norms' interchangeably. See Gretchen Helmke and Steven Levitsky, *Informal Institutions and Democracy: Lessons from Latin America* (JHU Press 2006) 5 for a discussion of the notion of political norms and conventions. See Neil S Siegel, 'Political Norms, Constitutional Conventions, and President Donald Trump' (2018) 93 Indiana Law Journal 177; Keith E Whittington, 'The Status of Unwritten Constitutional Conventions in the United States Symposium: Constitutional Traditions: Akhil Amar's America's Unwritten Constitution' (2013) 5 University of Illinois Law Review 1847; Albert V Dicey, *Introduction to the Study of the Law of the Constitution* (Macmillan and Company 1889) 422.

[96] See eg Jorge Carpizo, *El Presidencialismo Mexicano* (Siglo XXI 2002) 190–99; Weldon (n 2); Alonso Lujambio, 'Adiós a la Excepcionalidad: Régimen Presidencial y Gobierno Dividido en México' in Jorge L Lanzaro (ed), *Tipos de Presidencialismo y Coaliciones Politicas en America Latina* (CLACSO 2001) 254.

[97] Elkins, Ginsburg, and Melton (n 94) 194–95; Carpizo (n 96); Joy Langston, 'The Birth and Transformation of the Dedazo in Mexico' in Gretchen Helmke and Steven Levitsky (eds), *Informal Institutions and Democracy: Lessons from Latin America* (JHU Press 2006) 143.

[98] Weldon (n 2) 244–52.

To be sure, this is not to say that the president had absolute authority in the exercise of the metaconstitutional powers. For example, as Joy Langston has shown, candidate selection under the hegemonic PRI involved different degrees of centralization. For instance, the selection of local candidates tended to be more decentralized than federal ones, with the president delegating an important part of the selection process to the governors who at the same time had to negotiate with different sectors before making a decision.[99]

Roughly since the founding of the PNR (1929), party discipline within the official party in Congress was created through three methods: centralized party leadership, a closed-list system, and the lack of incentives for deputies to act in line with the interests of their constituencies.[100] Since then, the structure of the party tended towards a centralized party leadership. Party members were willing to delegate authority to the person who was perceived as the most (or one of the most) powerful individual in the organization, which at the time was Calles.[101] Candidate selection was originally determined by a decentralized mechanism akin to a primary election. However, in practice, it worked like a closed-list system due to the (ir)regular intervention of the Comité Ejecutivo Nacional (the executive committee of the party) (CEN) in vote counting and certification processes.[102] Being selected guaranteed that the candidate in question would win by any necessary means (eg through fraud or by taking advantage of the majorities held in the Electoral College to certify victories or overturn adverse elections).[103] The selection rules were modified in 1937 to formally increase centralization by introducing party conventions and the power of higher committees to veto nominations.[104] The candidate selection system under the hegemonic PRI regime developed into one where 'candidates for federal legislative posts were chosen by national party leaders (not party members or voters) with subnational input, while those for subnational posts were selected by state party leaders (the governors) with national supervision and input'.[105] Writing in 1997, Weldon points out that the party had a closed-list system of nominations and 'complete control over access to the ballot under the banner of the PRI'.[106] Moreover, until 1994, the national leadership of the party had the de facto veto power over Congress and

[99] Joy K Langston, *Democratization and Authoritarian Party Survival: Mexico's PRI* (OUP 2017) 129–37.
[100] Weldon (n 2) 246.
[101] ibid 247.
[102] ibid.
[103] ibid.
[104] ibid.
[105] Langston (n 99) 123.
[106] Weldon (n 2) 247.

governorship nominations.[107] Unsurprisingly, the sheer power of the party disincentivized defections because until 1989 (the year it lost its first gubernatorial race to the PAN in the State of Baja California),[108] it was the party winning virtually every election.[109] Put differently, not belonging to the party entailed very high costs in terms of political career development options. The third contributor to party discipline was the lack of incentives for deputies to act in line with the interests of their constituencies (resulting in the abdication of their law-making and checking powers[110]). According to Weldon, this lack of incentives originated in the constitutional prohibition of immediate re-election of deputies, senators, governors, state legislators, and mayors introduced in 1933.[111] With no immediate re-election, popularly elected officers had no incentives to respond to their constituencies once in office. Instead, if they wanted their political careers to flourish, members of Congress had to be responsive and accountable to the national party leaders—that is to say, to those who controlled the nomination processes.[112]

Party discipline is a factor that has been largely present in some shape or form across the historical period covered in this chapter, which among other things has allowed access to the amendment mechanism. To be sure, this is not to say that factions did not exist and that there were no cases in which the president faced pushback in Congress and elsewhere.[113] For instance, as noted in Section II, Juárez decided to back down on his efforts to amend the Constitution outside institutional means due to the pushback he experienced both in Congress and from the governors who refused to publish the relevant part of the *convocatoria*. From the 1940s onwards, the PRI was characterized by its high discipline.[114] A historical precedent to the workings of party discipline and centralization of decision-making under the hegemonic party system can be found in the Díaz regime (1876–1911). The Porfirian regime was personalist and decision-making was highly centralized.[115] Díaz's strategy was one of co-optation and negotiation. The opposition in the late nineteenth century

[107] ibid.
[108] ibid 244.
[109] ibid 247.
[110] María Amparo Casar, 'Executive–Legislative Relations: The Case of Mexico (1946–1997)' in Scott Morgenstern and Benito Nacif (eds), *Legislative Politics in Latin America* (OUP 2002) 121.
[111] Weldon (n 2) 247–48.
[112] ibid 248.
[113] For a well-documented account of the pushback presidents experienced from Congress between 1857 and 1940, see ibid 228–34. I thank José Antonio Caballero for pointing this out to me.
[114] ibid 246.
[115] See Knight (n 23) 15 (arguing, '[a] liberal by affiliation, Díaz displayed more appetite for power than adherence to principle and, once president, he resolved to curb factionalism, to blur the liberal-conservative battle-lines, and to create a strong, centralized regime around his own person').

was limited by personal stakes.[116] Charles Hale describes how most men of ideas in Mexico and those with available means to criticize the regime (eg with a voice in the media) had a personal stake in the system, either as elected officials or governmental appointees.[117] Instead of challenging the regime, the dominant intellectual group (the *Científicos*) of the time focused on justifying the permanence of Díaz in power as a necessary step for the realization of the liberal project and, most importantly, economic progress (even if that required the deployment of authoritarian practices).[118] Díaz also reduced the military to prevent other ambitious individuals from trying to take power violently as he had attempted to do.[119] In this way, he secured a subservient legislative branch and prevented the rise of potential candidates wanting to run for the presidency.[120] Candidate selection was also highly centralized: 're-elections and replacements only went ahead after Díaz had weighed local reports and petitions, exercising the ultimate veto of the "centre"'.[121] As Alan Knight puts it, under Díaz:

> Loyalty, rather than civic responsibility, was the chief desideratum. Hence, a large proportion of Porfirian governors—maybe 70%—were presidential favorites, imported into alien states, where their prime allegiance was to their president and maker, rather than to their provincial subjects.[122]

By enabling the centralization of decision-making, party discipline also had an impact on the workings of Mexico's constitutional order—including easy access to the amendment mechanism. Put differently, party discipline was an important unwritten rule that helped keep the PRI machine going for so long and guaranteed access to constitutional amendment if necessary. In Weldon's view, the extraordinary centralization of decision-making within the hegemonic party, which allowed the president to exercise virtually unchecked powers, 'cut across the branches of government, "violating" Article 49, which is supposed to guarantee the separation of powers'.[123] Although constitutional entrenchment rules were in place and formally observed, the power of the president was effectively unbound. Party discipline precluded all possibilities of formal

[116] Charles A Hale, *The Transformation of Liberalism in Late Nineteenth-Century Mexico* (Princeton UP 1989) 92.
[117] ibid.
[118] For a discussion of *Científicos*' politics, see ibid 25–63.
[119] Meyer (n 19) 139.
[120] ibid.
[121] Knight (n 23) 16.
[122] ibid 17.
[123] Weldon (n 2) 255.

constitutional veto points working properly. The president was able to amend the Constitution at will because the hegemonic party had control over the three branches of government, both at the federal and state level. As Benito Nacif puts it:

> [F]ormally, the Mexican Constitution provided for the separation of the executive and legislative branches of government, but in practice Congress was subordinated to the presidential authority. [. . .] The Presidency had the ability to deliver 'policy shocks' in response to critical situations. Under normal circumstances the chief executive had the power to bring about substantive policy change even when this involved amending the constitution.[124]

This situation meant that, if the president deemed it necessary, constitutional amendment would be available for political entrenchment. Until 1997, most constitutional amendments had been the result of proposals by the president.[125]

When discussing the political conditions that allowed the centralization of power under the hegemonic party system, Weldon identifies a basic problem: the gap between what the Constitution prescribes and the reality of constitutional and party politics. In this way, his work illuminates the implications of a governing elite subculture, its practices and behaviours, on the workings of the constitutional system. In particular, under the hegemonic party system, the source of the disproportionate power of the president was not the Constitution but 'the extraordinary centralization of decision-making within the party'.[126] That is, the power of the president relied less on the constitutional design of the presidential system than on unwritten aspects of the organization of the party and the centralization of power based on which it functioned. Given that in Weldon's model the centralization of power (ie the metaconstitutional powers of the president) was an issue of a political nature rather than one of institutional design, the assumption was that with democratization, the metaconstitutional powers of the president would disappear and the system of separation of powers would begin to function properly.[127] For instance, as will be seen in Chapter 7, in such conditions, the Supreme Court was expected to become a powerful political actor able to control the

[124] Benito Nacif, 'The Fall of the Dominant Presidency: Lawmaking under Divided Government in Mexico' in Roderic Ai Camp (ed), *The Oxford Handbook of Mexican Politics* (OUP 2012) 234.
[125] Weldon (n 2) 235.
[126] ibid 255.
[127] ibid 254–55.

political branches. That is, with democratization, the unwritten rules that had formed throughout a century would disappear and the Constitution would effectively constrain power.[128] Once the political conditions enabling the metaconstitutional powers of the president ceased to be present, the president would be left only with their formal constitutional powers, thus the gap between the Constitution and reality would be narrowed. This naturally meant that the constitutional amendment mechanism would cease to be readily available. However, even though the informal institutions that allowed the president to exercise unchecked political power mostly disappeared as the PRI hegemonic rule unravelled,[129] the patterns of amendment in the decades that followed suggest that new ones (inevitably influenced by old ones) emerged.

IV. Political Entrenchment Post-1988: The Cross-Party Entrenchment Regime

Just by looking at the volume of amendments discussed in Chapter 4, one can confirm that the amendment mechanism not only remained available in Mexico's economy of constitutional change but that it became a prominent tool for political entrenchment after the PRI lost its supermajority in the Chamber of Deputies and therefore the ability to amend the Constitution on its own in 1988. Over 60 per cent of the modifications to the Constitution have taken place since then. The change in the power structure meant that the norms of interaction among political actors (ie political parties) would change.[130] Constitutional amendment in the transitional years (ie between roughly 1988-2000) was determined by the interdependence of the weakened PRI and the growing opposition, namely the PAN and the newly founded PRD. The weakened hegemonic party had to bargain with the opposition and vice versa should they want to pass an amendment. While the PRI needed to surmount a legitimacy crisis and prove itself a viable political option, the opposition needed a series of amendments to secure its access to power. Like Juárez, Díaz, Calles, Cárdenas, López Portillo, and De la Madrid, post-1988 key political actors (eg presidents, party chairpersons, party leaders, and representatives) continued to see the amendment mechanisms as a tool for political entrenchment and

[128] Lujambio (n 96).
[129] Helmke and Levitsky (n 3) 92.
[130] Cansino (n 93) 10. See also Guillermo O'Donnell, Philippe C Schmitter, and Laurence Whitehead, *Transitions from Authoritarian Rule: Comparative Perspectives* (JHU Press 1986); Guillermo O'Donnell, Philippe C Schmitter, and Laurence Whitehead, *Transitions from Authoritarian Rule: Tentative Conclusions about Uncertain Democracies* (JHU Press 2013).

found new ways to make access to it possible. In a context of political fragmentation, it is evident that the trend of formal constitutional change discussed in Chapter 4 is the result of successful constitutional bargaining and cooperation across party lines.[131] In particular, from 1997 to 2018, constitutional amendments were the result of the cooperation between the three major political parties: PRI, PAN, and PRD. Whereas from 2018 to 2024, they were the result of the cooperation between MORENA as the party with the most seats in both chambers of Congress with its allies Partido del Trabajo (PT), Partido Encuentro Social (PES), PVEM, and PRI, or PAN, or PRD.[132]

In the regime that emerged after the end of the PRI hegemony, political parties found an alternative solution for dealing with political power-sharing through cross-party entrenchment. What we saw between 1988 and 1997 was a change from a regime in which a hegemonic party was the main beneficiary of direct political entrenchment to one in which multiple parties benefit from

[131] María Amparo Casar and Ignacio Marván, 'Pluralismo y Reformas Constitucionales en México 1997–2012' in María Amparo Casar and Ignacio Marván Laborde (eds), *Reformar sin Mayorías: La Dinámica del Cambio Constitucional en México: 1997–2012* (Penguin Random House 2014) 14.

[132] As seen in Table 4.2 in Chapter 4, from 2018 to 2021, MORENA held 250 out of 500 seats in the Chamber of Deputies and 61 out of 128 seats in the Senate. In that period, MORENA found a relatively stable coalition with PT, PES, and PVEM which held forty-two, twenty-three , and eleven seats in the Chamber of Deputies; and six, four, and six seats in the Senate, respectively. That is, together these parties held 326 seats in the Chamber of Deputies and 77 in the Senate. But that was not enough to reach the two-thirds majority required by the amendment rule (ie 334 out of 500 in the Chamber of Deputies and 86 out of 128 in the Senate). Accordingly, if MORENA wished to access the amendment mechanism, it needed the cooperation of the opposition—which it found to pass, for example, the Judicial Reform of 2021 and the expansion of *prisión preventiva* (pre-trial detention) scheme in 2019 dicussed at the end of this chapter and in Chapter 7, respectively. From 2021 to 2024, after the mid-term elections, MORENA held 200 seats in the Chamber of Deputies and 57 in the Senate. Its allies, PT and PES, held thirty-four and lost all its twenty three seats; however, PVEM went from eleven to thirty-nine in the Chamber of Deputies. Working together MOR-PT-PVEM held 273 votes in the Chamber of Deputies. In the Senate, PT, PES, and PVEM held six, four, and eight seats, respectively. Together, MOR-PT-PES-PVEM held 75 votes in the Senate. That was insufficient to reach the qualified majority of 334 and 86 in either chamber of Congress. In other words, in this period, in addition to the cooperation of its allies (PT, PES, and PVEM), MORENA more than ever needed the cooperation of either the PRI (which held 68 seats) or the PAN (which held 112) to reach the qualified majority. Whereas between 2018-2021, it was possible to sail through eighteen constitutional amendment processes, between 2021-2024 (31 July), this was the case in six ocassions. In the latter period, for the first time in recent history, a constitutional amendment was blocked while being 'deliberated' on the floor of a chamber of Congress. In April 2022, López Obrador's Reforma Electrica initiative (which sought to roll back important aspects of the Energy Reform of 2013 (discussed in Chapter 4) was blocked after the opposition (PRI-PAN-PRD) refused to cooperate with the government to push the reform through Congress. Similarly, in November of that year the PRI refused to partner with the government to pass López Obrador's Reforma Electoral initiative (that, among other things, sought to replace the electoral commissioners selection system for a popular election system, reduce the budget of the electoral watchdog INE, and reduce the membership of the chamber of deputies), after having agreed to do so. See 'Reforma Eléctrica: la iniciativa de AMLO fue rechazada con 275 votos a favor y 222 en contra' (*infobae*, 17 April 2022) <https://www.infobae.com/america/mexico/2022/04/17/reforma-electrica-en-vivo-diputados-de-morena-se-trasladan-a-la-camara-de-diputados/> accessed 2 April 2025; Guadalupe Irízar, Natalia Vitela and Martha Martínez, 'Y tras la marcha... rechaza PRI aprobar reforma electoral' *Reforma* (Mexico, 15 November 2022) <https://www.elnorte.com/y-tras-la-marcha-rechaza-pri-aprobar-reforma-electoral/ar2504372> accessed 27 February 2023.

it—namely, what I call the cross-party entrenchment regime (CPER). The formation of this new regime came with the formation of new unwritten rules of political interaction that allow access to direct political entrenchment even in times of divided government. In particular, what I call the rule of cooperation has been essential to ensure continued access to the amendment mechanism in a context of political fragmentation. As will be discussed in detail in Chapter 6, during the transitional years, the PRI set the conditions for the rule of cooperation to emerge.[133] By negotiating with the opposition and gradually conceding their long-standing demands to make the electoral system fair and competitive, the PRI ensured the opposition would keep cooperating. All of this was done while legitimizing its own existence and securing a loyal opposition.

At first glance, the possibility of cross-party entrenchment could be viewed as a positive development for democracy insofar as it is not only able to put politics in motion and provide political stability but it also allows frequent constitutional amendments, which could be read as a sign of a thriving democracy. A rapidly changing constitution, under such a view, would suggest that representatives are successfully fulfilling their roles by responding to the public will, reducing agency costs of representation by allowing the people to genuinely exercise their right to self-government. In Mexico, however, cross-party entrenchment comes with associated problems that affect the workings of constitutional democracy. The dynamics of formal constitutional change identified in Chapter 4 (ie the fast-track processes in Congress and rubber-stampings by state legislatures) indicate the parties' deal-making ability, strict party discipline, and, at the same time, centralization of constitutional decision-making where, in the best-case scenario, decisions are taken in legislative commissions and in the worst-case scenario secretly behind closed doors.[134] In particular, cross-party entrenchment has negative implications for the separation of

[133] In an illuminating article, Jean-François Prud'homme analyses the electoral legislative reforms adopted during the Salinas administration and argues that during said administration a new system of interaction between parties was formed. This is shown through the analysis of the three electoral reforms adopted between 1988 and 1994. Chapter 6 builds on this main argument and extends it to Zedillo's administration. In footnote 35, Prud'homme leaves an open question regarding to what extent the cooperation of the PAN with the PRI meant perpetuating old practices or actually meant the beginning of new game rules. The theory I build here answers this question. Unlike Prud'homme, I do not think the answer to his question should be an either/or answer. Instead, new rules of the game were formed and these rules are cemented in old practices. The rule of cooperation is crucial to understanding why the amendment mechanism remained available in Mexico's economy of constitutional change. Jean-François Prud'homme, 'La Negociación de Las Reglas Del Juego: Tres Reformas Electorales (1988–1994)' (1996) 3 Politica y Gobierno 93.

[134] As we saw in Chapter 4 with the *Pacto por México* and we will see in Chapter 6, this is not always the case.

powers, checks and balances, public deliberation, and the principle of non-arbitrary power. I will return to this point in Chapter 7.

The malfunction of vertical and horizontal mechanisms of accountability is explained by the fact that the political fragmentation that began to take place in 1989 neither entailed the disappearance of the PRI as a relevant political force nor the sudden disappearance of unwritten rules (such as party discipline), practices, and understandings that became part of Mexican constitutional culture since at least the late nineteenth century. Crucially, for example, when it comes to candidate selection and party discipline, what once belonged mainly to the president shifted to the party/ies after democratization.[135] Yet, that does not mean that candidate selection became open and decentralized in the long run. The tendency towards decentralization in candidate selection methods that characterized the 1990s and 2000s (in Mexico as well as globally) was reversed in the country after 2010 for most elected positions.[136] According to Langston, writing in 2022, '[o]ver the past 10 to 15 years, candidate selection in all of Mexico's major parties has transitioned from somewhat open and decentralized to almost completely closed and centralized to the national or state levels'.[137] While not largely exclusively in the hands of the president, candidate selection remains highly centralized, thus strong party discipline remains. Describing the internal dynamics created by such an arrangement within MORENA, the party in government during 2018–24, Langston portrays an image akin to the dynamics under the hegemonic PRI described above:

> In both the 2018 and 2021 elections, Morena's leaders only allowed a small number of PR candidacies to be chosen through democratic means, in this case, using the 'tombola' or by lot. The SMD candidates were designated almost entirely through top-down methods. Thus, we have no doubts that factions play a major role in MORENA as they do in the nation's three largest traditional parties.
>
> These factions help their members reach higher posts in return for loyalty to their leader; and many times, members stay for years as 'Politician X's' person, following the group's leaders and depending on them for their political positions, so we believe that this type of relationship is relevant for politicians to better construct long-term career paths, and therefore, party leaders

[135] See Casar (n 110) 141 (arguing, 'the conditions are being set for the party to assume the role of determining who the candidates will be, and thus transforming its prior subordination to the president').

[136] Joy K Langston, 'Legislative Candidate Selection and Incumbent Renomination in Mexico' (2022) 42 Revista de Ciencia Política 565, 568.

[137] ibid.

> choose a high percentage of candidates for elected offices who belong to their intra-party group because then these elected figures will owe their loyalty to that leader.[138]

Up to this point, two things in particular allow us to understand why after the hegemonic party unravelled, formal constitutional change continued to be available in Mexico's economy of constitutional change. On the one hand, the shared understandings about and preference for constitutional amendment as an effective means for political entrenchment that likely developed throughout a century; and, on the other, the continued centralization of candidate selection across the party system (which is also a result of practices that have been present in that country's constitutional history) is essential to understanding the parties' high discipline and consequently their ability to access the amendment mechanism. These two factors likely helped the PRI, as the party that had been the main beneficiary of direct political entrenchment for over six decades and the party that got to dictate the new norms governing party interaction (ie the rule of cooperation), to successfully dictate them—as will be discussed in Chapter 6.

V. Conclusion

In this chapter, I illustrated how, since the late nineteenth century, the Constitution (specifically the amendment mechanism) played a central role in entrenching policy agendas, consolidating political power, coping with a rising opposition, and even symbolically dealing with legitimacy crises. There are at least five features that can be identified in the different periods covered in this chapter and that are present in contemporary constitutional politics. First, since the late nineteenth century, the Constitution has played a central role in the public discourse as well as in protecting the interests of the ruling elite. Second, there is a long-standing tradition of using the amendment mechanism for political entrenchment instead of resorting to non-institutional means. This could be interpreted, on one hand, as part of the legacy of the historical precedent set by President Juárez's unsuccessful attempt to amend the Constitution by referendum. On the other hand, it may also be interpreted as a result of the influence of the *Científicos* as a legal movement favouring the idea of continuous constitutional reform. Third, constitutional amendment was used not only to address policy needs but also as a billboard. Similar to De la Madrid's

[138] ibid 573.

amendment for the *Renovación Moral* (moral renovation) to combat corruption and squandering, in 2021, President López Obrador (2018–24) and his party MORENA passed a wide-ranging judicial reform that was supposedly intended to end nepotism and corruption within the judicial branch.[139] In reality, it did little to nothing to address such a problem—which could have been dealt with through ordinary legislation.[140] The hidden agenda behind the judicial reform of 2021 came to light with the attempt to extend the term of Justice Arturo Zaldívar as chief justice (who had already proved himself as a government collaborator) through the hasty inclusion of a transitory provision in the occasion of the adoption of the secondary legislation implementing the constitutional amendment.[141] Fourth, candidate selection has remained highly centralized across constitutional history. Thus, party discipline has remained present as well. Fifth, the use of political manifestos during the revolutionary period also stands out—in particular, the centrality that the Constitution of 1857 (ie constitutional amendment) had in these documents as the main tool to bring about the necessary changes for the realization of the revolutionary ideals. These documents and their focus on constitutional change may be understood as the predecessors of the practice of written agreements (akin to the *Pacto por México* discussed in Chapter 4) between political parties to ensure smooth and efficient constitutional amendment processes—which played an important role in the formation of the rule of cooperation, which I discuss in the next chapter.

[139] This amendment should not be confused with the judicial overhaul of 2024 which I referred to at the outset of this book. Incidentally, both amendments (2021 and 2024) were justified as measures to end nepotism within the judiciary. Yet, none of them introduced measures that could reasonably be understood as means to tackle such a problem. Among other things, the judicial reform of 2021 changed the precedent rules for individual constitutional complaints (*amparo*) and created multi-member appellate courts. Similarly, it is unclear how exactly the popular election of judges could tackle the problem of nepotism and corruption on which the government attempted to justify the overhaul of the judiciary in 2024. Corruption and nepotism are a common feature in the political branches in Mexico and it is these branches that are now in control of the judicial candidate selection. See José Antonio Caballero Juárez, *La Reforma Judicial de 2021. ¿Hacia dónde va la Justicia?* (IIJ-UNAM 2021) 30–40 <https://biblio.juridicas.unam.mx/bjv/id/6578> accessed 15 August 2024. See also Mariana Velasco-Rivera, 'La Reforma Judicial que no Necesitamos' *Animal Político* <https://animalpolitico.com/analisis/invitades/la-reforma-judicial-que-no-necesitamos> accessed 16 August 2024; Mariana Velasco-Rivera, 'A Democratic Mandate to Overhaul Mexico's Judiciary?' (*Verfassungsblog*, 24 July 2024) <https://verfassungsblog.de/a-democratic-mandate-to-overhaul-mexicos-judiciary/> accessed 4 August 2024..

[140] Velasco-Rivera (n 139).

[141] The extension of the term of the chief justice was eventually struck down by the Supreme Court. For a discussion on the adoption of both the constitutional amendment to the judiciary and this particular episode, see Velasco-Rivera (n 53).

6

Actors, Choices, Decisions, and the Formation of Political Norms

I. Introduction

> Precedents created during an extended period of dysfunction do not go away once a new regime is consolidated. Expansion of presidential lawmaking powers is simply too valuable a tool to discard.[1]

Chapter 4 showed that most amendments to the Mexican Constitution have been adopted since 1988, the year the PRI lost its ability to amend the Constitution on its own. That chapter also identified a trend in the constitutional amendment processes from 1997 to 2024: *fast-track approvals* in both chambers of Congress and a *lack of opposition* in state legislatures. As previously discussed, such a trend can be explained as the product of strong party discipline across levels of government and sustained cooperation across party lines (ie cross-party entrenchment). The presence of these two elements facilitates the centralization of decision-making in constitution-amending processes in ways that go well beyond the design of the amendment rule. Chapter 5 explained the dynamics of constitutional change identified in Chapter 4 in light of Mexico's constitutional culture. By examining different episodes in that country's constitutional history, I argued that Mexico's constitutional culture has been shaped in important ways by the continuous use of constitutional amendments for political entrenchment. In so doing, I showed the place that the amendment mechanism has in Mexico's constitutional culture and illustrated the political norms that have developed and can still be found in contemporary constitutional politics. Against this backdrop, it should not be a surprise that after the transition to democracy at the turn of the century, the relevant political actors found ways to keep accessing the amendment mechanism. But how is all that possible in a context of political power fragmentation?

[1] Jack M Balkin, 'The Last Days of Disco: Why the American Political System Is Dysfunctional' (2014) 94 Boston University Law Review 1159, 1195.

The Politics of Constitutional Rigidity. Mariana Velasco-Rivera, Oxford University Press.
 DOI: 10.1093/9780191981876.003.0006

This chapter sheds light on the third element of the economy of constitutional change: the *choices made by key political actors*. In particular, the chapter seeks to show how the choices made during the period between 1988 and 1996 had a lasting impact on the trajectory of constitutional change in Mexico. One decision was key: the deployment of what I call the *consensus rationale*. By so doing, the PRI managed to gain the cooperation of the opposition parties when needed,[2] to maintain a predominant position vis-à-vis its counterparts,[3] and to dictate the terms and conditions of the transition. Most importantly, the PRI set the ground for perpetuating the centralization of constitutional decision-making, and in that way secured the continued access to constitutional amendment for political entrenchment. Through this still-privileged position, as discussed in Chapter 4, the PRI maintained a relevant position to effect formal constitutional change well into the twenty-first century: until 2015, the year when the PRI lost control of the majority of the state legislatures, its cooperation was necessary to pass any constitutional amendment. The choice of deploying the consensus rationale resulted in the formation of a new political norm; that is, the rule of cooperation—which, at the same time, has been the main driver of the cross-party entrenchment regime (CPER) I introduced in Chapter 5. The rule of cooperation operates through party discipline and its effect is the centralization of decision-making—which allows the continued use of the amendment mechanism for political entrenchment despite political fragmentation. Besides maintaining the amendment mechanism available in Mexico's economy of constitutional change, at the time of its emergence, the rule of cooperation had an important advantage: it smoothed out the amendment processes and created an image of consensus and stability—signalling that the country was on the right track to becoming a full democracy.

The chapter proceeds as follows. Section II lays out the social and political conditions that allowed the PRI to keep a dominant position between 1988 and 1996 in the realm of formal constitutional change despite its electoral debilitation. Section III traces the formation of the rule of cooperation by shedding light on the choices and decisions made by key political actors (including but not limited to the last two PRI presidents before the transition to democracy: President Salinas and President Zedillo) to deal with the new political reality—namely, the deployment of the consensus rationale. I will do so

[2] Jean-François Prud'homme, 'La Negociación de Las Reglas Del Juego: Tres Reformas Electorales (1988–1994)' (1996) 3 Politica y Gobierno 93.

[3] See Alberto Diaz-Cayeros and Beatriz Magaloni, 'Party Dominance and the Logic of Electoral Design in Mexico's Transition to Democracy' (2001) 13 Journal of Theoretical Politics 271 (arguing that electoral rules facilitated party dominance by disproportionately rewarding existing majorities and, at the same time, discouraging coordination among opposition parties).

through an analysis of the electoral and judicial reforms adopted between 1989 and 1996 to show the different moments in which the relevant political parties chose to accept the rule of cooperation. In Section IV, I offer an explanation as to why the deployment of the consensus rationale and the formation of rule of cooperation succeeded. Finally, Section V concludes.

II. The Political Conditions Pushing for Regime Change

Between 1988 and 1996, a number of factors made the PRI voluntarily tie its hands through successive constitutional amendments. The party was ousted from the presidency in 2000 after more than seventy years of hegemonic rule.[4] The inability of the PRI to tame factionalism within the party, the party split that followed, the formation of a strong movement with anti-regime tendencies, the economic collapse,[5] the changing balance of power after the elections of 1988, and the serious legitimacy crisis that followed are among the most important factors that led to the fall of the hegemonic party regime.[6] Despite the regime's unravelling, the PRI maintained an influential position in Mexican politics, especially regarding formal constitutional change. As I will explain, the co-optation of the rising opposition allowed the PRI to lead the transition

[4] Todd A Eisenstadt, *Courting Democracy in Mexico: Party Strategies and Electoral Institutions* (CUP 2004) 58–59 (arguing, 'The regime was forced to concede a series of electoral reforms leading to this point for a combination of reasons: the weakening of the electoral power of the PRI and internal divisions within the party, the rise of the opposition, and the influence of the international community. But the single most important event in establishing the imperative for electoral reforms was clearly the 1988 federal election and Salinas's subsequent efforts to rectify his credibility gap by complicity with PAN postelectoral mobilization, provided it stayed local and helped promote the PRI-state's national policy agenda'). Importantly, note that the constitutional and legal changes necessary to enable the democratic transition in Mexico began in 1977. As discussed in Chapter 5, in that year the Constitution was amended to, among other things, introduce the first iteration of the system of proportional representation in the Chamber of Deputies, whereby 25 per cent of the chamber would be elected through that system. The changes also included access to public party finance as well as the political party *registro condicionado* (conditional registry), which allowed small organizations to conditionally register as political parties subject to getting 1.5 per cent of the vote share in the relevant election. The effects of these changes, as reported by Lorenzo Córdova Vianello, were immediate. In the eight years that followed, several new political parties were formed, and the opposition consistently obtained seats in the Chamber of Deputies—1979: 106 seats; 1982: 101; and 1985: 108, out of 400 seats. See Lorenzo Córdova Vianello, 'El financiamiento a los partidos políticos en México' in Pablo Gutiérrez and Daniel Zovatto (eds), *Financiamiento de los partidos políticos en América Latina* (UNAM/IDEA/OEA 2011) 657–59.

[5] For a discussion of the PRI's *Corriente Democrática* (Democratic Current), the defection of its members after the selection of Carlos Salinas as presidential candidate, and what this meant for Mexican politics, see eg Luis Javier Garrido, *La ruptura: la Corriente Democrática del PRI* (Grijalbo 1993); Andrew Reding, 'The Democratic Current: A New Era in Mexican Politics' (1988) 5 World Policy Journal 323.

[6] For a discussion on Mexico's protracted transition, see Julio Labastida and Miguel Armando López Leyva, 'México: Una Transición Prolongada (1988–1996/97)' (2004) 66 Revista Mexicana de Sociología 749; Eisenstadt (n 4).

and dictate the new rules of the game while remaining an influential political force in the years to come.

In 1987, a split in the PRI over a disagreement on how to select presidential candidates was perhaps the final straw that triggered the end of the hegemonic party system. The practice until then had been what was called *dedazo*—the unilateral selection of the next president by the outgoing executive.[7] The leaders of the party's group, *Corriente Democrática* (Democratic Current), Cuauhtémoc Cárdenas and Porfirio Muñoz Ledo, called for the replacement of *dedazo* with a democratic and transparent process in which party members could participate. The proposal, however, was rejected during the XIII PRI National Assembly.[8] As a result, the members of *Corriente Democrática* decided to leave the PRI and, in turn, were able to rapidly form the *Frente Democrático Nacional* (National Democratic Front) (FDN) —an anti-PRI electoral coalition comprising several left-leaning parties[9] that would run against the PRI in the elections of 1988 with Cárdenas as their candidate.[10] After the presidential election of 1988, for the first time in history, the PRI had reason to fear losing its hold on power.[11] The PRI lost the qualified majority to unilaterally amend the Constitution and was ten seats short of losing the absolute majority in the Chamber of Deputies.[12]

The PRI not only lost the needed majority to amend the Constitution on its own. It is also widely believed that the government engaged in electoral fraud to retain the presidency.[13] The night of the election and its aftermath plunged the PRI into a legitimacy crisis that needed to be overcome not only in order to hold onto power for as long as possible but also because the election proved

[7] Joy Langston, 'The Birth and Transformation of the Dedazo in Mexico' in Gretchen Helmke and Steven Levitsky (eds), *Informal Institutions and Democracy: Lessons from Latin America* (JHU Press 2006) 143.

[8] Juan Molinar and Jeffrey Weldon, 'Elecciones de 1988 en México: Crisis del Autoritarismo' (1990) 52 Revista Mexicana de Sociología 229–62.

[9] PARM, PPS, PFCRN, and PMS.

[10] See Ann L Craig and Wayne A Cornelius, 'Houses Divided, Parties and Political Reform in Mexico' in Scott Mainwaring and Timothy Scully (eds), *Building Democratic Institutions: Party Systems in Latin America* (Stanford UP 1995) 249, 277 (arguing, 'The FDN worked to support Cardenas' campaign for the presidency and to present a unified, nationalist challenge to the PRI'); Stephen Haber and others, *Mexico since 1980* (CUP 2008) 132–33.

[11] Molinar and Weldon (n 8).

[12] As reported by Molinar Horcasitas and Weldon, the PRI won 260 out 500 seats in the Chamber of Deputies: Juan Molinar Horcasitas and Jeffrey A Weldon, 'Reforming Electoral Systems in Mexico' in Matthew Soberg Shugart and Martin P Wattenberg (eds), *Mixed-Member Electoral Systems: The Best of Both Worlds?* (OUP 2003) 218.

[13] Soledad Loaeza, 'La Crisis Electoral del 6 de Julio de 1988' (1999) 61 Revista Mexicana de Sociología 163; Haber and others (n 10) 133; Molinar Horcasitas and Weldon (n 12) 216; Aida Castro, 'El día en que "se cayó el sistema" y ganó Salinas' *El Universal* (Mexico, 1 August 2018) <www.eluniversal.com.mx/colaboracion/mochilazo-en-el-tiempo/nacion/sociedad/el-dia-en-que-se-cayo-el-sistema-y-gano-salinas> accessed 15 August 2024.

the hegemonic regime was indeed falling apart. The PRI needed to find a new narrative to present itself as truly committed to democratic values, and thus as a legitimate political option. The question was, how to do it? In a context where critics of the regime saw the electoral system as an obstacle to a true democracy, changing the narrative required changing the Constitution. If the PRI wanted to pass a constitutional amendment, the now weakened hegemonic party had to negotiate with the opposition and vice versa. From the very beginning, the Salinas administration and the PRI found themselves at a political crossroads: they could either choose to resist the inevitable fall of the hegemonic regime or reach out to the opposition and be able to continue accessing the amendment mechanism.

To be sure, President Salinas could have opted for the former and chosen indirect means of entrenchment. Even though the PRI lost the qualified majority to amend the Constitution on its own, it retained the absolute majority necessary to pass ordinary legislation in Congress. As for constitutional amendments, the opposition became important at the congressional level but the PRI maintained control of the state legislatures (which would allow it to pass or block amendment proposals adopted by Congress). This new balance of power meant that amending the Constitution was only possible through cooperation among political parties. The PRI, however, maintained a bargaining advantage because it was the only truly indispensable party to meet the requirements of the amendment rule. Additionally, at any moment it could opt for indirect means of entrenchment. These new political conditions, specifically the interaction required between the opposition and the PRI to bring forward constitutional amendments, provided the setting for the formation of new political norms and, eventually, a new regime.[14]

[14] As Joy Langston put it, 'the PRI regime, led by Salinas, was forced to adopt a new strategy of negotiating far-reaching electoral reforms with the center-right National Action Party (PAN) designed to make the elections more fair and transparent and at the same time, to create credible electoral outcomes, in order to keep mass protests against dirty elections from creating conditions of political chaos' (Joy Langston, 'Elite Ruptures: When Do Parties Split?' in Andreas Schedler (ed), *Electoral Authoritarianism: The Dynamics of Unfree Competition* (Lynne Rienner Publishers 2006) 71). The PRI was going through changes as well. The internal struggle over nominations did not end with the departure of the group led by Cárdenas and Muñoz Ledo. Between 1988 and 2000 there were attempts by lower-level actors within the party to change the statutes of the party to decentralize nominations. After a failed attempt during the Salinas administration, the first presidential primary election in the history of the PRI was held in 1999 during the Zedillo administration, the year before the hegemonic party lost a presidential election for the first time (see Joy Langston, 'Why Rules Matter: Changes in Candidate Selection in Mexico's PRI, 1988–2000' (2001) 33 Journal of Latin American Studies 486–90). The changes to candidate selection methods, however, do not seem to have had an impact on the discipline of party members for the passage of constitutional amendments in this period. Generally speaking, electoral law gives significant discretion to political parties to decide their methods of candidate selection. On paper, political parties' statutes have tended to democratize their candidate selection

Socially and politically, things were also complicated. For example, the Ejército Zapatista de Liberación Nacional's (EZLN's) uprising on 1 January 1994, the day the North America Free Trade Agreement (NAFTA) came into force, called into question the government and Salinas' neoliberal project, and laid out specific demands for 'the creation of a more just and democratic Mexico'.[15] Salinas' market opening agenda was a government priority seeking to, among other things, set the adequate conditions to bring NAFTA forward.[16] The social and political instability produced by the *Zapatista* uprising was simply not a good advertisement for a country that sought to attract foreign capital. The potential overlapping interests of the EZLN (as an anti-regime movement) and the PRD likely made the PRI realize that it had to include the latter in constitutional bargaining and make concessions.[17] On top of this, 1994 (a general election year) brought more instability with two political assassinations and a severe economic crisis.

As we will see in Sections III and IV, Salinas opted for a conciliatory approach to the opposition. Soon after the election of 1988, first the PAN and then several smaller parties opted to cooperate with the PRI to bring democratizing constitutional amendments forward.[18] (The PRD would take longer to cooperate and remained alienated in the meantime.) The way in which the PRI chose to handle the constitutional amendment processes and how it managed to get the opposition to cooperate with, rather than challenge, the regime are fundamental to understanding constitutional change in the post-hegemonic period.

processes. Yet, in practice, high-ranking decision-making bodies within the parties retain control and influence over rank-and-file party members (J Esteban Manteca Melgarejo, 'Métodos de Selección de Candidatos en México, 1994–2018' in Luis Carlos Ugalde and Saíd Hernández (eds), *Elecciones, justicia y democracia en México. Fortalezas y debilidades del sistema electoral, 1990–2020* (TEPJF) 207, 222).

[15] Shannon I Mattiace, '"Zapata Vive!": The EZLN, Indigenous Politics, and the Autonomy Movement in Mexico' (1997) 3 Journal of Latin American Anthropology 32, 32–33; Consuelo Sánchez, 'Breve Historia del EZLN' [1998] Boletín de Antropología Americana 127.

[16] See Haber and others (n 10) 16 (arguing, 'Carlos Salinas de Gortari [1988–94] accelerated the process of market opening—privatizing the banks and other major public firms, liberalizing restrictions on foreign direct investment, and, most dramatically, negotiating the North American Free Trade Agreement [NAFTA] with Canada and the United States. The NAFTA in particular represented a bold effort by the government to regain the confidence of investors by making it more difficult for a future administration to revert to trade protectionism and by establishing mechanisms that firmly safeguarded the property rights of foreign investors').

[17] Prud'homme (n 2) 120.

[18] Soledad Loaeza, 'El Partido Acción Nacional: La Oposición Leal en México' (1974) 14 Foro Internacional 352–74. See also Roderic Ai Camp, 'Democratizing Mexican Politics, 1982–2012' [2015] Oxford Research Encyclopedia of Latin American History <http://oxfordre.com/view/10.1093/acrefore/9780199366439.001.0001/acrefore-9780199366439-e-12> accessed 16 August 2024.

III. The Formation of the (Unwritten) Rule of Cooperation

The political conditions described in the previous section required key political actors to make decisions and choices that would allow them to deal with the new political reality. President Salinas and then President Zedillo chose to appeal to an idea of consensus that implicitly rejects the legitimacy of (a non-cooperating) political opposition and, perhaps most importantly, facilitated the centralization of constitutional decision-making—in a way that largely resembled the workings of the hegemonic party regime. In his first public appearance after the election and in the midst of demonstrations by the opposition, the virtual winner of the election, PRI Carlos Salinas de Gortari, opted for a conciliatory discourse acknowledging the rising political opposition and the need to change the forms of political interaction, stating that: '[Today] the single-party regime ends and we enter a new political stage [. . .] with a majority party [the PRI] and very intense competition from the opposition.'[19] A few months later, in his inauguration address, President Salinas adopted the discourse of 'unity', 'negotiation', 'consensus', and 'dialogue' and acknowledged the rising opposition:

> [A]fter the democratic contest, it is time to strengthen national unity through the path of dialogue, respect and good faith. That will be the attitude of this government in the new stage that we are starting today. We will move forward and strengthen electoral transparency. I hereby call for legal reforms to the current electoral code. I am determined to carry out a democratic reform, I have invited political parties to dialogue; here I ratify my invitation, I know that it is a matter of interest to all the political forces of the country, we are all concerned [. . .] let's work together on that task. The depth and pace of reform will be a consequence of the degree of consensus that the various political forces will build.[20]

A cooperating opposition would surely provide the legitimacy the government needed and that could hardly be achieved otherwise.[21] For the years to

[19] Antonio Caño, 'Cárdenas, Virtual Triunfador en la Capital Mexicana' *El País* (Madrid, 7 July 1988) <https://elpais.com/diario/1988/07/08/internacional/584316005_850215.html> accessed 16 August 2024; Loaeza (n 13) 173.

[20] Carlos Salinas de Gortari, 'Discurso de Toma de posesión' (1 December 1988) <http://revistas.bancomext.gob.mx/rce/magazines/193/16/RCE16.pdf> accessed 25 October 2024.

[21] Paulina Fernández Christlieb, 'El partido político en el discurso del gobierno mexicano' in Margarita Favela Gavia and Julio Muñoz Rubio (eds), *Jornadas Anuales de Investigación 2005* (Centro de Investigaciones Interdisciplinarias en Ciencias y Humanidades, UNAM 2006) 100.

come, this official discourse would shape the government's approach to its engagement with the opposition. I call this form of engagement the *consensus rationale*. From the perspective of the hegemonic party, the political instability of the time, the general distrust in the electoral system, and previous election fraud scandals made the idea of consensus an end in itself. Underscoring the need for peace and maintaining the rule of law was very important. The promotion of the conciliatory narrative entailed only one acceptable political behaviour: the transition to democracy could only be achieved through agreements and negotiation.[22] The underlying message of the official discourse, in this sense, was that consensus was inherently and democratically valuable. The consensus rationale was successfully positioned. As will be illustrated below, by 1996 (the year when the CPER was consolidated), the idea of consensus stopped being only an end in itself: President Zedillo started portraying it as a *sine qua non* for democracy.

In practice, the effect of the political opposition's acceptance of the consensus rationale was the formation of the rule of cooperation and, consequently, the availability of the amendment mechanism in Mexico's economy of constitutional change despite the context of political fragmentation. The rule of cooperation can be defined as an unwritten political norm or convention that allows political parties to strike deals across party lines to preserve their interests through institutional mechanisms of constitutional change that otherwise would not be available in the economy of constitutional change (eg constitutional amendments). All of the reforms during this period (1988–96) were adopted as a result of *ex ante* negotiations and agreements among party leaders before activating the amendment mechanism established in Article 135 of the Constitution. The rule of cooperation became the driving force of constitutional change.

In what follows, I analyse four electoral reforms and two judicial reforms that came into effect between 1989 and 1996 to illustrate the emergence of the rule of cooperation and, thus, the formation of the CPER. This set of reforms and their context showcase two important factors explaining the emergence of the rule of cooperation and the CPER. First, they show how the weakened PRI dictated the terms and conditions in which the transition took place. Second, they exemplify how the constitutional pre-understandings around the function of constitutional amendments discussed in Chapter 5 were inherited by this new political regime. The effect was that, just like in the PRI hegemonic

[22] Bertha Lerner de Sheinbaum, 'El Estado Mexicano y el 6 de Julio de 1988' (1989) 51 Revista Mexicana de Sociología 199–237, 213. For a speech synthesizing Salinas' view on democracy, see Carlos Salinas de Gortari, *El Reto* (Editorial Diana 1988) 37–58.

days, constitutional decision-making remained highly centralized—which in turn explains the continued access to the amendment mechanism illustrated in Chapter 4.

The electoral reform of 1990

It is perhaps unsurprising that the first amendment after the fraught elections of 1988 was an electoral reform partially conceding one of the PAN's most important long-standing demands: the democratization of the electoral system. Article 41 of the Constitution was amended to create the Instituto Federal Electoral (IFE)—an autonomous body in charge of organizing and overseeing elections to guarantee legal and transparent electoral processes, and to establish an electoral justice system, which included an Electoral Tribunal (initially conceived as an autonomous body but incorporated into the judicial branch in 1996).[23] This reform was only a partial victory because even though it meant taking away both the power to certify elections from Congress and the power to organize and oversee them from the executive,[24] the latter did not entirely lose its grip on the organization of elections. The IFE's highest decision-making body, the Consejo General, was presided over by the minister of the interior.[25] As for the minor parties, once part of the FDN, they were granted the possibility of winning ten seats (instead of the seven they could win before) in the Chamber of Deputies when getting a minimum of 1.5 per cent of the total votes in an election.[26]

These gains, however, did not come without compromise. The amendment also included two important institutional features that created an electoral distortion in favour of the PRI: the governability clause with a sliding-scale system.[27] The governability clause[28] allocated the majority of seats in the Chamber of Deputies to the party obtaining 35 per cent of the votes in the general election, 'creating an artificial absolute majority for the benefit of

[23] For a general overview of this amendment, see Lorenzo Córdova Vianello, 'La Reforma Electoral y el Cambio Político en México' in Daniel Zovatto and José de Jesús Orozco Henríquez (eds), *Reforma Política y Electoral en América Latina 1978–2007* (IIJ-UNAM/IDEA 2008) 653–704.

[24] Before this amendment, elections were organized and oversighted by the Federal Electoral Commission, an administrative agency formally dependent of the secretary of the interior. See ibid 660, 661–62.

[25] For an explanation of the integration of the first iteration of the IFE's general council, see ibid 662.

[26] Molinar Horcasitas and Weldon (n 12) 216.

[27] Córdova Vianello (n 23) 664.

[28] As seen in Chapter 5, the first iteration of this clause was adopted before the elections of 1988. As argued by Molinar Horcasitas and Weldon, the clause was adopted because the PRI feared losing control of the Chamber of Deputies. See Molinar Horcasitas and Weldon (n 12) 214–15.

the official party'—namely, the PRI.[29] Additionally, 'if the winning party won more than 35% but no more than 60% of the vote',[30] the sliding-scale system would assign two additional seats in the Chamber of Deputies for each percentage point above the 35 per cent threshold. Additionally, the prohibition of cross-endorsements and the onerous requirements to form party coalitions for the presidential race precluded the possibility of repeating the experience with the FDN in 1988.[31] This measure translated into the pulverization of the anti-regime movement, avoiding precisely what had put the PRI in danger of losing the presidency one year before.[32] Unsurprisingly, in the mid-term elections of 1991, the PRI recovered fifty-nine seats in the Chamber of Deputies.[33]

Trade-offs between the parties are clear in this set of reforms. The PAN scored a partial victory towards free and fair elections with the creation of the IFE and the smaller parties got a deal to get more seats in Congress. The PRI secured not only both an insurance against electoral coalitions and the control of the Chamber of Deputies with the governability clause and the sliding-scale mechanism but also the future cooperation of the PAN. If the PAN wanted to achieve its long-standing demands regarding a constitutional and legal framework able to guarantee free and fair elections, it needed to keep cooperating with the PRI. Given the clear distortions that this reform created in favour of the PRI, for some scholars it is not clear why the PAN cooperated with the once hegemonic party.[34] What the PAN's cooperation reveals, in my view, is that the government's effort to appeal for consensus and cooperation worked and that the opportunities it entailed for the opposition (ie direct entrenchment) were very hard to resist. The PAN's cooperation also reveals the privileged bargaining position the PRI held to pass constitutional amendments. As noted earlier, the PRI hegemony was still very much alive at the local level, and no constitutional amendment would pass without its acquiescence. The PAN seems to have settled with a 'better than nothing' approach, perhaps foreseeing that the PRI would continue to need its support.[35]

[29] Córdova Vianello (n 23) 687; Labastida and López Leyva (n 6) 772.

[30] Molinar Horcasitas and Weldon (n 12) 219.

[31] See Prud'homme (n 2) 107–08 (arguing these measures both guaranteed staying in power and avoided the risk of another strong anti-system alliance); Molinar Horcasitas and Weldon (n 12) 220.

[32] Alberto Diaz-Cayeros, Beatriz Magaloni, and Barry R. Weingast, 'Tragic Brilliance: Equilibrium Party Hegemony in Mexico' (2003) <https://papers.ssrn.com/abstract=1153510> accessed 16 August 2024.

[33] It went from 262/500 to 321/500 seats. See Atlas Electoral <http://siceef.ine.mx/camdiputados.html?página=1> accessed 16 August 2024.

[34] See Molinar Horcasitas and Weldon (n 12) 219–20 (arguing, 'The PAN's decision can be understood only under the premise that they gave much more salience to the issue of clean elections than to considerations of the electoral formula').

[35] Others have referred to this as the PAN's 'gradualist' approach. See ibid 218; Loaeza (n 13).

Indeed, the Salinas administration was able to bring forward an agenda that sought to restore the confidence in the government but perhaps most importantly in the PRI.[36] In so doing, it implemented several measures to reignite the stagnated economy by attracting foreign investment. Sweeping neoliberal reforms included, among other things, deregulation measures and the privatization of state-owned companies (eg banks, airlines, and the telephone monopoly)[37]—many of which would not have been possible without the support of the PAN (eg the constitutional amendment for the privatization of banks in 1990).[38] These reforms may be understood as contributions to the creation of an appropriate environment for NAFTA.[39] In line with the consensus rationale that was being championed by the government at the time, both the electoral reform and Salinas' neoliberal reforms were adopted through the cooperation of the PAN—marking the rise of what would eventually become the rule of cooperation and the CPER.

The electoral reform of 1993

This reform was adopted after the mid-term elections of 1991 (where, as mentioned above, the PRI recovered electoral strength in the Chamber of Deputies[40]) and immediately before the ratification of NAFTA in November 1993. Although the elections took place in much better circumstances than before, the stark asymmetric results in favour of the PRI[41] most likely gave reasons for the opposition to choose to continue cooperating and pushing for further reforms. Even though the PRI had the needed majority in the Senate to ratify NAFTA, there were enough incentives to make more concessions in favour of the opposition. The eyes of the United States were on Mexico and a general election was coming soon. Amid the debate over the ratification of NAFTA in

[36] See Haber and others (n 10) 73 (arguing, 'The economic and political reality of Mexico in the late 1980s—economic stagnation and widespread discontent with the PRI—compelled the Salinas de Gortari administration [1988–94] to go beyond the steps that de la Madrid had taken to reignite growth and restore confidence in the government').

[37] ibid 16, 74.

[38] For a study on the privatization of the bank industry in Mexico, see Francisco A Ibarra Palafox, *La Privatización Bancaria en México: Reforma Jurídica, Política y Financiera* (Siglo XXI 2014).

[39] Haber and others (n 10) 73–75.

[40] It went from 262/500 to 321/500 seats. See Atlas Electoral <http://siceef.ine.mx/camdiputados.html?página=1> accessed 16 August 2024.

[41] For the Chamber of Deputies, 58.47 per cent of the votes were for the PRI, 16.82 per cent for the PAN, and 7.91 per cent for the PRD; for the Senate, 58.66 per cent for the PRI, 16.87 per cent for the PAN, and 3.61 per cent for the PRD. See Instituto Nacional Electoral, Atlas de Resultados Electorales Federales 1991–2015 <www.ine.mx/archivos3/portal/historico/contenido/Historico_de_Resultados_Electorales> accessed 5 February 2017.

the US Congress, Vice President Al Gore stated that Mexico was not yet a full democracy and that it still lacked full protection of human rights.[42] The PRI had a good impression to make and needed to prove that, if not quite there yet, the country was on the correct path towards becoming a full democracy.[43]

In this context, important changes were made that catered to long-standing opposition demands to improve the proportional system. The governability clause was replaced by a linked two-tier system to elect the members of the Chamber of Deputies through an amendment to Article 54 of the Constitution. The new two-tier system limited the number of seats a party could win overall (no party could hold more than 315 out of 500 seats, 35 seats fewer than before).[44] On paper, this new system was more proportional than the earlier iteration, but was designed in such a way that it would produce an absolute majority for the winning party in most cases.[45] Additionally, the amendment to Article 56 of the Constitution modified the size of the Senate and implemented a plurality rule to distribute seats.[46] The number of senators increased from 64 to 128, which meant doubling the number of senators per state from 2 to 4. The new distribution formula consisted of allocating three seats to the party with most votes and one to the second runner-up.[47] This meant 32 out of the 128 senators would be from opposition parties. Although this amendment secured the presence of the opposition in the Senate, the new formula put a significant burden on opposition parties to acquire relevance: they needed to become the

[42] On 9 November, days before the vote in Congress to pass the trade agreement, these doubts were confirmed by Vice President Al Gore's opinion that Mexico was 'not yet a full democracy [and still lacked] full protection of human rights'. See Larry King Show, 'The NAFTA Debate' (CNN 1993) <http://edition.cnn.com/videos/politics/2016/09/02/nafta-debate-1993-al-gore-ross-perot-entire-larry-king-live.cnn/video/playlists/larry-king-live-interviews> accessed 16 August 2024; see also David E Rosenbaum, 'The Free Trade Accord: The Overview; Gore and Perot Dual on TV over the Trade Pact' *The New York Times* (10 November 1993) <www.nytimes.com/1993/11/10/us/the-free-trade-accord-the-overview-gore-and-perot-dual-on-tv-over-the-trade-pact.html> accessed 16 August 2024.

[43] See Wayne A Cornelius, 'Mexico's Delayed Democratization' [1994] Foreign Policy 53, 70 (arguing, 'While the Mexican government was able to keep "democracy" off the NAFTA negotiating table, it is inevitable that, with the agreement in place, Mexico's domestic politics will be scrutinized by U.S. officialdom as never before. Unrepentant critics of NAFTA, like Senator Ernest Hollings [Democrat for South Carolina], contend that the growing U.S. need to export goods should not constrain it from exporting American values to countries with questionable records on human rights and democracy, including Mexico. Having made important economic concessions to Mexico by approving NAFTA, the argument goes, the United States now has the "right" to insist on basic changes in its neighbor's political system').

[44] Molinar Horcasitas and Weldon (n 12) 222.

[45] ibid 221.

[46] Córdova Vianello (n 23) 666; Joseph L Klesner, 'Electoral Reform in Mexico's Hegemonic Party System: Perpetuation of Privilege or Democratic Advance?' (Annual Meeting of the American Political Science Association, Washington, DC, 28–31 August 1997) <www2.kenyon.edu/Depts/PSci/Fac/klesner/Electoral_Reform_in_Mexico.htm> accessed 16 August 2024.

[47] Jorge Alcocer, 'Recientes Reformas Electorales' in Riordan Roett (ed), *El Desafío de la Reforma Institucional en México* (Siglo XXI 1996) 91.

first political force in at least fifteen states for this to translate into forty-five seats in the Senate (ie the needed seats for the PRI to lose the qualified majority to, among other things, pass or block constitutional amendments proposals or make judicial appointments on its own).

Another important partial concession by the PRI in this reform is related to the limits of party and campaign finance. A new paragraph was introduced to Article 41 stating that 'the law will establish the rules to which political parties and campaign finance will be subject'.[48] The lack of specificity in this constitutional provision reflects the limited leverage the PAN had, while showing once again the PRI's privileged bargaining position. The PAN wanted to settle the issue in the constitutional text because it was at this level that they had leverage vis-à-vis the PRI. The PRI logically preferred to leave it open and defer the decision to ordinary legislation—as it still had comfortable control of both chambers of Congress and, if needed, could unilaterally determine party and campaign financing limits. As we will see in Section IV, this issue re-emerged during the adoption of the electoral reform of 1996, when the PAN again failed to achieve its goal. Consequently, campaign finance limits were unilaterally included by the PRI in the electoral code.

Just as in the electoral reform of 1990, the limited concessions granted by the PRI show how, led by President Salinas, the party was setting the new norms of interaction among political parties to achieve constitutional change. Most importantly, the acquiescence of the PAN (ie a choice by a key political actor) against the backdrop of the consensus rationale being championed by the government was essential for the emergence and consolidation of the rule of cooperation. The trade-off dynamic behind the consensus rationale (and later the rule of cooperation) is well illustrated in the preamble of the constitutional amendment initiative that the PRI, PAN, and Partido Auténtico de la Revolución Mexicana (PARM)[49] passed jointly. The text of the initiative contains a revealing statement by the PAN:

> The PAN deputies who have been part of the Plural Commission hereby leave on record that the progress contained in the *present initiative does not*

[48] 'Decreto por el que se Reforman los Artículos 41, 54, 56, 60, 63, 74 y 100 de la Constitución Política de los Estados Unidos Mexicanos' Diario Oficial de la Federación (3 September 1993) (article 41 paragraph 6) <www.diputados.gob.mx/LeyesBiblio/ref/dof/CPEUM_ref_128_03sep93_ima.pdf> accessed 16 August 2024.

[49] As discussed in Chapter 2, this was a small party founded in 1954 that in theory was an opposition party but in practice never acted as such. For example, it traditionally endorsed PRI presidential candidates and supported the PRI in Congress.

> *imply any capitulation by their parliamentary group and that they will insist on improving it during the legislative process* and will continue to promote the substantial improvement of the secondary law in all those aspects that have been repeatedly mentioned.
>
> It is pertinent to point out that *the present initiative only addresses the constitutional reforms that have reached the consensus of the political forces subscribing it*, and that the commitment to continue the plural effort to obtain additions and modifications to the regulatory law in all those aspects that would favour the consolidation of electoral democracy remains.[50]

This disclaimer confirms the approach the PAN chose to follow. In their role as the largest opposition party,[51] they were willing to play by the PRI's rules for constitutional change and get the most out of them. Although the disclaimer states that the PAN was not capitulating and that representatives would continue to push for their original demands in the formal amendment process that was being activated with the initiative, the truth is that, in terms of that specific process, there was nothing left to fight for—neither regarding the content of the amendment nor regarding ordinary legislation to implement it. As admitted in the second paragraph of the disclaimer, the initiative contained only the modifications for which there was consensus (ie the necessary votes to pass). Thus, it is difficult to see how the PAN would have been able to achieve in an ordinary legislation process, where it had significantly less leverage, what it was not able to achieve in the negotiations over the constitutional amendment. As mentioned earlier, the PRI still had control in both chambers of Congress to unilaterally pass ordinary legislation. Remarkably, though, the disclaimer suggests the PAN was already committed to continuing to take any opportunity offered by the PRI to advance their agenda. In that specific amendment process, they were in fact renouncing their demands and, perhaps, hoping for further opportunities to engage in constitutional bargaining, while embracing the rule of cooperation in the context of formal constitutional change. After activating the amendment mechanism, it took only fifteen days (from 19 August 1993 to 3 September 1993) for the initiative to go through both chambers of Congress and twenty-four state legislatures, and to be published.

[50] Cámara de Diputados, 'Iniciativa de Reforma Constitucional Presentada por los Diputados Coordinadores de los Grupos Parlamentarios del PRI, PAN y PARM' (19 August 1993) <http://cronica.diputados.gob.mx/Iniciativas/55/166.html> accessed 16 August 2024 (emphasis added).

[51] The PAN had 89 out of 500 seats in the Chamber of Deputies. PRI 321, PRD 41, PPS 11, PFCRN 23, PARM 15. See Atlas Electoral <http://siceef.ine.mx/camdiputados.html?página=1> accessed 16 August 2024.

The electoral and judicial reform 1994

The year 1994, a general election year, brought the perfect political conditions and opportunities for the opposition to engage in further constitutional bargaining. Importantly, for the first time, Cárdenas and the PRD participated in a political agreement to bring about constitutional change together with the PAN and PRI, marking the beginning of a regime of cooperation between these three political parties.[52] On 1 January 1994 (the day on which NAFTA officially came into force), the *Zapatista* guerrilla movement rose against the backdrop of centuries of discrimination against indigenous peoples and against Salinas' neoliberal project. The social and political instability that the *Zapatista* uprising produced seen parallel to the social mobilization that Cárdenas and the PRD had managed to ignite after the 1988 election alleged fraud is perhaps what, at least partly, explains the PRI openness to new negotiations to reform the electoral system and to include the PRD in them.[53] The PRI probably—and understandably—wanted to avoid any escalation of the already unstable social and political situation, or the threat that contested electoral results later that year could mean in terms of the image the country could project at the international level (one should not forget the government's efforts to attract foreign investment).

On 27 January, in the midst of the *Zapatista* uprising, all the presidential candidates (including the PRI, PAN, and PRD) signed the *Pacto por la Paz, la Democracia y la Justicia* (National Pact for Peace, Democracy and Justice) (PPDJ), which, according to President Salinas, was the basis for the electoral reform that took place months later.[54] Confirming the PRI's new negotiation approach and what was already consolidating as the consensus rationale of the regime, in his memoirs former President Salinas recalls: 'we opted for deepening political dialogue and *consensus as a method*'.[55]

In the PPDJ, the political parties and their respective presidential candidates agreed, among other things, to contribute to the creation of a social and political climate of stability and trust for the general elections that would take place in August of that year (naturally, this included accepting the result of the election) and to take action to make the electoral system reliable, fair, and impartial

[52] Carlos Salinas de Gortari, *México, un Paso Difícil a la Modernidad* (Penguin Random House Grupo Editorial México 2013).

[53] Prud'homme (n 2) 120–23.

[54] Jorge Carpizo, 'La reforma electoral de 1994' in Jorge Alcocer, Jorge Carpizo, and Eugenia Huerta (eds), *Elecciones, Diálogo y Reforma, México, 1994* (Nuevo Horizonte Editores 1995) 85; Javier Moctezuma Barragán, 'La justicia electoral y las reformas constitucionales y legales de 1994' (1994) 14 Cuadernos Constitucionales México-Centroamérica 53, 65-67.

[55] Salinas de Gortari (n 52) (emphasis added).

(eg to give citizens control over elections by including them in the IFE's general council and to revise the voter census).[56] The last point of the agreement stated that if any of its clauses needed legal adjustments, *they would take place only after reaching consensus among the signatories.*[57] Led by the secretary of the interior, Jorge Carpizo, the negotiation group—formed by the presidential candidates of the PRI, Luis Donaldo Colosio, and PAN, Diego Fernández de Cevallos, as well as Porfirio Muñoz Ledo as representative of the PRD and representatives of the Salinas administration—reached an agreement by 8 March.[58] Accordingly, on 22 March, an extraordinary legislative period was convened in Congress to modify Article 41 of the Constitution. The constitutional amendment was enacted on 19 April.[59]

Article 41 was amended to modify the composition of the IFE's general council to include six 'citizen councillors' that would be nominated by the parliamentary groups of the Chamber of Deputies and confirmed by a two-thirds vote in that chamber. Although the executive retained its presiding seat (via the secretary of the interior) in that decision-making body, from the perspective of the opposition this was an important step towards making the electoral authority an impartial and non-partisan decision-making body.

The judicial reform: consensus and cooperation during the Zedillo administration

Against all odds and fears of violence, the presidential election took place peacefully in August 1994. The contenders accepted the victory of PRI Ernesto Zedillo,[60] who claimed the presidency with 50.2 per cent of the vote.[61] Zedillo and his party retained the majority of seats in both chambers of Congress.[62] Yet, this does not mean that the transition months (August to November) would come without challenges. On top of the already complicated social and political climate caused by the *Zapatista* movement and the assassination of PRI's presidential candidate (the previously mentioned Luis Donaldo Colosio)

[56] Fernando Orgambides, 'Pacto Por La Paz, La Democracia y La Justicia' *El País* (Mexico, 29 January 1994) <https://elpais.com/diario/1994/01/29/internacional/759798004_850215.html> accessed 16 March 2020; Córdova Vianello (n 23) 667; Carpizo (n 54).

[57] Orgambides (n 56) (emphasis added).

[58] Eduardo Huchim, *México 1994: La Rebelión y el Magnicidio* (Nueva Imagen 1994) 172; Salinas de Gortari (n 52); Carpizo (n 54).

[59] John M Ackerman, *Organismos Autónomos y Democracia: El Caso de México* (Siglo XXI 2007) 66; Molinar Horcasitas and Weldon (n 12) 223.

[60] As reported by Haber and others, the PRD initially refused to accept the election results, claiming the presence of the same fradulent tactics employed by the PRI in 1988. Although election observers recognized the presence of vote buying and coercion, they agreed the election and vote count were clean overall but that the playing field was not even. See Haber and others (n 10) 139.

[61] Córdova Vianello (n 23) 668; Haber and others (n 10) 139–40.

[62] Haber and others (n 10) 139.

on 23 March 1994, the PRI was soon after involved in yet another scandal of murder and corruption. On 28 September, José Francisco Ruiz Massieu, the secretary-general of the PRI and former governor of the State of Guerrero, was assassinated in Mexico City. The deputy attorney general investigating the murder, Mario Ruiz Massieu (who happened to be the brother of the victim), resigned shortly after the launch of the investigation, alleging that officials at the higher ranks of the PRI were attempting to block the inquiry.[63] This situation put President-elect Ernesto Zedillo in a compromising position. This was in addition to the financial crisis that unravelled soon after his inauguration and that resulted in an economic recession worse than the one endured during De la Madrid administration in the 1980s—a blow that was inevitably taken by the PRI.[64] In this context, Zedillo's vow to maintaining a *sana distancia* (healthy distance) between his administration and the PRI is hardly surprising.[65] Perhaps the clearest example of his declared intention of distancing his administration from the party was that in the first months of his presidency, Raúl Salinas de Gortari (the older brother of the former president and brother-in-law of the victim) was charged (and eventually condemned) for being the mastermind behind Ruiz Massieu's murder.[66]

Despite the 'healthy distance' trope, President Zedillo continued to champion the consensus rationale that his predecessor had popularized. In his inauguration address, Zedillo declared:

> To a great extent, the advancement of democracy depends on the strength of our party system. It depends on our ability to privilege consensus over difference, the cohesion of purposes [*propósitos*] over disagreements, unity over confrontation. [. . .] Mexico demands a reform that, supported by a broad political consensus, eradicates suspicions, recriminations [. . .] that tarnish electoral processes.[67]

[63] ibid 140; Phill Gunson, 'Mario Ruiz Massieu' *The Guardian* (20 September 1999) <www.theguardian.com/news/1999/sep/20/guardianobituaries1> accessed 16 August 2024.

[64] Haber and others (n 10) 141. For in-depth studies on the economic crisis of that year, see eg, Guillermo A Calvo and Enrique G Mendoza, 'Mexico's Balance-of-Payments Crisis: A Chronicle of a Death Foretold' (1996) 41 Journal of International Economics 235–64; and Harold L Cole and Timothy J Kehoe, 'A Self-Fulfilling Model of Mexico's 1994–1995 Debt Crisis' (1996) 41 Journal of International Economics 309–30.

[65] Miguel González Compeán, 'La distancia necesaria y lo inevitable de la cercanía' in Miguel González Compeán, Leonardo Lomelí, and Pedro Salmerón Sanginés (eds), *El Partido de la revolución: institución y conflicto, 1928–1999* (Fondo de Cultura Económica 2000) 636–70; Rogelio Hernández Rodríguez, 'Ernesto Zedillo. La Presidencia Contenida' (2003) 43 Foro Internacional 39, 54–55.

[66] Haber and others (n 10) 140.

[67] Ernesto Zedillo, 'Discurso de toma de posesión' [1995] Revista Mexicana de Política Exterior 274, 281. See also Labastida and López Leyva (n 6) 787–88.

In that same address, President Zedillo vowed to bring about a '*definitive electoral reform* to make democracy part of every aspect of social life'[68] and a judicial reform to strengthen the judiciary and balance the three branches of government.[69] Even though Zedillo was rhetorically distancing his administration from the PRI, in practice he enjoyed the party's support to bring about his government agenda in general[70] and this constitutional amendments in particular. The judicial reform was adopted shortly after Zedillo's inauguration and took effect on 1 January 1995—exactly a month after inauguration day.[71] The 'definitive' electoral reform, as will be discussed in the following section, would materialize in 1996.

The judicial reform[72] was promoted by the government as a measure to transform the Supreme Court into an 'authentic' Constitutional Tribunal and was seen by scholars as a prelude to the judicialization of politics in Mexico.[73] It reduced the membership of the Supreme Court from twenty-six to eleven; reestablished the judicial appointment mechanism President Calles had introduced in 1928, giving the president a central role in the process; abolished life tenure and replaced it with fifteen-year terms; empowered the Supreme Court with new judicial review powers to exercise abstract review and to solve disputes regarding the allocation of power among branches of government (ie *acciones de inconstitucionalidad* and *controversias constitucionales*);[74] and established a federal judicial council.[75]

[68] ibid 280 (emphasis added).

[69] Labastida and López Leyva (n 6) 787–88.

[70] As Hernández Rodriguez argues, what Zedillo ambiguously called 'healthy distance' consisted of the government not granting any privileges to the PRI outside the law, but it would still expect 'reasonable' support from the party. See Hernández Rodríguez (n 65) 55.

[71] Stephen Zamora and José Ramón Cossío, 'Mexican Constitutionalism after Presidencialismo' (2006) 4 International Journal of Constitutional Law 411.

[72] See Ernesto Zedillo Ponce de Leon, 'Iniciativa de Reforma Constitucional' (5 December 1994) (the reform initiative to the Senate, stating it aimed at 'transforming the judiciary into an independent and strong power [. . .] for the better equilibrium of the Powers of the Union').

[73] See eg Miguel González Compeán and Peter Bauer, *Jurisdicción y Democracia: Los Nuevos Rumbos del Poder Judicial en México* (Cal y Arena 2002) 171, 394, 465; Jodi S Finkel, *Judicial Reform as Political Insurance: Argentina, Peru, and Mexico in the 1990s* (University of Notre Dame Press 2008); Zamora and Cossío (n 71). But see Silvia Inclán Oseguera, 'Judicial Reform in Mexico: Political Insurance or the Search for Political Legitimacy?' (2009) 62 Political Research Quarterly 753 (arguing that the amendment was adopted due to the reformers' need to legitimize their rule in a context marked by political competition and a discredited Supreme Court).

[74] As discussed by Zamora and Cossío, *controversias constitucionales* were provided in the Constitution since 1917. The judicial reform of 1994, however, expanded the Supreme Court's authority to settle disputes among government authorities across levels of government. See Zamora and Cossío (n 71) 421–22.

[75] For an overview of this judicial reform, see Stephen Zamora and others, 'Judicial Procedures to Enforce the Constitution' in Stephen Zamora and others (eds), *Mexican Law* (OUP 2005) 274–86; Zamora and Cossío (n 71) 421; Inclán Oseguera (n 73); Silvia Inclan Oseguera, 'Judicial Reform and Democratization: Mexico in the 1990s' (PhD, Boston University 2004).

This sweeping amendment was adopted through a *fast-track* process by a PRI–PAN coalition. It took only *five days* for the amendment proposal to go through both chambers of Congress and *nine days* to get the ratification of the majority of the state legislatures.[76] Given that its implementation entailed the replacement of all sitting Supreme Court judges, a few voices denounced the reform as a coup d'etat[77] (a measure that today would likely be interpreted as a 'constitutional coup' in Kim Lane Scheppele's[78] terms or as 'abusive constitutionalism' in David Landau's,[79] and that is also reminiscent of President Cárdenas' judicial overhaul discussed in Chapter 5).[80] In fact, PRD senators—still hesitant to submit to the PRI rules of engagement—left the Senate floor before the vote took place as a statement of their disagreement with passing the amendment through a fast-track process while preventing the inclusion of experts' opinions on the proposal.[81] Yet, as we know, this action had no consequences because the PRI only needed the cooperation of the PAN to have the qualified majority to pass the amendment (quorum rules only require simple majority for the chambers of Congress to function).[82] By 31 December, the Supreme Court had brand-new powers of competence allocation and abstract review, and all sitting members were to be replaced in thirty days.[83] The new court was installed on 1 February 1995.

[76] The days are counted from the moment the relevant committee in the Senate (as the chamber of origin) issued its report on the amendment proposal (16 December 1994) to the day it was approved in the Chamber of Deputies (21 December 1994). The following eight days are counted from the moment the Chamber of Deputies approved the amendment (21 December 1994) to the day the majority of the state legislatures ratified it (29 December 1994). The amendment was enacted on 31 December 1994. , working with the information available at <www.diputados.gob.mx> and <www.senado.gob.mx> accessed 16 August 2024.

[77] Miguel Ángel Granados Chapa, 'La reforma (per)judicial' *Reforma* (Mexico, 12 December 1994); Héctor Fix-Fierro, 'La Reforma Judicial en México: ¿De Dónde Viene? ¿Hacia Dónde Va?' (2003) 1 Reforma Judicial. Revista Mexicana de Justicia 259–66; Guillermo Ruiz Morales and Alberto Rocha Arrieta, 'La reforma al Poder Judicial de 1994, ¿Un Golpe de Estado?' [2012] El Cotidiano 18.

[78] Kim Lane Scheppele, 'Constitutional Coups and Judicial Review: How Transnational Institutions Can Strengthen Peak Courts at Times of Crisis (With Special Reference to Hungary)' (2014) 23 Transnational Law and Contemporary Problems 51.

[79] David Landau, 'Abusive Constitutionalism' (2013) 47 UC Davis Law Review 189.

[80] Reminiscent both of Presidents Cárdenas and Zedillo, in February 2024 President López Obrador sent a set of wide-ranging constitutional amendment initiatives to, among other things, reduce the membership of the Supreme Court from eleven to nine and introduce the popular election of federal judges, including Supreme Court Justices. The adoption of such measures would imply the replacement of all sitting judges in 2025. See Alejandro I López, 'Las 20 Reformas Constitucionales que Propone López Obrador' *El País* (Mexico, 6 February 2024) <https://elpais.com/mexico/2024-02-06/las-20-reformas-constitucionales-que-propone-lopez-obrador.html> accessed 21 February 2024; Javier Martín Reyes, 'Plan C: purgar, capturar y obradorizar el poder judicial' (2022) <https://eljuegodelacorte.nexos.com.mx/plan-c-purgar-capturar-y-obradorizar-el-poder-judicial> accessed 21 February 2024.

[81] Fix-Fierro (n 77) 260.

[82] Constitution of 1917, Art 63, 135; Reglamento del Senado de la República 2010 Art 59; Reglamento de la Cámara de Diputados 2010 Art 46.

[83] See SCJN, XV Años de la Consolidacion de la Suprema Corte como Tribunal Constitucional <http://sistemabibliotecario.scjn.gob.mx/sisbib/CST/80011/80011.pdf> accessed 25 October 2024.

Scholars have offered different accounts to explain the different motivations that could have been behind the adoption of this amendment. For instance, while Jodi Finkel argues that the amendment was purely the result of a political insurance tactic from a debilitating ruling party that was uncertain about its ability to remain in power,[84] Silvia Inclán argues that it was part of Zedillo's strategy of establishing a 'healthy distance' between the PRI and the State as an attempt to regain legitimacy and credibility in a context of democratization.[85] The amendment was, of course, multifactorial. What should be clear, however, is that both the PRI and the PAN had an interest in accessing direct entrenchment on this matter. On the one hand, the Zedillo administration and the PRI were dealing with an unravelling financial crisis less than a year after NAFTA took effect. This was on top of an increasing perception of lack of independence of and corruption within the judiciary—the Supreme Court included.[86] If anything, the government could not afford to have a questionable judiciary when it was trying to attract foreign investment. It this sense, it is reasonable to think that more than ever, it was necessary to show to the world that changes were being made to have trustworthy independent institutions and to send a clear message that the country was truly committed to the rule of law (understood as a key component of a mature democracy) and, thus, was a safe place to invest.[87] A judicial reform of this kind and breadth was a good way of signalling Mexico's commitment to join the wave of *new constitutionalism* that was taking place across the world.[88]

As discussed above, the PAN embraced the consensus rationale as soon as it was offered the opportunity to take part in constitutional bargaining, and, in so doing, it made an important contribution to the emergence of the rule of

[84] Jodi Finkel, 'Judicial Reform as Insurance Policy: Mexico in the 1990s' (2005) 47 Latin American Politics and Society 87.

[85] See Inclán Oseguera (n 73) 762 (arguing, 'Judicial reform in Mexico was designed and launched as a campaign promise to present Zedillo as a . . . different PRI candidate with an aim to separate the PRI from the state and ready to promote government accountability. After Zedillo's victory, the campaign promise was soon turned into a presidential initiative because the Supreme Court, long associated as under PRI control, faced public exposure as a corrupt and inefficient body').

[86] Fix-Fierro (n 77) 261–62; José Ramón Cossío Díaz, *La Teoría Constitucional de La Suprema Corte de Justicia* (Fontamara 2008) 131; Silvia Inclán Oseguera, 'La Reforma Judicial En México: ¿Seguro Político o Búsqueda de Legitimidad?' in Camilo Saavedra (ed), *Veinte años no es nada: la Suprema Corte y la justicia constitucional antes y después de la reforma judicial de 1994* (SCJN/CEC 2018) 365, 383-386.

[87] For an in-depth discussion on the interest and efforts of the government to attract foreign investment, see Haber and others (n 10) 66–94.

[88] For one of the most influential accounts explaining the origins of the new constitutionalism, see Ran Hirschl, *Towards Juristocracy: The Origins and Consequences of the New Constitutionalism* (Harvard UP 2004).

cooperation. In the context of the judicial reform of 1994–95, for example, the creation of the Consejo de la Judicatura Federal (federal judicial council) (CJF) reflects a PAN demand—the original idea of its creation was included in the 1994–2000 PAN electoral platform.[89] By contrast, as illustrated above, the PRD took longer to fully embrace the rule of cooperation.[90] In fact, one could argue that the PRD had more liberty to be inconsistent because the value of its cooperation in the emerging CPER was, more than anything, symbolic. As noted earlier, the PRI only needed the cooperation of the PAN to reach the qualified majority to amend the Constitution. Yet, this doesn't mean that the PRD did not benefit from direct entrenchment. As mentioned earlier, it may be argued that in previous amendments the PRD indirectly benefited from the PRI–PAN cross-party cooperation because there was an overlap of interests with the PAN's long-standing pro-democracy demands.[91] It was during the electoral reform of 1996 that the PRD finally submitted to the rule of cooperation.

The electoral and judicial reform 1996: the consolidation of the rule of cooperation

On 17 January 1995, two weeks after the judicial reform was enacted, the leaders of the PRI, the PAN, the PRD, and the government signed the *Acuerdo Político Nacional* (National Political Agreement), a written agreement to formalize their will to consolidate the democratic reform in Mexico.[92] In a speech delivered at the signing ceremony of the agreement, President Zedillo added a layer to the consensus rationale discussed above. Zedillo portrayed the idea of *consensus*, unity, and absence of confrontation as a *sine qua non* for democracy. In his words,

> The construction of democracy must satisfy everyone so that it is respected and cared for by all.
>
> Therefore, the *commitments signed today mark the beginning of a political agreement that will only be reached through perfect consensus.* Only a perfectly

[89] Fix-Fierro (n 77) 260. Cf Andrea Pozas-Loyo and Julio Rios-Figueroa, 'The Politics of Amendment Processes: Supreme Court Influence in the Design of Judicial Councils' (2010) 89 Texas Law Review 1807, 1815.

[90] For a discussion on the PRD's strategy of confrontation and cooperation with the PRI, see Prud'homme (n 2).

[91] ibid 115.

[92] Labastida and López Leyva (n 6) 788–89; Ricardo Becerra, Pedro Salazar, and José Woldenberg, *La Mecánica Del Cambio Político En México: Elecciones, Partidos y Reformas* (Cal y Arena 2000) 377–80; Sergio Aguayo, *La Transición en México, Una historia Documental 1910–2010* (Fondo de Cultura Económica 2010).

> constructed consensus guarantees respect for rules and political contest in a climate of social tranquility.
>
> From now on *the advancement of democracy will be based on a national dialogue* for the reform of power, a reform that will lead us to a presidential regime better balanced by the other power branches of the State and by the strict observance of the Constitution; a reform [. . .] where the relations between the executive, legislative, and judicial powers are based on a *genuine autonomy and on invariable respect*; a reform to move towards a new federalism *where states and municipalities are stronger by their ability to make decisions.*
>
> [...]
>
> On behalf of the government [. . .] I make a special acknowledgement to the party leaderships of Partido de Acción Nacional, Partido de la Revolución Democrática, Partido del Trabajo, and Partido Revolucionario Institucional *for their commitment to democracy.*
>
> [...]
>
> *Now and here, a historic era ends and another begins.* It is in our hands that future generations may remember the signing of these commitments for a *National Political Agreement as the foundation of the new Mexican democracy.* I am absolutely sure we will not let them down.[93]

With this speech, President Zedillo implied a set of rules of interaction among political parties to achieve constitutional change that closely resembled the rules the PRI already had in place and that facilitated the centralization of decision-making. In turn, the signing of the agreement is symbolically powerful in that it meant all parties formally agreed to be bound by the same set of rules. At the same time, the notion of consensus was presented by Zedillo as an essential element of a democracy; disagreement between political parties, rather than signalling a healthy democratic culture, would, under Zedillo's conception, appear as a sign of institutional weakness.

Since then, smooth amendment processes became almost a necessary condition to regard a reform as legitimate and as proof of the democratic commitment of political parties. Even though in the speech President Zedillo mentioned the importance of having independent governmental branches and a federal system where states are able to make their own decisions for the

[93] Ernesto Zedillo Ponce de León, 'Firma del Acuerdo Político Nacional entre los Principales Partidos Políticos del País, Ceremonia Efectuada en el Salón Adolfo López Mateos de la Residencia Oficial de Los Pinos' (17 January 1995) <http://zedillo.presidencia.gob.mx/pages/disc/ene95/17ene95.html> accessed 23 March 2017 (emphasis added).

advancement of democracy, when it comes to formal constitutional change (as illustrated by the amendment dynamics identified in Chapter 4), the distinguishing feature is the centralization of constitutional decision-making. The fast-track patterns in Congress and the rubber-stamping function of state legislatures in the adoption of constitutional amendments discussed in Chapter 4 leaves no space for independent governmental branches or strong federalism. The centralization of constitutional decision-making and strong party discipline runs counter to the idea of members of Congress and members of state legislatures performing their role as veto players when Article 135 is activated. Under Zedillo's logic of consensus as a *sine qua non* for democracy, anything or anyone running counter to it would not only be hindering the foundation and realization of the 'new Mexican democracy' but would also be showing a lack of commitment to democracy itself.[94]

Just like with the *Pacto por México* in 2012, discussed in Chapter 4, the negotiations on the electoral reform of 1996 took place before activating Article 135. A smooth amendment process would symbolize the commitment of all parties to the new rules of the game for the first time ever. The aim was to reach consensus to prevent challenges to the legitimacy of electoral rules and therefore any distrust of the electoral results as much as possible.[95] Before that happened and a joint constitutional amendment proposal could be sent to Congress, the real negotiations took place among the leaders of the PRI, PAN, and PRD behind closed doors at the Ministry of the Interior.[96] The negotiations went on for an eighteen-month period due to setbacks caused by local electoral disputes in the states of Chiapas, Tabasco, Yucatán, and Puebla.[97] Neither the PAN nor PRD were hesitant to use their leverage. As reported by different commentators, both parties left the negotiation table on multiple occasions to negotiate the concession of governorships and the settlement of local electoral disputes.[98]

On 25 July 1996, the three parties jointly submitted the constitutional amendment initiative, which was enacted in less than thirty days. In the Chamber of Deputies, the amendment was approved *without debate* by 455

[94] To be sure, this is not to say everything is only about the power of narratives. As discussed in Chapter 5, candidate selection plays an important role in explaining why the deployment of the consensus narrative was so effective.

[95] Felipe Gonzalez, Dieter Nohlen, and Daniel Zovatto, 'Análisis del Sistema Electoral Mexicano: Informe de un Grupo de Expertos' (Oficina de Servicios para Proyectos de las Naciones Unidas 1997) 4.

[96] Hernández Rodríguez (n 65) 56–57.

[97] Labastida and López Leyva (n 6) 792; Hernández Rodríguez (n 65) 57.

[98] Labastida and López Leyva (n 6) 792; Hernández Rodríguez (n 64) 57; Becerra, Salazar, and Woldenberg (n 92) 387.

votes out of 500, 6 days after the initiative was presented.[99] That is, it took only six days for the relevant legislative committees to assess the amendment and produce a report to present it to the floor of the chamber. The Senate was even faster: the next day, on 1 August, the amendment was passed by a unanimous vote of 124 senators.[100] Twenty days later, 28 state legislatures had ratified it.[101] The passage of this amendment (and the decision of the PRI, the PAN, and, most importantly, the PRD to support it) illustrates that the rule of cooperation was already in place.

Among the many important modifications, four stand out. First, the membership of the IFE general council would no longer include members from the executive branch and those from the legislative branch (one representative for each parliamentary group) lost their right to vote. Instead, the general council would only be composed of citizens appointed by a two-thirds majority in the Chamber of Deputies.[102] Moreover, the IFE's political finance oversight power was strengthened.[103] Second, the incorporation of the Electoral Tribunal (created in the electoral reform of 1990, discussed above) to the judicial branch came with new judicial review powers.[104] Namely, all electoral constitutional complaints would now be settled by it, except for those involving the constitutionality of the federal and state electoral laws.[105] In turn, the amendment granted the power of judicial review of federal and state electoral laws to the Supreme Court. Additionally, the system of judicial appointments to the Electoral Tribunal would be handled by the Senate together with the Supreme Court. The latter would be in charge of nominations and the former of confirmations. Third, the modification of the party and campaign finance system, which I discuss in more detail in the following section, provided that party finance should be predominantly based on public funding.[106] Fourth, the changes to the electoral system related to the integration of the chambers of Congress consisted of limits to the number of seats a party could hold. In the

[99] Labastida and López Leyva (n 6) 793.

[100] In both chambers of Congress, the amendment was approved without votes against. ibid.

[101] The twenty-eight state legislatures approving the amendment were: Aguascalientes, Baja California Sur, Campeche, Chiapas, Chihuahua, Coahuila, Colima, Durango, Guanajuato, Guerrero, Hidalgo, Jalisco, México, Morelos, Nuevo León, Oaxaca, Puebla, Querétaro, Quintana Roo, San Luis Potosí, Sinaloa, Sonora, Tabasco, Tamaulipas, Tlaxcala, Veracruz, Yucatán, and Zacatecas. For the complete legislative process, see <http://legislacion.scjn.gob.mx/Buscador/Paginas/wfProcesoLegislativoCompleto.aspx?q=b/EcoMjefuFeB6DOaNOimNPZPsNLFqe0s7fey1Fqrifa3mZNTFB9uPdFekY38OAk9MxZQwPtxl9rjI4b1Li9bQ> accessed 16 August 2024.

[102] Córdova Vianello (n 23) 669.

[103] ibid.

[104] ibid 670.

[105] ibid.

[106] ibid 692–93; Labastida and López Leyva (n 6) 793.

Chamber of Deputies, no party could hold more than 300 out of 500 seats (15 seats fewer than before), regardless of their total share of the vote, and an 8 per cent limit of over-representation was established.[107] In the Senate, on the other hand, proportional representation was introduced. From the 128 seats, each state would elect 3 senators (2 would be assigned to the plurality party and 1 to the runner-up), and the remaining 32 would be distributed among parties in proportion to their national vote.[108] As reported by Juan Molinar Horcasitas and Jeffrey Weldon, the quid pro quo in this amendment was very clear:

> the PRI demanded a complete overhaul of the General Council of IFE, because it did not trust several of the IFE members. In return for this overhaul, the opposition negotiators won most of their demands, including a more proportional electoral formula, the extrication of government from the electoral agency, and stronger regulations of political financing.[109]

Even taking into account the opposition's important gains, the PRI's privileged bargaining position was again revealed in this process. The regulation of campaign finance was deferred to ordinary laws, which meant the PRI had the power to unilaterally decide on this matter. In fact, the modifications to the electoral code were passed by members of the PRI only, which still held a majority in Congress.[110]

Despite disagreements over the regulation of campaign finance in ordinary legislation, the electoral reform of 1996 is generally considered as having secured the final rupture with the PRI authoritarian structures and the advent of electoral democracy.[111] In the mid-term elections that took place the following year, the PRI lost the absolute majority in the Chamber of Deputies and three years later the PAN won the presidential election in 2000.[112] More importantly, the *Acuerdo Político Nacional* and the constitutional amendment materializing it in 1996 consolidated the CPER, which for decades to come would allow the amendment mechanism to remain available in Mexico's economy of constitutional change. This specific agreement and this specific constitutional amendment,

[107] Molinar Horcasitas and Weldon (n 12) 225; Córdova Vianello (n 23) 672.

[108] Córdova Vianello (n 23) 672.

[109] Molinar Horcasitas and Weldon (n 12) 226.

[110] In the Chamber of Deputies, the ordinary piece of legislation on campaign financing (COFIPE) was approved solely by the PRI with 288 votes—142 representatives (from PAN, PRD, and PT) voted against. Similarly, in the Senate the piece of legislation was passed solely by the PRI with eighty-nine votes; twenty-three PAN representatives voted against it (PRD representatives were not present). See Labastida and Miguel López Leyva (n 6) 794.

[111] See eg ibid 798; Córdova Vianello (n 23) 677.

[112] Beatriz Magaloni, *Voting for Autocracy: Hegemonic Party Survival and Its Demise in Mexico* (CUP 2006) 195.

not earlier ones, consolidated the rule of cooperation and the CPER for two main reasons. First, even though the consensus rationale had been deployed by President Salinas and materialized in previous constitutional amendments, this time all major political parties acquiesced to the conventions around constitutional change (ie the consensus rationale, the rule of cooperation, and party discipline). All key political actors (ie the leaders of the major political parties) agreed that the centralization of decision-making for constitutional amendment was effective for entrenching their interests, setting a fertile ground to resemble the hegemonic PRI model of decision-making in a new political context (as the discussion regarding the *Pacto por México* in Chapter 4 illustrates). Second, with the benefit of hindsight we know that, as seen in Chapter 4, cross-party entrenchment continued to take place in the following decades, even though no party has had the power to amend the Constitution on its own.

With the consolidation of the rule of cooperation in 1996 and the electoral results of 1997 (where the PRI lost the absolute majority in the Chamber of Deputies), the CPER was ready to work. Trade-off practices to adopt constitutional amendments had already proven a boon for all parties, thus the incentives to continue the trend were in place. Although the distribution of power seemed to be ideal for the system of checks and balances to work properly, the path of constitutional change was set to resemble the working of the hegemonic party regime, allowing the Constitution to become a central tool for political entrenchment.

IV. Why Did the Choice for Consensus Work?

The choice by key PRI political actors to promote the consensus rationale that eventually transformed into the rule of cooperation worked because the right incentives were in place. To be sure, things could have developed differently from the outset. The PAN could have opted for not cooperating and becoming an anti-regime opposition party. Yet the power constellation resulting from, on the one hand, the 1988 election and, on the other, factionalism within the anti-regime coalition set the right incentives for the PRI to compromise while keeping a privileged position, and for the opposition to cooperate instead of advancing an anti-regime strategy. The Salinas administration needed to avoid any further conflict that could challenge its legitimacy, and the government's economic agenda included a considerable number of liberalizing reforms that could not be brought into existence without the cooperation of at least part of the opposition. As Julio Labastida and Armando López point out, 'Salinas needed an ally to legitimate his office, a partner to accompany him in the Chamber of Deputies in order to be able to bring forward his government project.'[113] As for the opposition parties, they found the right incentives to opt for cooperation.[114] Importantly, as seen in Chapter 4, despite its electoral debilitation, the PRI remained strong both at the federal Congress and State level: its votes were necessary to pass any constitutional amendment.[115] At that point, cooperating with the PRI meant that the opposition could secure amendments to guarantee free and fair elections and thus enable their access to power.

As seen in the previous section, soon after the 1988 election, the PAN entered into a trade-off dynamic with the PRI. The cooperation of the PAN is particularly important to understand the dynamics of constitutional change because it remained a constant in the decades to come.[116] The PAN's decision to cooperate with the PRI is hardly surprising as it had long seen itself as a loyal opposition.[117] Plus, as reported by Haber and others, the PRI leadership offered a back-room deal: should the PAN work with the PRI, the government would respect the PAN's victories in gubernatorial, mayoral, and municipal elections.[118] Moreover, as the small parties that supported Cárdenas in the presidential election encountered new possibilities to negotiate with the Salinas administration and entrench their interests as well,[119] the consensus rationale also neutralized the threat the FDN represented.

For Cárdenas' PRD (created in the spring of 1989),[120] it took longer to accept the consensus rationale. The dilemma Cárdenas and his party faced was

[113] Labastida and López Leyva (n 6) 765.

[114] See Haber and others (n 10) 133 (arguing, 'Legitimizing the outcome of the 1988 presidential election was a complicated and delicate affair. Indeed, the egregious fraud that took place was one of the reasons why the FDN became the PRD. Even though the PRI still controlled the newly elected Chamber of Deputies [which, along with the Senate, served as an electoral college constitutionally responsible for certifying the election results] and therefore had the capacity to certify Salinas's victory, it needed political support from the PAN. Had the PAN, whose candidate placed third in the presidential election, continued to side with Cárdenas's supporters in denouncing electoral fraud and seeking to block the certification process, the elections might have been viewed as completely illegitimate by both Mexican citizens and the international community. PRI leaders, however, offered the PAN a backroom deal: If the PAN would work with the PRI, then in exchange the government would henceforth respect the PAN's victories in gubernatorial, mayoral, and municipal council elections').

[115] Molinar Horcasitas and Weldon (n 12) 217–18.

[116] The PAN was ready to cooperate and let Salinas bring forward his policy agenda perhaps because ideologically these two parties are not very far apart, but also because after having lost its place as the second political force (obtaining only 17 per cent of the votes in the general election), the PAN needed to position itself as a relevant political force and most importantly secure reforms aiming to bring electoral democracy to secure its access to power. Prud'homme (n 2) 101.

[117] Loaeza (n 18) 352–74.

[118] Haber and others (n 10) 133.

[119] Prud'homme (n 2) 101–02.

[120] Kathleen Bruhn, *Taking on Goliath: The Emergence of a New Left Party and the Struggle for Democracy in Mexico* (Pennsylvania State UP 2010) 7; Kathleen Bruhn, 'The PRD and the Mexican Left' in Roderic Ai Camp (ed), *The Oxford Handbook of Mexican Politics* (OUP 2012) 188.

that any cooperation with the government would seem like a capitulation to the PRI. Throughout the Salinas administration (1988–94), the approach of the PRD towards the government was antagonistic. As Prud'homme argues, the refusal to engage in negotiations with the government was the most important expression of resistance to one of the mechanisms on which the PRI regime rested: legitimation through the co-optation of opposition forces.[121] The refusal to cooperate would result in the alienation of the party from the negotiations and therefore in the lack of influence over the content of the amendments. But the PRD indirectly benefited from the PRI–PAN agreed reforms on electoral matters (in the end, the PAN and the PRD shared a desire for fair electoral processes), and at the same time remained willing and able to attack and question the legitimacy of the government.[122] Eventually, on the occasion of the reform to the system of political party finance (ie the Electoral reform of 1996), the PRD embraced the consensus rationale. It was then that the *rule of cooperation* emerged—which would in turn allow the centralization of constitutional decision-making and, thus, access to the amendment mechanism for direct entrenchment.

The practice that developed was to activate the amendment mechanism only after agreements with the leadership of the opposition parties were reached and the necessary votes were secured. In order to be able to strike an agreement, the PRI had to make piecemeal concessions. Since the PRI retained its strongholds locally, it still had a better negotiating position vis-à-vis its counterparts. The PRI's core strategy for building consensus was top-down: bargain with the leaders of the opposition parties, aiming to reach cross-party agreements for constitutional reform. In turn, opposition leaders would make sure sitting party members in Congress voted in favour of the amendment at hand. Eventually, as the constitutional amendment dynamics discussed in Chapter 4 illustrate (ie the fast-track pattern in Crongress and the lack of opposition by state legislatures), the rule of cooperation became embedded in the party system.

Another element that explains the formation of the rule of cooperation: money

During the transitional years, public party finance was seen as a fundamental issue to guarantee fair electoral processes. In particular, after the 1994 general election the issue became more pressing after it came to light that despite the

[121] Prud'homme (n 2) 106.
[122] ibid 101–02.

already existing party and campaign finance regulations, the PRI had an unfair and significant budgetary advantage.[123] In this sense, the modification can be read as a major victory for the opposition.[124] Yet, this does not mean that the PRI acted selflessly. It also had incentives for the adoption of a public party finance system. As Green and Sánchez-Talanquer argue, with privatizations, the public funds once available to fund the PRI shrank dramatically.[125] Public party finance, in this sense, would guarantee the PRI funds that were otherwise not available anymore. Moreover, Paulina Fernández Christlieb discusses how important for the PRI public party finance was for the formation of a new political regime:

> [i]t was necessary to reinforce the parties' dependency [. . .], [to] consolidate their integration into the political regime they had once opposed and that now they were part of, to definitively complete its dissociation from the needs of the general population and, for that, public [party] finance was a key tool. [. . .] Zedillo's legacy, which to this day no political party wants to give up, was the enlargement of [party] prerogatives and the constitutionalization of the basis to calculate public [party] finance [. . .] which has reached amounts that have little to do with democracy and nothing to do with justice.[126]

As already noted, the PRD's choice to embrace the consensus rationale took longer than it did for the PAN. We saw in the previous section that all constitutional amendments in this period were the result of cross-party cooperation between the PRI and PAN except for the electoral reform of 1996 whereby Article 41-II of the Constitution was amended to establish a formula that would ensure that political party finance was predominantly public.[127] It is not a minor detail that the decision of the PRD to embrace the consensus rationale was the amendment that dealt with establishing rules of party finance that in practice would translate into a significant increase in all parties' budgets. The constitutional modification regarding party and campaign finance, among

[123] According to a report by the IFE general council, the PRI spent 71.4 per cent of the public funding availaible for the presidential election of 1994. Becerra, Salazar, and Woldenberg (n 92).

[124] For a detailed analysis of the implications of the electoral reform of 1996 for the 1997 mid-term elections, see ibid 458–82.

[125] Kenneth F Greene and Mariano Sanchez-Talanquer, 'Authoritarian Legacies and Party System Stability in Mexico' in Scott Mainwaring (ed), *Party Systems in Latin America: Institutionalization, Decay, and Collapse* (CUP 2018) 222–24.

[126] Fernández Christlieb (n 20) 102–03.

[127] Becerra, Salazar, and Woldenberg (n 92) 378 (arguing, 'in 1994, after the uprising in Chiapas, the rule of inclusion and consensus became necessary to adequate the legal framework but in 1996 it was unavoidable: it was necessary to design an electoral framework with the participation of, at least, the three main national political groups: PRI, PAN, and PRD').

other things, consisted in the establishment of a formula to determine the annual budget for political parties (70 per cent of which would be proportionately distributed by vote share while 30 per cent would be equally distributed) and restrictions to private money in politics.[128] In electoral years, additional funds (equivalent to the annual budget for their ordinary activities) would be available.[129]

Two things happened with the adoption of the party finance formula: on the one hand, the necessary funds were injected to level the playing field so that the main opposition parties stood a chance of winning elections and most likely facilitated the transition in 2000. At the same time, however, in line with what Katz and Mair have called the cartelization of political parties, the major political parties ensured their long-term preservation by formally and practically removing themselves from society and becoming part of the State.[130] The practical effect of the modification was to increase 'public party financing by 600%, making Mexico's elections among the most expensive per capita in the world'.[131] As of the presidential elections of 2012, party dependency on public funding in Mexico was 95 per cent, one of the highest dependency rates in Latin America.[132] Katz and Mair assert that cartel parties are characterized by the 'interpenetration of party and state, and also by a pattern of inter-party collusion'.[133] Importantly, 'this development depends on collusion and cooperation between ostensible competitors, and on agreements which, of necessity, require the consent and cooperation of all, or almost all, relevant participants'.[134] Katz and Mair contend that cartel parties develop in contexts where

[128] Córdova Vianello (n 23) 671, 693.

[129] ibid 671.

[130] Richard S Katz and Peter Mair, 'Changing Models of Party Organization and Party Democracy: The Emergence of the Cartel Party' (1995) 1 Party Politics 5; Richard S Katz and Peter Mair, *Democracy and the Cartelization of Political Parties* (OUP 2018).

[131] Greene and Sanchez-Talanquer (n 125) 223.

[132] Elin Falguera and others (eds), *Funding of Political Parties and Election Campaigns: A Handbook on Political Finance* (IDEA 2014) 140–41; Fransje Molenaar and others, 'Legitimising Political Party Representation: Party Law Development in Latin America' (2014) 35 International Political Science Review 324.

[133] Katz and Mair (n 130) 7 (arguing, 'For the principal-agent model to be appropriate for describing the relationship between citizens and parties requires that ultimate power rests with the citizens as principal.... As translated into the electoral sphere, this means at least that, on the one hand, the electorate must have a substantial choice among competing parties, and, on the other hand, that the cost of the potential sanction of electoral defeat to a party is sufficiently high as to "concentrate the mind wonderfully".... The essence of our argument ... is that these conditions are not well met in modern democracies: the choice offered to electors by the "mainstream parties" [ie those with a realistic chance of being in government in the medium term] has become progressively less substantial in the sense that changes of government are less directly tied to changes in policy or outcomes, and the cost to parties in the mainstream of losing an election [the difference in pay-offs between being a winner and being a loser] has been significantly reduced').

[134] Katz and Mair (n 130) 17.

party finance is predominantly based on state subventions. According to them, public party finance results in parties increasingly becoming part of the state and removed from society. The increased removal from society, naturally, has problematic implications for democratic representation.[135] The function of political parties in the cartel party model is less about the representation of the popular will, in Balkin and Levinson's terms, than it is about their own preservation.[136] Competition is contained,[137] ideological commitments are blurred, and so is the distinction between parties and policy preferences.[138] As Carlos Leonhardt Álvarez has shown, Mexico's party system is consistent with Katz and Mair's model.[139] Greene and Sánchez-Talanquer have reached a similar conclusion, focusing on the impact that the new electoral and party financing regulations had on privileging existing parties over new potential ones in the Mexican party system.[140]

Both Katz and Mair's notion of cartel parties, as well as Leonhardt Álvarez's and Greene and Sánchez-Talanquer's analyses, mainly focus on electoral rules and, in particular, on party finance to explain why and how parties collude to prevent the entrance of new competitors (and, in the case of Katz and Mair, the effects this has on the quality of democracy). That is to say, the emphasis is on cross-party cooperation or collusion to design rules that would contribute to the existing parties' material preservation. Party cartelization not

[135] See ibid 5 (arguing, 'With the development of the cartel party, the goals of politics become self-referential, professional, and technocratic, and what substantive interparty competition remains becomes focused on the efficient and effective management of the polity. Competition between cartel parties focuses less on differences in policy and more—in a manner consistent with Bernard Manin's notion of "audience democracy"—on the provision of spectacle, image, and theater').

[136] Richard S Katz and Peter Mair, 'The Cartel Party Thesis: A Restatement' (2009) 7 Perspectives on Politics 753, 757 (arguing, 'A very important part of their shared interest is to contain the costs of losing, and in this sense to find an equilibrium that suits all of their own "private" interests. This also means cooperation, even if this cooperation need not be overt or conscious. That is, even if parties might be disinclined to rely heavily on overt deals with one another, their mutual awareness of shared interests, and their sense of all being in the same boat and relying on the same sorts of resources, means that we can conclude by hypothesizing collusion [or its functional equivalent] and cartel-like behavior').

[137] Katz and Mair, 'Changing Models of Party Organization and Party Democracy' (n 130) 17; Katz and Mair, *Democracy and the Cartelization of Political Parties* (n 130) 7.

[138] See Katz and Mair (n 136) 757 (arguing, 'these parties increasingly resemble one another; in terms of their electorates, policies, goals, styles, there is less and less dividing them—their interests are now much more shared, and this also facilitates cooperation').

[139] Carlos Leonhardt Álvarez, 'Partidos y Sistemas de Partidos en México ¿Cártel en una Nueva Democracia?' (doctoral thesis, Universidad Complutense de Madrid 2015) 175–222 <http://eprints.ucm.es/32872> accessed 11 June 2018.

[140] See Greene and Sánchez-Talanquer (n 125) 203, 224 (arguing, '[s]ubsequent negotiations between the then-dominant PRI and its two primary challengers over electoral rules and party finance regulations locked in advantages for these existing parties at the onset of fully competitive democracy, helping them survive and dissuading potential new competitors. [. . .] the new system advantaged existing parties over potential entrants. [. . .] due mainly to public financing, the three main parties accounted for 83% of total licit funding in the 1997 elections and 78% in 2000, with the remainder spread across numerous small competitors').

only affects the quality of democracy in general. The analysis provided in this and Chapter 4 sheds light on the negative implications of party cartelization in constitutional politics and processes. As political parties become detached from the public and therefore less accountable, the centralization of constitutional decision-making is facilitated. The logic of trade-offs within the CPER, where all cartel parties benefit from their ability to strike deals regardless of whether they are in government or not, provides little incentives for political parties to oversee and/or challenge each other. In a context of party cartelization, genuine commitments to constitutional democracy are not necessary.

V. Conclusion

This chapter analysed the decisions and choices made by key political actors as the third dimension of Mexico's economy of constitutional change. In so doing, I shed light on the process by which the rule of cooperation came into being. I emphasized two aspects of such process: the deployment of the consensus rationale and the cartelization of the party system. The rule of cooperation allowed continuous access to direct political entrenchment through constitutional amendment for three decades despite the fragmentation of political power. The rule of cooperation has had lasting effects on how constitutional change takes in place in Mexico. Chief among these is the centralization of constitutional decision-making in a context of power fragmentation.

By underscoring the important role that President Salinas and President Zedillo had in the formation of the rule of cooperation (through the deployment of the consensus rationale), this chapter showed how choices and decisions by key political actors contribute to the present and future workings of constitutional systems. Had Salinas and Zedillo not opted for the consensus rationale approach, Mexico's economy of constitutional change would likely have evolved very differently. Constitutional amendments would probably simply not have been available for political entrenchment and the amendment rate would look very different today. Without the electoral reforms adopted in the transitional years, it would have taken much longer for an opposition party to win the presidency or the transition would simply not have been peaceful. At the political crossroads at which the PRI found itself after the 1988 election, its leaders could have decided not to reach out to the opposition and instead choose indirect means of entrenchment. In the end, as illustrated by the passage of the electoral code (COFIPE) in 1996, the PRI maintained control of Congress to pass ordinary legislation on its own. The formation of the rule of cooperation not only allowed the parties to negotiate electoral and party finance rules in their favour. As seen in Chapter 4, it also allowed them to access the constitutional amendment mechanism to directly entrench their interests in a wide array of subject matters.

The rule of cooperation and the consequent centralization of constitutional decision-making have clear negative implications for the workings of constitutional democracy when it comes to formal constitutional change; in particular, for the system of checks and balances, separation of powers, deliberation, and transparency. Chapter 7 unpacks these negative implications. It also shows how the Supreme Court, instead of checking and addressing these issues, has exacerbated them. In so doing, has created incentives for the continuous use of the amendment mechanism through two constitutional doctrines: the non-justiciability of constitutional amendments doctrine and the constitutional restrictions doctrine. The Supreme Court is the remaining factor that explains the availability of constitutional amendment in Mexico's economy of constitutional change.

7

The Supreme Court in Mexico's Economy of Constitutional Change

I. Introduction

Chapter 6 sought to show how choices and decisions by key political actors played a crucial role in the formation of the rule of cooperation as the norm that has facilitated the centralization of constitutional decision-making to access the amendment mechanism. The centralization of decision-making in this context has negative implications in terms of the values and principles that, in a liberal constitutional democracy, the state is supposed to guarantee and protect. Chief among these are the separation of powers, the system of checks and balances, transparency, non-arbitrary state action, and accountability. This chapter explores the role that Mexico's Supreme Court has played in that country's economy of constitutional change. In theory, under a 'new constitutionalism' and juristocracy logic, the Court would be the constitutional actor in a position to enforce those principles. Far from it: since the fall of the PRI hegemonic regime, the Court's doctrines have played an important role in shaping the preferences of political parties and the government for direct political entrenchment. In particular, the non-justiciability of constitutional amendments doctrine and the constitutional restrictions doctrine, which are largely based on the notion of a 'permanent constituent power', shield the amendment power from scrutiny and accountability, making such power arbitrary. In this way, the Court has played a central role in informing the understandings, attitudes, and beliefs of key political actors about the scope and limits of the amendment power, contributing to explaining the continuous availability of the amendment mechanism in Mexico's economy of change.

Section II of this chapter discusses the negative implications of the rule of cooperation and the CPER on the workings of Mexico's constitutional system. Far from addressing the vices created by the rule of cooperation, the Supreme Court has arguably exacerbated them through the non-justiciability and

The Politics of Constitutional Rigidity. Mariana Velasco-Rivera, Oxford University Press.
 DOI: 10.1093/9780191981876.003.0007

constitutional restrictions doctrines, which are briefly described in Section III. Section IV places the development of these doctrines in context and discusses their effects on Mexico's constitutional democracy—namely, the disempowerment of citizens and informing the understandings, attitudes, and beliefs of politicians about the scope and limits of the amendment power.

II. Negative Implications of the Rule of Cooperation and the CPER

As discussed in Chapter 2, in constitutional theory and comparative constitutional studies, there are pervasive assumptions regarding the normative implications of amendment rules on the quality of amendment processes and the adopted texts. For instance, Levinson and Jackson assume that constitutional amendment processes are deliberative and transparent. Albert assumes that changes in the master-text Constitution reflect the will of the people. As seen in the preceding chapters, the case of Mexico sheds light on the limitations of such assumptions. The centralization of constitutional decision-making (which manifests in fast-tack approvals in Congress and the absence of opposition by state legislatures—the trends identified and substantiated in Chapter 4) has negative implications for the values and principles that liberal constitutional democracies are supposed to protect and guarantee. Chief among these are the separation of powers, the system of checks and balances, and deliberation and transparency. These negative implications, at the same time, create an additional problem which is making constitutional amendments prone to arbitrariness.

Separation of powers and checks and balances

As discussed in Chapter 4, works explaining the dysfunction of the constitutional system during the PRI hegemonic regime, such as Jeffrey Weldon's, consider that vertical and horizontal mechanisms of accountability (ie separation of powers and the system of checks and balances) in Mexico did not function properly because the constitutional system was co-opted by one party within which decision-making was highly centralized. For Weldon, the PRI hegemonic regime relied on four necessary conditions: '(1) a presidential system based in the constitution; (2) a unified government, where the ruling party controls the presidency and both houses of Congress; (3) discipline within the ruling party; and (4) a president who is the acknowledged leader of the ruling party'.[1] In that regime, access to the amendment mechanism was ensured by party discipline—an unwritten rule that was enforced by corporatist politics that resulted in the lack of incentives to exercise the veto points established in the Constitution. Constitutional entrenchment rules were in place and formally observed, but the power of the president was effectively unbound. The implicit assumption is that if any of the four conditions ceased to exist, the equilibrium of *presidencialismo* would begin to break down and eventually disappear. Accordingly, the fall of the PRI as a hegemonic party should have allowed the mechanisms of vertical and horizontal accountability to begin to work properly as expected by the conventional wisdom of the time.

Mexico seemed to fall right into the trend associated with the new constitutionalism wave which, in the last decades of the twentieth century, saw the empowerment of apex courts around the world.[2] Theories of judicial review in third-wave democracies reveal the emergence of entrenched written constitutions, rights' charters, and judicial review as means to deal with power-sharing in contexts of political fragmentation. In such contexts, on the one hand, entrenched constitutions are understood as pre-commitment devices that aim at limiting political discretion to protect basic commitments to democracy. Judicial review, on the other hand, confers constitutional courts with policy-making power to ensure the continued protection of the once hegemonic power's interests,[3] political stability,[4] and/or the enforcement of constitutional commitments, principles, and values such as the protection of human rights.[5] Regardless of the cause, end, or purpose of the adoption of judicial review, there are two common correlated assumptions throughout the scholarship: that once the constitution-making or constitution-amending moment passes (where constitutional judicial review is adopted), the constitutional text will remain stable, with all disputes on constitutional meaning settled by the constitutional court, giving way to a model of judicial supremacy where courts are powerful actors able to control the political branches.

[1] Jeffrey Weldon, 'Political Sources of Presidencialismo in Mexico' in Scott Mainwaring and Matthew Soberg Shugart (eds), *Presidentialism and Democracy in Latin America* (CUP 1997) 227.

[2] Stephen Zamora and José Ramón Cossío, 'Mexican Constitutionalism after Presidencialismo' (2006) 4 International Journal of Constitutional Law 411.

[3] Tom Ginsburg, *Judicial Review in New Democracies: Constitutional Courts in Asian Cases* (CUP 2003); Ran Hirschl, *Towards Juristocracy: The Origins and Consequences of the New Constitutionalism* (Harvard UP 2004).

[4] Samuel Issacharoff, *Fragile Democracies: Contested Power in the Era of Constitutional Courts* (CUP 2015)

[5] Alec Stone Sweet, 'Constitutional Courts' in Michel Rosenfeld and András Sajó (eds), *The Oxford Handbook of Comparative Constitutional Law* (OUP 2012) 816.

For some, said assumptions are coupled with the idea that the purpose of peak courts is to be agents of democratization.[6] As such, they are expected to be consequential actors in the protection of the Constitution, democracy, and democratic values.[7] For instance, Alec Stone Sweet views the adoption of judicial review by third-wave democracies almost as a *sine qua non* for the transition to constitutional democracy.[8] His theory of constitutional politics assumes that the adoption of a constitutional review mechanism would necessarily translate into a virtuous circle where courts review the constitutionality of statutes and those decisions would eventually become part of constitutional discourse as the legislatures take them into account when making public policy.[9] Similarly, Samuel Issacharoff understands judicial review as indispensable to establishing constitutional democracy[10] and attributes constitutional courts a 'democratic hedging' function. Issacharoff's view relies on the need for strong constitutional courts to prevent the concentration of power and provide political stability across time. In his view, strong courts are a 'necessary check on excessive concentration of political power under conditions that are unforeseeable at the time of constitutional ratification or whose terms cannot be specified under the strategic uncertainties of the installation of democracy'.[11] More recently, the expectations of apex courts as guardians of democracy have

[6] See eg Tom Gerald Daly, *The Alchemists: Questioning Our Faith in Courts as Democracy-Builders* (CUP 2017) 21; Karl Klare, 'Legal Culture and Transformative Constitutionalism' (1998) 14 South African Journal on Human Rights 146; Alec Stone Sweet, *Governing with Judges: Constitutional Politics in Europe* (OUP 2000); Siri Gloppen, Roberto Gargarella, and Elin Skaar (eds), *Democratization and the Judiciary: The Accountability Function of Courts in New Democracies* (Frank Cass 2004); Gretchen Helmke and Julio Ríos-Figueroa (eds), *Courts in Latin America* (CUP 2011); Samuel Issacharoff, *Fragile Democracies: Contested Power in the Era of Constitutional Courts* (CUP 2015); Bruce Wilson and others, *Courts and Power in Latin America and Africa* (Springer 2016); Wojciech Sadurski, *Constitutional Justice, East and West: Democratic Legitimacy and Constitutional Courts in Post-Communist Europe in a Comparative Perspective* (Springer 2002); Wojciech Sadurski, *Rights before Courts: A Study of Constitutional Courts in Postcommunist States of Central and Eastern Europe* (Springer Science & Business Media 2005); Víctor Ferreres Comella, *Constitutional Courts and Democratic Values: A European Perspective* (Yale UP 2009); Rosalind Dixon, *Responsive Judicial Review: Democracy and Dysfunction in the Modern Age* (OUP 2023).

[7] Issacharoff (n 6); Oscar Vilhena Vieira, Upendra Baxi, and Frans Viljoen, *Transformative Constitutionalism: Comparing the Apex Courts of Brazil, India and South Africa* (PULP 2013); Daniel Bonilla Maldonado (ed), *Constitutionalism of the Global South: The Activist Tribunals of India, South Africa, and Colombia* (CUP 2013); Armin von Bogdandy and others (eds), *Transformative Constitutionalism in Latin America: The Emergence of a New Ius Commune* (OUP 2017); Diana Kapiszewski, Gordon Silverstein, and Robert Kagan (eds), *Consequential Courts: Judicial Roles in Global Perspective* (CUP 2013); Detlef Nolte and Almut Schilling-Vacaflor (eds), *New Constitutionalism in Latin America: Promises and Practices* (Ashgate 2012); Klare (n 6). But see Daly (n 6).

[8] Stone Sweet (n 5).

[9] ibid 202–03. Similary, for a normative account on the need of collaboration between branches of government for the protection of human rights and democracy see Aileen Kavanagh, *The Collaborative Constitution* (CUP 2023).

[10] Samuel Issacharoff, 'Constitutional Courts and Democratic Hedging' (2010) 99 Georgetown Law Journal 961, 986.

[11] ibid 987.

extended to the imposition of limits to formal constitutional change through the development of unconstitutional constitutional amendment doctrines.[12]

Two transformations fed into the conventional wisdom that placed Mexico as part of the trend towards juristocracy and mirrored the normative assumptions regarding the role of the Supreme Court: one political and one constitutional. The political transformation consisted of the increasing political power fragmentation that resulted from the crumbling of the PRI regime (1988–2000). The constitutional transformation resulted from the empowerment of the Supreme Court with new constitutional judicial review powers in 1994–95, in combination with the electoral reforms adopted between 1990 and 1996 that facilitated the transition to democracy (discussed in Chapter 6). The general expectation was that the system of separation of powers would start working properly. In particular, it was thought that the Mexican Supreme Court would become an effective independent organ to check other branches of government due to the increasing fragmentation of political power.[13]

In the context of formal constitutional change, a correct functioning of the separation of powers and of the system of checks and balances should have translated into a drop in the amendment rate. Political power fragmentation would make it difficult to amend the entrenched Constitution and the Supreme Court would be able to exert its power over and control the political branches through its constitutional review powers. Such an assumption is pervasive in the scholarship documenting the transition to democracy as well as the empowerment of the Supreme Court in 1994–95, both in political science and law.[14] Delivering what Benito Nacif calls 'policy shocks' through constitutional

[12] Yaniv Roznai, *Unconstitutional Constitutional Amendments: The Limits of Amendment Powers* (OUP 2017).

[13] Julio Ríos-Figueroa, 'Fragmentation of Power and the Emergence of an Effective Judiciary in Mexico, 1994–2002' (2007) 49 Latin American Politics and Society 31.

[14] See eg Jorge A Vargas, 'The Rebirth of the Supreme Court of Mexico: An Appraisal of President Zedillo's Judicial Reform of 1995 Recent Developments' (1996) 11 American University Journal of International Law and Policy 295, 339 (arguing, 'one may construe these changes as the first constitutional initiative in the political history of that nation expressly drafted to provide its Supreme Court of Justice with a new and more vigorous official profile. This constitutional transformation was designed to produce a "political rebirth" of Mexico's highest tribunal'); Pilar Domingo, 'Judicial Independence: The Politics of the Supreme Court in Mexico' (2000) 32 Journal of Latin American Studies 705—Domingo underscores how the judicial reform of 1994 triggered an 'undisputable process of judicialization politics' through which the relationship between the executive and the Supreme Court was significantly altered when the ruling parties accepted delegating political decision-making power to the judicial branch; Jodi Finkel, 'Judicial Reform as Insurance Policy: Mexico in the 1990s' (2005) 47 Latin American Politics and Society 87; Zamora and Cossío (n 2) (arguing, 'after decades of exercising relatively little impact on the development of law in Mexico, the Mexican Supreme Court has finally assumed a key role in a system that is learning to live with the checks and balances that have been the hallmark of the U.S. constitutional model'); Ríos-Figueroa (n 13); Karina Ansolabehere, 'Jueces, Política y Derecho: Particularidades y Alcances de La Politización de La Justicia' (2005) 22 Isonomía: Revista de Teoría y Filosofía Del Derecho 39, 45 (arguing that the Mexican Supreme Court can be understood as an 'assumed arbiter' in that it does not hesitate in exercising its new constitutional

amendment would become more difficult and, together with a lower amendment rate, the country would see a shift from formal to informal constitutional change.[15] According to political scientist Beatriz Magaloni:

> [t]he constitution is no longer endogenous to the president's will since no party holds the necessary supermajority to amend it. Nomination procedures also changed, since a two-thirds vote in the Senate is now required for approval and the PRI no longer controls such a supermajority. Finally, the Supreme Court now has the power to interpret the constitution. [. . .] The constitutional reform of 1994 produced a profound change in the relationship between the president and the judiciary and a revitalization of the Supreme Court within the system of checks and balances. The significance of these changes should be underscored, particularly considering the prevailing constitutional doctrine, dating back to the turn of the century. The Supreme Court had played no role in interpreting the constitution and controlling legislative decisions. Rather the Court had become an agent of the president and legislators.[16]

Similarly, Elkins, Ginsburg, and Melton argue that during the PRI hegemonic regime constitutional amendments served as a tool that provided political goods that allowed for the co-optation of interest groups and the creation of the necessary loyalty to make bargaining possible.[17] Moreover, in line with the assumption of a shift to a model of judicial supremacy, Elkins, Ginsburg, and Melton assumed that 'with the decline of the PRI supermajority, the primary mechanism of constitutional change . . . shifted from a formal constitutional amendment toward informal judicial amendment through interpretation'.[18]

review powers or show any preoccupation in limiting its jurisdiction on political matters); Issacharoff (n 6) 224 (arguing, 'in Mexico, the emergence of strong challengers to the PRI's hegemony and the possibility of electoral reversals created an incentive for the ruling PRI to institute reforms granting real measures of autonomous judicial authority').

[15] Benito Nacif, 'The Fall of the Dominant Presidency: Lawmaking under Divided Government in Mexico' in Roderic Ai Camp (ed), *The Oxford Handbook of Mexican Politics* (OUP 2012) 234.

[16] Beatriz Magaloni, 'Authoritarianism, Democracy and the Supreme Court: Horizontal Exchange and the Rule of Law in Mexico' in Christopher Welna and Scott Mainwaring (eds), *Democratic Accountability in Latin America* (Oxford Scholarship Online 2005) 303–04.

[17] Zachary Elkins, Tom Ginsburg, and James Melton, *The Endurance of National Constitutions* (CUP 2009) 197 '[C]onstitutional amendment during the PRI regime was frequent, and amendments provided political goods. The PRI used the Constitution to incorporate social insurgencies and political dissidents while limiting their effective power'.

[18] ibid 198; see also Beatriz Magaloni, 'Enforcing the Autocratic Political Order and the Role of Courts: The Case of Mexico' in Tom Ginsburg and Tamir Moustafa (eds), *Rule by Law: The Politics of Courts in Authoritarian Regimes* (CUP 2008) 182; Julio Ríos-Figueroa and Andrea Pozas-Loyo, 'The Transformations of the Role of the Mexican Supreme Court' in Andrea Castagnola and Saul

Three decades after the fall of the hegemonic party regime and the empowerment of the Supreme Court, it is clear that the change from a single-party to a multi-party system did not make the Constitution more difficult to amend. Instead, the frequency of constitutional amendments more than doubled after the PRI lost the power to amend the Constitution on its own in 1988. In the context of formal constitutional change, Mexico faces problems in terms of separation of powers and checks and balances that do not look very different from those faced during the PRI regime. As seen in the preceding chapters, in the CPER, constitutional decision-making remains highly centralized and, as the relevant parties have access to the benefits of direct political entrenchment, regardless of whether they are in government, there are few incentives among parties within Congress, among co-equal branches of government (ie executive–legislative), and across levels of government, to check on each other. The fast-track processes and the lack of opposition by state legislatures identified in Chapter 4 suggest that under the CPER the exercise of power may go unchecked. As in Weldon's account of the PRI regime, the cause for the centralization of decision-making in the CPER (ie the rule of cooperation) is political in nature and not a question of institutional design. Note that from the four conditions that Weldon proposes, party discipline is the one factor that remained after the fall of the hegemonic party. As seen in Chapter 6, in the CPER, the unwritten rule of cooperation, which allows access to direct political entrenchment, also requires party discipline—which among other things is facilitated by the cartelization of the party system.

A reasonable expectation in this context would be for the judiciary, in particular the Supreme Court, to function as a check and address the vices created by the CPER. However, as we will see, this has not been the case. Instead, far from performing its role as a check on power, the Mexican Supreme Court has played a central role in shaping the preferences of political parties and the government for formal constitutional change by informing their understandings, attitudes, and beliefs about the scope and limits of the amendment power. In so doing, it has contributed to the availability of the amendment mechanism in Mexico's economy of constitutional change.

Lopez Noriega (eds), *Judicial Politics in Mexico: The Supreme Court and the Transition to Democracy* (Routledge 2016) 8–40.

Lack of deliberation and transparency

The rule of cooperation also negatively impacts amendment processes in that it enables the lack of democratic deliberation and transparency, which at the same time opens the door to arbitrariness and abuse.[19] The lack of deliberation and transparency is perhaps best illustrated by what has become a common practice deliberately aimed at avoiding public scrutiny: the *madruguete* or *albazo*. The terms refer to actions in the very early hours while everyone is asleep—that is to say, taking someone off guard. *Madruguetes* normally entail decisions taken behind closed doors, with no real public deliberation and expedited approvals. The less time for public consideration, the better. In particular, in the case of constitutional amendments, fast-track processes, and acquiescent state legislatures is what hinders the possibility of deliberation, transparency, and public scrutiny more generally. A good example is the Energy Reform of 2013, discussed in Chapter 4, which took seventy-two hours to wend through all stages in both chambers of Congress (from the presentation of the amendment initiative to approval) and seven days to get ratified by the majority of state legislatures. The amendment was initially secretly agreed to by President Peña Nieto's administration and the (non-democratically elected) leaders of the PRI, PAN, and PRD as part of the *Pacto por México*. Not only did the negotiations take place behind closed doors and without prior notice to party members[20] but also the expeditious process suggests that the needed majorities were secured even before activating Article 135.

[19] For a discussion on the importance of public deliberation in constitution-making processes, see Jon Elster, 'Deliberation and Constitution Making' in Jon Elster and Adam Przeworski (eds), *Deliberative Democracy* (CUP 1998) 111 (arguing, 'the effect of an audience is to replace the language of interest by the language of reason and to replace impartial motives by passionate ones. The presence of a public makes it especially hard to appear motivated merely by self-interest. Even if one's fellow assembly members would not be shocked, the audience would be. In general, the civilizing force of hypocrisy is a desirable effect of publicity' (citation omitted) (emphasis omitted)). For a discussion on the importance of public discussion for the legitimacy of political decisions, see James D Fearon, 'Deliberation as Discussion' in Jon Elster and Adam Przeworski (eds), *Deliberative Democracy* (CUP 1998) 62 ('if we all deliberated privately, the losers in a vote would not know exactly what reasons and arguments the winners had judged to be stronger in deciding the meets of the case. Thus, it would not be clear why the decision would be legitimate for them, if they had no grounds for understanding why the majority thought this is the most reasonable thing to do. Now, if people were assumed to be unboundedly rational calculators, then they could simply infer from losing a vote that a majority must have judged arguments x, y, and z to be stronger, and the effect would be the same if they had held a discussion. But if people are, boundedly rational [. . .] then losing the vote may leave the losers perplexed as to exactly why they should view the decision as legitimate. Further without public discussion, the losers not have a complete confidence that members of the majority had thought of and carefully weighed the minority's arguments against the decision. Hence discussion rather than private deliberation would be necessary to put on the table the various reasons and arguments that different individuals had in mind, and this to ensure that no one could see the result as arbitrary rather than reasonable and justifiable, even if not what he or she happened to see as most justifiable').

[20] Claudia Guerrero, 'Fraguan el Pacto durante Dos Meses' *Reforma* (28 November 2012).

Coupled with the number and scope of constitutional amendments, the lack of genuine deliberation and transparency produced by fast-track processes and the lack of opposition by state legislatures, make the amendment power prone to abuse and arbitrariness, as things can go easily unnoticed. The adoption of the Energy Reform produced a massive mobilization that resulted in violent clashes between police forces and protestors. But not all amendments are as high profile as the Energy Reform, which dealt with one of the most divisive questions in Mexican society (ie the ownership of oil). The public is ready to protest unpopular measures taken under the CPER, but this only comes up in the context of high-profile cases. As the number and scope of constitutional amendments grow, it would be unrealistic to expect the general public to follow all constitutional changes and processes. In this context, it is possible for things to go unnoticed, which allows the government and political parties to act under very little, if any, public scrutiny. At the same time, this opens the possibility of adopting policy measures through amendments without having to offer robust reasons to justify them. In this way, the amendment power under the CPER is prone to arbitrariness and abuse.

Arbitrariness

In the CPER, the principle of non-arbitrary power is also ineffective. Constitutional amendment is prone to arbitrariness from a procedural point of view[21] and to arbitrariness as 'deliberative isolation'.[22] From a procedural point of view, according to Frank Lovett, for power not to be arbitrary, it needs *effective* external constraints.[23] When it comes to constitutional amendment, we can think of external constraints in two ways. On the one hand, where the amendment rule establishes a layered process where multiple veto players are involved, from the point of view of each player, the external constraints can be understood as the power of the other veto players to decline the proposed change. On the other hand, people can contest decisions made through amendment processes through the institutional means available, such as judicial review.[24] Note that, for Lovett, whether power is non-arbitrary depends on the effectiveness of the constraints, not just on their mere existence. As

[21] Frank Lovett, 'What Counts as Arbitrary Power?' (2012) 5 Journal of Political Power 137.
[22] Christopher McCammon, 'Domination: A Rethinking' (2015) 125 Ethics 1028.
[23] Lovett (n 21).
[24] Mariana Velasco-Rivera and Joel I Colón-Ríos, 'On the Legal Implications of a "Permanent" Constituent Power' (2023) 12 Global Constitutionalism 269.

discussed above, in the CPER, due to the rule of cooperation (which produces a high centralization of decision-making), there is no effective constraint to the power exercised through the amendment process. In other words, procedures are followed but the power exercised through them is not effectively constrained. This would not necessarily be a problem if other external constraints were available, which brings us to the power of the people to contest those exercises of power. The most obvious mechanism to do so would be through judicial review. However, in the CPER this option is not available either. As will be seen in the next section, the Supreme Court's doctrines on the non-justiciability of constitutional amendments and constitutional restrictions have, for all practical purposes, shielded formal constitutional change from any kind of contestation or scrutiny.

The second way in which constitutional amendment tends to arbitrariness in the CPER is what Christopher McCammon describes as 'deliberative isolation'.[25] Deliberative isolation refers to the possibility of wielding power without accountability to any other sense of practical reason than one's own.[26] According to McCammon, power's arbitrariness is a function of its deliberative isolation.[27] When deliberative isolation is absolute, 'the empowered person [or group] isn't accountable to anyone else when it comes to how they use their power'.[28] This is to say that those who wield power in deliberative isolation (ie arbitrarily) may impose their will[29] without accountability to those who will be affected by it (that is, regardless of their needs or wants). When it comes to formal constitutional change, deliberative isolation means that those who have the legal power to activate the amendment mechanism can decide on the content of the master-text Constitution, regardless of what citizens think. That is to say, constitutional decision-making can take place without democratic accountability. Note that McCammon's emphasis, in contrast to Lovett's, is on accountability. Importantly, in his account, reducing or taming arbitrary power wielded by groups (ie making the empowered pay attention to what the subjugated group thinks or wants) requires the people to have some kind of say-so on how the power will be used.[30] In the context of formal constitutional change, having a say-so may come in the form of referendums or other means of popular participation including elections. But where the amendment rule

[25] McCammon (n 22).
[26] ibid 1047.
[27] ibid 1050.
[28] ibid 1046.
[29] This is what McCammon understands as 'impositional power' in domination relationships. For a discussion on this point, see ibid 1041.
[30] ibid 1050.

does not provide for such an option and the political parties are increasingly detached from society, as is the case of Mexico, the most obvious means to allow the citizens a say-so is judicial review;[31] in particular, through individual constitutional complaints mechanisms, such as the *amparo* in Mexico. In the CPER, however, individual constitutional complaints through *amparo*, as will be seen, were initially precluded by judicial doctrines and later statutorily banned.[32]

In the CPER, the exercise of power is not constrained or accountable, and is shielded from any form of scrutiny, which allows for abuse. I will return to this point later in this chapter. Before doing so, in the following section I explain the flawed Supreme Court doctrines that enable the arbitrariness of the constitutional amendment power in Mexico.

III. On the Limits of the Amendment Power: The Non-Justiciability of Constitutional Amendments and the Constitutional Restrictions Doctrines

In theory, the judiciary, particularly the Supreme Court, would be the constitutional actor in the best position to address and correct the negative implications of the CPER on the separation of powers, the system of check and balances, and the principle of non-arbitrary power. Apex courts around the world have endeavoured to control and evaluate the power that is exercised through the constitutional amendment mechanism.[33] Although the development of unconstitutional constitutional amendment doctrines has not gone without objections as to their legitimacy, it is a practice that has become increasingly common. Mexico is not part of that trend. The reason is found in two Supreme Court doctrines that through the notion of a 'permanent constituent power' have shut down the possibility of effectively constraining and holding to account the amendment power, therefore enabling arbitrariness: the non-justiciability of constitutional amendment doctrine and the constitutional restrictions doctrine.

The question of judicial review of constitutional amendments has been brought before the Mexican Supreme Court, both in original jurisdiction (ie *controversias constitucionales*, the competence allocation mechanism, and

[31] For a discussion on other possible mechanisms allowing the people a say-so regarding constitutional change, see Velasco-Rivera and Colón-Ríos (n 24).
[32] Ley de Amparo, Art 61-I, Diario Oficial de la Federación (2 April 2013).
[33] Roznai (n 12).

acciones de inconstitucionalidad, the abstract review mechanism) and appellate jurisdiction (ie *amparo*, the individual constitutional complaints mechanism), on several occasions over the last four decades in cases that have dealt with questions of violations of political rights,[34] the right of indigenous peoples to be consulted,[35] freedom of expression, and principles of fair electoral competition.

The non-justiciability of constitutional amendments doctrine in original jurisdiction

The non-justiciability of constitutional amendments doctrine in original jurisdiction cases is primarily based on the concept of a 'permanent constituent power'. Originally coined by Felipe Tena Ramírez in the 1940s and despite the otherwise changing political conditions in Mexico, the concept has been and remains very influential in both Mexican legal academia and constitutional doctrine.[36] In a nutshell, for Tena Ramírez, the constitutional amendment rule in Article 135 blurred the line between constituent and constituted powers by establishing an organ (comprising the Federal Congress and state legislatures)

[34] Soon after formal empowerment of the Supreme Court as a constitutional tribunal in 1994, the question of judicial review of constitutional amendments was brought to the Court in the context of the *Amparo Camacho Solis*. The case was brought against the backdrop of the *Acuerdo Político Nacional* (National Political Agreement) that brought forward the Electoral Reform in 1996 discussed in Chapter 6. Former Mexico City's mayor Manuel Camacho Solis (1988–93) was specifically interested in challenging the section of Article 122 which impeded him to run for mayor of Mexico City in 1997. Camacho Solis was only able to challenge the constitutional amendment under procedural grounds and not for violating his political rights because according to the Court's doctrine, the former are not subject to judicial review through *amparo* (María C Alanis Figueroa, 'La Protección Constitucional de los Derechos Politco-Electorales y el Juicio de Amparo' in Eduardo Ferrer Mac-Gregor and Alfonso Herrera García (eds), *El Juicio de Amparo en el Centenario de la Constitución Mexicana de 1917*, vol 2 (IIJ-UNAM 2017) 195–200). The Supreme Court, sitting *en banc*, unanimously decided that when a constitutional amendment process is challenged, it does not challenge the substance of the amendment itself but the set of acts comprising the legislative procedure that culminates in the amendment. Therefore, it was possible to exercise judicial review of constitutional amendments through *amparo* in that the normative hierarchy of the proposed amendment cannot cancel the possibility to access the constitutional protection of rights through judicial review (SCJN, 9 September 1999, AR 1334/98). Judicial review of constitutional amendments, however, would only have the purpose of verifying the formal rules and that the 'essence' of the procedure was duly observed. Although this interpretation did not include the possibility of substantive review, the shift in the doctrine of the Court in a pluralizing political context could have been interpreted as a positive sign in the direction of its consolidation as a constitutional tribunal. However, that did not last very long. Three years later, in 2002, the Court precluded the possibility of judicial oversight of constitutional amendments based on the idea that they are the only channel through which the 'permanent constituent power' is exercised (SCJN, 6 September 2002, CC 82/2001).

[35] SCJN, 6 September 2002, Controversia Constitucional [CC] 82/2001.

[36] For a detailed discussion on the origins of the concept of a 'permanent' constituent power in Tena's work and its relation with classic works in constitutional theory, see Velasco-Rivera and Colón-Ríos (n 24) 272–78.

capable of modifying the Constitution without specifying its limits or competencies.[37] Accordingly, such an organ 'must participate in some way in the sovereign function: its function is, therefore, constituent'.[38] As it survives the author of the Constitution, in Tena's view, the organ created by Article 135 merited the name of the 'permanent constituent power'.[39]

The Supreme Court's non-justiciability doctrine reflects Tena's conception. The Court has established that the amending power is not subject to any type of judicially enforceable limits because when acting under Article 135, the Federal Congress and state legislatures act as the 'direct successor' of the original constituent power.[40] What is more, the Supreme Court has gone so far as to say that Article 135 creates an organ that is above the constituted powers in that it exercises a sovereign function not subject to judicial review.[41] In the view of the Court,

> [o]nce the basic foundational task is fulfilled, the original [c]onstituent [p]ower disappears and the newly created political organization will act through the constituted powers . . . In this context, it may be argued that the body in which the amendment function is placed . . . is the only and direct depository of the sovereign function of modifying and adding norms to the Fundamental Law [and as such] it is above the three branches of government.[42]
>
> [. . .]
>
> the Constituent power cannot be subject to juridical limits or restrictions, because according to Article 39 of the Constitution, the people exercise its sovereignty through the Original Constituent power and, thereafter, by the Permanent Constituent power, which is comprised by the Congress of the Union and the State Legislatures.[43]

Of course, it did not go unnoticed by the Court that such an interpretation creates problems from the point of view of the most basic notion of constitutional democracy in that, for all practical purposes, it authorizes the exercise of an unlimited power. But the Court considered that given the fact that the amending power comprises different organs (ie each of the chambers of the Federal Congress and a majority of state legislatures), it contains the necessary

[37] ibid 275.
[38] Felipe Tena Ramírez, *Derecho Constitucional Mexicano* (Editorial Porrúa 1978) 54.
[39] ibid.
[40] SCJN, CC 82/2001, 79.
[41] SCJN, 26 June 2008, AI 168/2007.
[42] SCJN, AI 168/2007, 205, 215–16.
[43] SCJN, AI 168/2007, 223.

features to control itself.[44] Based on its 'self-controlling' nature, according to the Court, the organ created by Article 135 is the only competent authority to check and constrain its own behaviour.

The non-justiciability doctrine of constitutional amendments in *amparo*

As will be discussed in detail in the following section, the development of the non-justiciability doctrine in *amparo* has taken place in parallel to the doctrine in original jurisdiction. The reason is that amendments had been challenged through the different judicial review mechanisms available. Therefore, it is no surprise that the doctrine in *amparo* does not differ from the idea that the amendment power, as the permanent constituent power, is incontestable.[45] But although the effect is the same (ie an unlimited amending power), the binding precedent for lower courts was set based on remedy-related reasons.[46]

The doctrine was built drawing on Article 73-XVIII in connection with Article 80 of the *Ley de Amparo*, the statute regulating *amparo* proceedings until 2013. Article 80 mandated that remedies in *amparo* should be inter-partes and Article 73 established the cases of non-justiciability (eg claims against Supreme Court decisions, cases that do not comply with standing rules). Article 73-XVIII established an open-ended non-justiciability clause to include 'every other case in which an inadmissibility cause arises from a legal provision'.[47] While in abstract review the effects of decisions are general (ie *erga omnes*), in *amparo* the effects of rulings are inter-partes only.[48] That is to say, remedies only apply to the claimant. In the view of the Court, granting remedies after declaring a constitutional amendment unconstitutional would

[44] SCJN, CC 82/2001, 79–82; Jurisprudencia P/J 39/2002, emitida por el Tribunal Pleno, publicada en el Semanario Judicial de la Federación y su Gaceta, Novena Época, tomo XVI, septiembre de 2002, 1136 (6 September 2002).

[45] In a dismissal of an individual constitutional complaint challenging the Indigenous Rights Reform of 2001, the unanimous decision states, 'there is no constitutional mechanism available to challenge the will of the amendment power'. SCJN, 4 October 2002, Amparo em Revisión[AR] 123/2002, 122.

[46] See SCJN, 28 March 2011, AR 2021/2009 (*Amparo Intelectuales*). The justices in the majority were Aguirre, Luna, Franco, Pardo, Aguilar, Valls, and Ortiz Mayagoitia. The disenting votes were by Cossío Díaz, Zaldívar, Sánchez Cordero, and Silva Meza. Seven months later, the Second Chamber of the Court unanimously decided the additional five cases needed to set precedent. See SCJN, 5 October 2011, AR 488/2010; SCJN, 5 October 2011, AR 2008/2009; SCJN, 5 October 2011, AR 1989/2009; SCJN, 5 October 2011, AR 1858/2009; SCJN, 5 October 2011, AR 896/2008.

[47] Ley de Amparo, Art. 73-XVIII, Diario Oficial de la Federación (10 January 1936).

[48] This was the case until 2011, when the possibility of *erga omnes* effects of decisions in *amparo* was introduced in the occasion of the constitutional and statutory reform regulating *amparo* proceedings, which I discuss in more detail later in this chapter.

be impossible without breaching the inter-partes mandate.[49] Therefore, the challenges against constitutional amendments should be considered non-justiciable. Notably, in 2013, on the occasion of the implementation of a constitutional amendment that sought to overhaul the mechanism of *amparo*, the judicial review of constitutional amendments was statutorily banned.[50] I will come back to this point later.

The constitutional restrictions doctrine

The Human Rights Reform of 2011, discussed in Chapter 4, incorporated the notion of a 'constitutional bloc'—that is, the incorporation of international human rights treaties as part of the Constitution. In so doing, it explicitly included human rights treaties as part of the constitutional order and recognized the *pro homine* principle, as follows:

> all individuals shall be entitled to the human rights granted by this Constitution and the international treaties signed by the Mexican State, as well as to the guarantees for the protection of these rights. Such human rights shall not be restricted or suspended, except for the cases and under the conditions established by this Constitution itself.
>
> Provisions relating to human rights shall be interpreted [. . .] working in favor of the broader protection of people at all times.[51]

In 2013, the question arose as to what the hierarchical relationship was between human rights treaties and the Constitution in the form of a *contradicción de tesis*.[52] Similar to circuit splits in the US, a *contradicción de tesis* arises when two or more appellate tribunals reach different conclusions on the same legal issue. According to precedent rules in *amparo*, the decision solving the conflicting conclusions becomes a binding precedent.[53] The inclusion of human rights treaties as part of the Constitution, coupled with the *pro homine* principle, established a hermeneutical rule that puts the Constitution and human rights treaties at the same hierarchical level (ie when interpreting provisions

[49] SCJN, 28 March 2011, AR 2021/2009 (*Amparo Intelectuales*).

[50] Ley de Amparo, Art 61-I, Diario Oficial de la Federación (2 April 2013).

[51] Constitution of 1917, Art 1, para 1-2, as amended, Diario Oficial de la Federación (10 June 2011).

[52] SCJN, 3 September 2013, CT 293/2011 and SCJN, 9 September 2013, CT 21/2011. See also José Ramón Cossío, Raúl Mejía Garza, and Laura P Rojas Zamudio, *La Construcción De Las Restricciones Constitucionales A Los Derechos Humanos* (Editorial Porrúa 2015).

[53] Ley de Amparo, Art 225–229, Diario Oficial de la Federación (2 April 2013).

related to human rights, those granting the best possible treatment to individuals should be favoured). In theory, the inclusion of this hermeneutical rule mandates all public authorities, including courts, to conduct what is known as 'conventionality control'—that is to say, interpret national domestic law in a way that is compatible with the American Convention on Human Rights (ACHR).[54] However, the Supreme Court significantly curtailed it. In a 10:1 decision,[55] the Supreme Court determined that while international and constitutional human rights were at the same hierarchical level, whenever the Constitution established a restriction on human rights, the constitutional provision should prevail over the international provision.[56]

The decision was a powerful message to the political branches regarding the scope and limits of the amendment power: the Supreme Court will not question rights restrictions as long as they are made part of the constitutional text, even in those cases when the restrictions may be in direct conflict with international standards. Effectively, the Supreme Court determined, and political parties and the government now knew, that as long as specific policy decisions are introduced in the Constitution, these will be shielded from judicial review.

IV. The Effects of the Supreme Court Doctrines on Non-Justiciability of Constitutional Amendments and Constitutional Restrictions

I have noted that when the PRI hegemonic regime unravelled, there was a pervasive assumption that the mechanisms of horizontal and vertical accountability would begin to work properly. That assumption naturally included the Supreme Court. By now, we have seen that when it comes to formal constitutional change, the mechanisms of separation of powers and checks and balances built into the amendment rule established by Article 135 of the

[54] Pablo González-Domínguez, *The Doctrine of Conventionality Control: Between Uniformity and Legal Pluralism in the Inter-American Human Rights System*, vol 11 (Intersentia 2018); Laurence Burgorgue-Larsen, 'Conventionality Control: Inter-American Court of Human Rights (IACtHR)', *Max Planck Encyclopedia of International Procedural Law* (Oxford Public International Law 2018) <https://opil.ouplaw.com/display/10.1093/law-mpeipro/e3634.013.3634/law-mpeipro-e3634> accessed 16 August 2024.

[55] The justices in the majority were Alfredo Gutiérrez Ortiz Mena, Margarita Luna Ramos, Fernando Franco González Salas, Arturo Zaldívar, Juan Silva Meza, Jorge Mario Pardo Rebolledo, Luis María Aguilar Morales, Olga Sánchez Cordero, Sergio Valls, and Alberto Pérez Dayán. The only dissenting vote was by Justice José Ramón Cossío Díaz.

[56] SCJN, 3 September 2013, CT 293/2011, 64–65.

Constitution do not work properly. In Mexico, when it comes to decision-making relating to constitutional amendment, decisions are incontestable. The Supreme Court doctrines on non-justiciability of constitutional amendments and constitutional restrictions have for all practical purposes shielded the amendment power from any kind of contestation or scrutiny. Put differently, the amendment power in Mexico is arbitrary in Lovett's and McCammon's terms inasmuch as citizens have been disempowered from having a say-so as to how the amendment power is wielded. The arbitrary nature of the amendment power, at the same time, has had a lasting impact on informing understandings, attitudes, and beliefs about constitutional amendments as an effective means of entrenchment. This reality has shaped the preferences of political parties and the government for formal constitutional change and contributed to the availability of the amendment mechanism in Mexico's economy of constitutional change.

Disempowering citizens

The non-justiciability and the constitutional restriction doctrines have rendered the amendment power arbitrary because they shield it from effective constraints and accountability, in Lovitt's and McCammon's terms, respectively. The disempowering effect of these doctrines is best illustrated if we think about them in terms of McCammon's 'deliberative isolation' of arbitrary power as explained in Section I. As noted above, for McCammon, those who wield power in deliberative isolation (ie arbitrarily) may impose their will[57] without accountability on those who will be affected by it. Importantly, taming arbitrary power wielded by groups necessarily entails that the people have some kind of say-so about how the power is used.[58] The disempowering effect of the non-justiciability doctrine rests on the fact that it allows for the imposition of the will of the political parties with access to the amendment mechanism over the citizens by removing the possibility for people to have a say-so on how the amendment power is exercised. The disempowering effect of the non-justiciability doctrine in the CPER is well illustrated by the challenges against the Indigenous Peoples Rights Reform of 2001, the Electoral Reform of 2007, and the Education and Energy Reforms of 2013. All of these episodes show,

[57] This is what McCammon understands as 'impositional power' in domination relationships. For a discussion on this point, see McCammon (n 22) 1041.
[58] ibid 1050.

on the one hand, the disempowerment of the people seeking to have a say-so on how the amendment mechanism had been exercised. On the other hand, they also show that the message from the Supreme Court was clear: the judiciary would not meddle with direct political entrenchment. As will be seen later in this chapter, such a message has had a lasting impact on the perceptions and understandings of key actors about the amendment power as an effective means of entrenchment, therefore shaping their preferences for it.

Challenges against the Indigenous Peoples Rights Reform of 2001

The Indigenous Peoples Rights Reform of 2001 was adopted in the context of the *Acuerdos de San Andrés* (San Andrés Accords) between the EZLN and the federal government in February 1996. The accords were the product of previous peace talks and marked the beginning of negotiations towards putting an end to Chiapas' armed conflict that rose amid the adoption of NAFTA discussed in Chapter 6. Roughly speaking, in these accords the government agreed to adopt a constitutional amendment and a legal framework recognizing the rights to self-determination, territory, political rights, social rights, economic rights, and cultural rights of indigenous peoples.[59] However, the government did not take the indigenous peoples into account in the following rounds of negotiations and largely ignored the specific commitments agreed upon in the accords for the constitutional amendment. Accordingly, soon after the enactment of the constitutional amendment in 2001, hundreds of constitutional claims were presented both through *controversias constitucionales* (ie the competence allocation mechanism) and *amparo* suits.

Indigenous municipalities from several states across the country (ie Oaxaca, Puebla, Guerrero, Morelos, Veracruz, Jalisco, Michoacán, Tabasco, and Hidalgo), the state legislature of Chiapas, and the governor of Tlaxcala brought 321 *controversias constitucionales* before the Supreme Court, which were all dismissed based on the reasoning laid out in CC 82/2001. In broad terms, the indigenous municipalities made a general claim arguing formal violations of the amendment process—that is, violations to Article 135 of the Constitution.[60] On the one hand, they argued that counting the votes of the state legislatures and formalizing the constitutional reform before having received the votes of the totality of the legislatures was a violation of the procedure established in

[59] Secretaría de Gobernación, 'Propuestas Conjuntas que el Gobierno Federal y el EZLN se Comprometen a Enviar a las Instancias de Debate y Decisión Nacional, Correspondientes al Punto 1.4. de las Reglas de Procedimiento', Documento 2 <http://zedillo.presidencia.gob.mx/pages/chiapas/docs/sanandres/p-conju-doc2.html> accessed 16 February 2016.

[60] SCJN, 6 September 2002, CC 82/2001, 8.

Article 135 in that it denaturalized and fragmented the reforming body. On the other hand, it was argued that according to Article 6 of the Indigenous and Tribal Peoples Convention of 1989 (No 169), for the constitutional reform to be valid, the indigenous peoples should have been consulted.[61] In an 8:3 decision, the Supreme Court dismissed the claims on the grounds that, as explained in section III, constitutional amendments are not subject to any kind of review because the amendment process itself is its own control.[62] One month after CC 82/2001 was decided, the Second Chamber of the Court dismissed an *amparo* against the indigenous peoples reform. As in CC 82/2001, the indigenous community bringing this claim pointed to irregularities in the amendment process as they had not been consulted and alleged an arbitrary reduction in their territory.[63] The Second Chamber unanimously decided in the same terms as CC 82/2001 decided the month before.

Note that the reasoning in CC 82/2001 effectively equates the amendment power with the constituent power. By giving the amendment power a special position vis-à-vis the constitutional order for its 'exclusive constitutional function', it puts the decisions taken in the context of a constitutional amendment out of the scope of any kind of scrutiny—that is, above the law. Given the volume of claims and the politically complex conflict they were addressing, the Supreme Court delivered a powerful political message with this massive dismissal: there would not be judicial meddling in those political agreements entrenched in the Constitution. The Supreme Court, in this sense, signed a blank check for the political elite to act with absolute discretion in the realm of constitutional amendments.

Challenges against the Electoral Reform of 2007

The constitutional reforms adopted in November 2007 were a response to the political turmoil created by the highly contested 2006 presidential election.

[61] Indigenous and Tribal Peoples Convention of 1989 (No 169), Article 6.1, 5 September 1990, ILO. Article 6.1 of this Convention states: 'In applying the provisions of this Convention, governments shall: (a) consult the peoples concerned, through appropriate procedures and in particular through their representative institutions, whenever consideration is being given to legislative or administrative measures which may affect them directly; (b) establish means by which these peoples can freely participate, to at least the same extent as other sectors of the population, at all levels of decision-making in elective institutions and administrative and other bodies responsible for policies and programs which concern them; (c) establish means for the full development of these peoples' own institutions and initiatives, and in appropriate cases provide the resources necessary for this purpose. 2. The consultations carried out in application of this Convention shall be undertaken, in good faith and in a form appropriate to the circumstances, with the objective of achieving agreement or consent to the proposed measures.'

[62] SCJN, 6 September 2002, CC 82/2001.

[63] SCJN, 4 October 2002, AR 123/2002, 15.

The election result was arguably heavily influenced by a PAN political campaign innovation: through TV spots, the incumbent party deployed a negative campaign against the PRD candidate, Andrés Manuel López Obrador.[64] The Electoral Reform of 2007 was adopted to ban negative campaigns and the acquisition of airtime by private parties for electoral matters, and to establish a scheme of free access to media that would be administered by the IFE.[65] Shortly after, the amendment was challenged both through abstract review and through *amparo*. The abstract review claim, AI 168/2007, was brought by the national leaders of two small political parties—Partido Convergencia and Partido Nueva Alianza. The main claim was that the system for distributing airtime violated the multi-party system constitutional principles enshrined in Article 41 of the Constitution by unduly harming newly created political parties. Under this system, in the view of the claimants, newly created parties would be at a disadvantage vis-à-vis the traditional political parties.[66] Applying the precedent established in CC 82/2001, in a 7:4 decision, the Supreme Court precluded the possibility of reviewing constitutional amendments in abstract review.[67] In this sense, the Supreme Court maintained the inadmissibility of the case based on procedural grounds. In short, the Supreme Court considered that the claims were inadmissible for two main reasons. On the one hand, the Court considered that abstract judicial review only applied to laws in a strict sense (ie laws issued under the ordinary legislative processes as opposed to the constitutional amendment process) and not to constitutional provisions—which as the 'supreme law' cannot be subject to the same kind of review as ordinary laws.[68] On the other hand, it determined that the Constitution did not expressly allow for the judicial review of constitutional amendments and that such power could not be inferred.[69] Therefore, the Supreme Court could not engage in reviewing the constitutionality of constitutional amendments.

[64] See eg Flavia Freidenberg and Luis González Tule, 'Estrategias partidistas, preferencias ciudadanas y anuncios televisivos: Un análisis de la campaña electoral mexicana de 2006' (2009) 16 Política y Gobierno 269; Ana Yely Pérez Dámazo, 'Campañas negativas en las elecciones 2000 y 2006 en México' (2014) 59 Revista Mexicana de Ciencias Políticas y Sociales 87.

[65] Broadly speaking, the amendment did two things: (i) established a system to distribute air time tied to previous electoral results—30 per cent of the time would be equally distributed between competing parties and 70 per cent would be proportionally distributed to the number of votes obtained in the previous mid-term election; (ii) established a general prohibition to privately acquire airtime for electoral ends. See CP 1917, Art 41(A)(g)(third clause), as amended, Diario Oficial de la Federación (13 November 2007).

[66] SCJN, 26 June 2008, AI 169/2007, 20.

[67] The majority was composed by Justices Luna, Franco, Gudiño, Azuela, Valls, Sánchez Cordero, and Ortiz Mayagoitia, the minority by Justices Aguirre, Cossío, Góngora, and Silva.

[68] SCJN, 26 June 2008, AI 169/2007, 246.

[69] SCJN, 26 June 2008, AI 169/2007, 254.

Several challenges were brought against the Electoral Reform of 2007 via *amparo*. The case based on which the precedent was later set for lower courts in 2011 came to be known as *Amparo Intelectuales*. The claimants argued that the constitutional amendment that established the general prohibition to acquire airtime for electoral purposes unduly restricted their freedom of expression. In a 7:4 decision, the Supreme Court dismissed the claim on the grounds that, as explained in section III, it was impossible to grant remedies without breaching the inter-partes mandate. According to the majority, allowing the claimants to acquire airtime for political propaganda would not only benefit them but also the person they decided to support electorally and the companies they would buy the airtime from. By June 2008, the state of affairs of the case law on the judicial review of constitutional amendments was that the latter were not reviewable through any of the judicial review mechanisms provided in the constitution. The political message was clear: the Supreme Court would not meddle in the CPER as long as cross-party bargains were introduced in the constitution.

Informing understandings, shaping preferences

The question of judicial review of constitutional amendments is, of course, one of judicial restraint that is not foreign in other latitudes. The Mexican Supreme Court surely is not the first or the last court to decide against reviewing the constitutionality of constitutional amendments. Yet, there are contexts in which the lack of such doctrines may be more problematic than in others. In the Mexican context, the absolute absence of judicial review of amendments is particularly problematic because of the prevalent use of constitutional amendments for political entrenchment. In the CPER, the lack of an unconstitutional constitutional amendment doctrine translates into allowing arbitrary power through the disempowerment of citizens. In this way, the non-justiciability and constitutional restrictions doctrines have also had a lasting effect on shaping preferences by informing the understandings, attitudes, and beliefs of public officials about formal constitutional change as an effective means of entrenchment. To determine the exact extent to which Supreme Court doctrines have shaped those understandings would require a separate book. There are, however, good reasons to believe that the doctrines discussed in this chapter played a fundamental role in the way political actors relate to the amendment rule.[70]

[70] Importantly, the preference for the amendment mechanism could change in time. Should the non-justiciability doctrine be reversed, it is reasonable to believe that this change would shape perceptions about the suitability of constitutional amendments to advance and entrench political agendas.

One of the most important functions of the Supreme Court doctrines analysed here is shielding cross-party agreements directly entrenched in the Constitution from scrutiny and accountability. The possibility of exercising arbitrary power enabled by the doctrines creates the perfect conditions for political parties and the government to use, and keep wanting to use, constitutional amendments as a means of political entrenchment. Assuming that politicians are rational actors, the possibility of exercising arbitrary power is very attractive to overlook simply because the survival of a given policy decision is guaranteed if directly entrenched in the master-text Constitution. In this way, the doctrines preventing the review of constitutional amendment play a crucial role in the CPER in that they facilitate its operation and stability. By preventing judicial oversight, the non-justiciability doctrine guarantees the insulation of cross-party agreements and, therefore, incentivizes the observance of the rule of cooperation while ensuring the stability and preservation of the regime. Should there be no guarantee of insulation of the cross-party agreements, opposing parties would have fewer incentives to cooperate with each other.

Two things showcase how much politicians value the insulation of policy decisions provided by the Supreme Court doctrines: the statutory ban on judicial review of constitutional amendments and the reaction of high-ranking public officials when the equilibrium provided by the doctrines was revisited. These two examples are instructive to see the ways in which the doctrines have informed the understandings, attitudes, and beliefs about formal constitutional change as an effective means of entrenchment.

Statutory ban on judicial review of constitutional amendments

The disempowering effect of the Supreme Court doctrines was later reflected in legislation adopted against the backdrop of the Public Education and Energy Reforms of 2013. Both reforms were brought forward along with much social unrest and both reached the judiciary through challenges to their constitutionality.[71] The constitutional reform on education brought 40,000 teachers from across the country to a strike in Mexico City that lasted for over a month. In addition to protests and strikes, around 100,000 teachers collectively filed *amparos* against the constitutional amendment claiming the violation of labour rights.[72] Incidentally, days before the filings were made, a statutory ban

[71] Notimex, 'Tribunal Desecha Amparo Contra Reforma Energética' *Milenio* (Mexico, 14 May 2014) <www.milenio.com/politica/reforma_energetica-amparo_contra_reforma_energetica_0_298770447.html> accessed 13 February 2025.

[72] Alfredo Méndez, 'Desechan Solicitudes de Amparo de 100 Mil Maestros Contra las Modificaciones' (30 April 2013) <www.jornada.com.mx/2013/04/30/politica/007n1pol> accessed 16 August 2024.

on judicial review of constitutional amendments in *amparo* had been introduced in a statute regulating *amparo* proceedings that replaced the one from 1936: the Nueva Ley de Amparo (NLA). The NLA was enacted in 2013, two years after the adoption of the widely celebrated constitutional amendment of 2011 that reformed important aspects of *amparo* proceedings. Among other things, the constitutional amendment to *amparo* proceedings was said to be expanding the constitutional protection of human rights by enlarging the scope of claims that could be brought to courts in *amparo* (ie it expanded the concept of authority and relaxed standing rules), and empowering the Supreme Court by including the possibility of giving general effects to *amparo* rulings. Yet, when the time came to issue the legislation implementing the constitutional amendment, a non-justiciability clause banning judicial review of amendments to the Constitution was introduced in Article 61-I. Accordingly, the lawsuits were dismissed by lower courts in application of the newly adopted statutory ban.[73] The inclusion of Article 61-I speaks against the argument that the constitutional amendment of 2011 aimed at expanding access to justice through *amparo* to better protect rights. Rather than expanding the scope of constitutional claims that can be brought to the judiciary, it clearly reduced it. However, no legislator publicly addressed or questioned its inclusion in the new law. Notably, the Second Chamber (ie a five-judge panel) of the Supreme Court denied a *certiorari* to review the constitutionality of the ban on the grounds that the non-justiciability clause in Article 61-I made challenges against constitutional amendments constitutionally irrelevant and that even before the clause was introduced, the Supreme Court had already established that constitutional amendments were incontestable.[74]

The Energy Reform was not vastly different. After the enactment of the reform privatizing the oil industry in 2013, around 65,000 people protested in Mexico City.[75] The amendment was unsuccessfully challenged in *amparo*.[76]

[73] SCJN, 14 August 2013, SEFA 222/2013; SCJN, 14 August 2013, SEFA 227/2013; SCJN, 14 August 2013, SEFA 228/2013; SCJN, 21 August 2013, SEFA 224/2013; SCJN, 21 August 2013, SEFA 225/2013; SCJN, 21 August 2013, SEFA 229/2013; SCJN, 28 August 2013, SEFA 221/2013; SCJN, 28 August 2013, SEFA 226/2013. See also La Redacción, 'Niega La Corte Amparos a Maestros Por La Reforma Educativa' *Proceso* (Mexico, 14 August 2013) <www.proceso.com.mx/350089/niega-la-corte-amparos-a-maestros-por-la-reforma-educativa> accessed 16 August 2024.

[74] SCJN, 14 August 2013, SEFA 222/2013, 24.

[75] 'Reforma Energetica Levanta Protestas en México' *Univision* (1 February 2014) <www.univision.com/noticias/noticias-de-mexico/reforma-energetica-levanta-protestas-en-mexico> accessed 16 August 2024.

[76] There was also a legal strategy that attempted to challenge the amendment via *consulta popular* (ie referendum). Since 2012, under Article 35-VIII of the Constitution, citizens are able to put a public issue to referendum if they represent at least 2 per cent of the people subscribed in the electoral registry (over 2,500,000 signatures are needed). A referendum can only be held on election day and the questions put forward have to be previously approved by the Supreme Court. The Supreme Court

Like with the challenges against the Education Reform, the claims against the Energy Reform were dismissed by a circuit court in application of the non-justiciability clause of constitutional amendments in *amparo* proceedings. Considering the rate of constitutional amendments and the fact that individuals were willing to bring claims against constitutional amendments to court, Article 61-I seems to have been a direct answer to those citizens trying to have a say-so on how power is exercised through constitutional amendment and defend their rights and the Constitution.

The legislative efforts to pass the NLA began long before the 2011 amendment was adopted. Different actors were pushing for a new and more protective law since the 1990s. In 1999, the Supreme Court created a commission charged with the drafting of a bill on this matter. The bill was then reviewed by the justices sitting *en banc* in 2001.[77] However, the legislative story of Article 61-I is considerably shorter. On 15 February 2011, PRI Senators Jesús Murillo Karam and Alejandro Zapata Perogordo presented a bill that considered the work done by the Supreme Court in 1999–2001 and allowed constitutional complaints against constitutional amendments but only for violations of the amendment procedure.[78] Months later, on 22 September 2011, PRD Senator Tomás Torres Mercado submitted a bill that included a clause with an blanket ban on individual constitutional complaints against constitutional amendments.[79] These legislative proposals came against the backdrop of the *Amparo Intelectuales* which was adjudicated in March 2011. Incidentally, the relevant legislative commission presented its report on the proposals to the Senate floor on 6 October, one day after the Second Chamber set the precedent on the inadmissibility of claims against constitutional amendments in *amparo* in the cases against the Electoral Reform of 2007.[80] The report adopted Senator Torres' proposal to include the blanket ban on judicial review of constitutional

denied the authorization to hold the referendum to ask the population whether they supported the Energy Reform. See Constitution of 1917, Art 35-VIII, as amended, Diario Oficial de la Federación (9 August 2012); Isabel González, 'SCJN le Dice "No" a Consulta Energética del PRD y Morena' *Excelsior* (Mexico, 30 October 2014) <www.excelsior.com.mx/nacional/2014/10/30/989737> accessed 16 August 2024.

[77] Arturo Zaldívar Lelo de Larrea, *Hacia una Nueva Ley de Amparo* (UNAM 2002).

[78] Senado de la República, Gaceta Parlamentaria, núm. LXI/2SPO-208-966, LXI Legislatura, Segundo Periodo Ordinario (15 February 2011) <www.senado.gob.mx/65/gaceta_del_senado/2011_02_15/966> accessed 16 August 2024.

[79] Senado de la República, Gaceta Parlamentaria, núm. LXI/3PPO-273-1066/31870, LXI Legislatura, Primer Periodo Ordinario (22 September 2011) <www.senado.gob.mx/65/gaceta_del_senado/2011_09_22/1066> accessed 16 August 2024.

[80] 'Los Hechos que Han Marcado las Protestas de la CNTE contra la Reforma Educativa' [2016] *Expansión* <https://expansion.mx/nacional/2016/06/02/los-hechos-que-han-marcado-las-protestas-de-la-cnte-contra-la-reforma-educativa> accessed 16 August 2024.

amendments, which was to become Article 61-I of the NLA.[81] The bill was passed by the Senate and submitted to the Chamber of Deputies on 13 October 2011, where it remained on standby until February 2013 amid the protests against the adoption of the Education Reform enacted in the same month. This legislative measure effectively put an end to the long-standing question of judicial review of constitutional amendments through *amparo*. It could be argued that the inclusion of Article 61-I technically incorporated the Supreme Court's doctrine on the matter. However, sitting *en banc*, the Supreme Court was still divided on the question of reviewability of constitutional amendment in *amparo* and, most importantly, had not issued a binding decision for the Second Chamber and lower courts.[82] Precluding the possibility of judicial review of constitutional amendments guarantees that policy decisions directly entrenched in the Constitution would not be subject to judicial review (which was later reinforced by the constitutional restriction doctrine). In this context, it is unsurprising that no one in Congress raised concerns about the inclusion of the clause.[83] Although the enactment of the NLA was overdue one year and four months, it came right on time before the filings against the Education and Energy Reform of 2013.

Regardless of the merits of the claims against the Indigenous Peoples Rights Reform, the Electoral Reform of 2007 previously discussed, and the Education and Energy Reforms, the problem is that both the Supreme Court doctrines and the statutory ban on individual constitutional complaints against constitutional amendments allow for the arbitrary exercise of the amendment power. In particular, the inclusion of the non-justiciability clause of constitutional amendments in the NLA is very telling in terms of how much the political parties and the government value arbitrary power. It is not that they simply took advantage of the insulation of policy choices provided by a given judicial doctrine; it is that deliberative isolation was actively sought with the adoption of the non-justiciability of constitutional amendments clause in Article 61-I of the NLA.

[81] Secretaría de Gobernación, Sistema de Información Legislativa, Decretos Publicados en el Diario Oficial de la Federación LXII Legislatura, Ley de Amparo (2 April 2013) <http://sil.gobernacion.gob.mx/Archivos/Documentos/2011/10/asun_2802816_20111006_1317913242.pdf> accessed 16 August 2024.

[82] The *Amparo Intelectuales* (SCJN, 28 March 2011, AR 2021/2009) was the last case on the matter decided by the Supreme Court sitting *en banc* (7:4). As mentioned earlier, according to the precedent rule in *amparo* proceedings, for the Supreme Court to set precedent it needs to rule five consecutive cases with the same outcome and by a qualified majority of eight votes. In this sense, the *Amparo Intelectuales* did not have any value to set a potential precedent or to argue the issue was settled.

[83] Senado de la Republica, Diario de los Debates, Sesión Ordinaria (11 October 2011) <www.senado.gob.mx/64/diario_de_los_debates/documento/2103> accessed 16 August 2024.

The reaction of high-ranking public officials when the non-justiciability and constitutional restriction doctrines were to be revisited

The second way to showcase how much arbitrary power is valued in the CPER is to analyse the reaction of high-ranking public officials when the equilibrium provided by the doctrines was to be revisited. Unsurprisingly, the possibility of insulating of policy choices provided by the Supreme Court doctrines has been abused. By abuse, I mean taking advantage of an amendment power that is shielded from scrutiny and accountability to entrench policy decisions that by domestic and/or international standards would otherwise be unconstitutional.[84] Perhaps the most instructive examples of this are the creation of constitutional regimes of exception when it comes to criminal procedure rights: the *arraigo* detention and *prisión preventiva oficiosa* (automatic pre-trial detention) (PPO), both of which were constitutionally entrenched as part of the Criminal Justice System Reform of 2008. These two examples are useful for two reasons. First, they show that the understandings of high-ranking officials about the scope and limits of the amendment power mirror the Supreme Court doctrines. This supports the claim that the non-justiciability doctrine and the constitutional restrictions doctrine have informed the preference for direct political entrenchment in the CPER. The second reason is that due to different circumstances and legal strategies, the *arraigo* and PPO mechanisms (and by implication the doctrines) have been under consideration by the Supreme Court and the Inter-American Court of Human Rights. The reaction of high-ranking public officials to the threat to the insurance provided by Supreme Court doctrines shows how much the arbitrary amendment of power is valued in the CPER.

The *arraigo* detention and *prisión preventiva oficiosa* were introduced as part of the widely celebrated Criminal Justice System Reform of 2008 that adopted an accusatory criminal justice system to replace the inquisitorial system and prioritize the presumption of innocence.[85] The *arraigo* detention allows prosecutors to detain suspects of organized crime for up to eighty days to gather

[84] To be sure, the amendment power would still be arbitrary if intentions were altruistic because for all practical purposes the amendment power is shielded from any form of scrutiny and accountability.

[85] Constitution of 1917, Art 16, para 8, as amended, Diario Oficial de la Federación (18 June 2008). This article states the following: 'In the case of organized crime, and at the request of the Public Prosecution Service, judicial authority can order to put a person into hold restraint, complying with the terms of time and place established by law and without exceeding forty days, whenever necessary for the success of the investigation, the protection of people or legal goods, or when there is reason to believe that the accused could avoid the action of justice. The forty days term can be extended, provided that the Public Prosecution Service proves that the causes that originate hold restraint still remain. In any case, the hold restraint shall not last more than eighty days' (translation by Constitute Project, 'Mexico').

evidence before bringing suspects before a judge and formally charging them with a crime 'to ensure the success of the investigation'. Once regulated in ordinary legislation, its constitutionalization came against the recommendations of several international human rights bodies, who favoured its elimination.[86] Its adoption also overruled a Supreme Court decision in abstract review that had declared it unconstitutional in 2005 in the State of Chihuahua for violating the right to personal liberty, the constitutional guarantees of due process in criminal proceedings[87] (eg no accused person can be detained by the public prosecution service for longer than forty-eight hours before being released or brought before a court of law and being formally charged with a crime within seventy-two hours after being brought before a judge), and the freedom of movement.[88]

The *prisión preventiva oficiosa* (automatic pre-trial detention) is a vestige of the inquisitorial system where pre-trial detention was the rule rather than the exception. Contrary to Inter-American standards that require, among other things, pre-trial detention to be treated as an exceptional measure, the PPO mandates judges to order it without evaluating its necessity when it comes to the crimes and categories of crimes included in the catalogue provided by Article 19 of the Constitution. As such, the PPO systemconstitutes a regime of exception to the accusatory system that is supposed to prioritize the presumption of innocence that was also introduced as part of the Criminal Justice Reform 2008 in Article 20. Since its adoption, members of civil society, non-governmental organizations, and international human rights bodies have advocated for its elimination for being against international human rights standards. But ever since, governments across the political spectrum have only doubled down in their commitment to such policy choice. Between 2008 and 2024, the catalogue in Article 19 was expanded twice: in 2011 and in 2019. As a result, when looking into the relevant secondary legislation, the catalogue in Article 19 of the Constitution translates into over 150 crimes that qualify for *prisión preventiva oficiosa*.[89] What is more, in February 2024, President López

[86] National and International Human Rights organizations and bodies, such as the UN Committee against torture, have long documented the connection of the *arraigo* detention with other violations of human rights such as torture and forced disappearances. See Lucía G Chávez Vargas and Javier Carrasco Solís, 'Amicus Curiae Inconvencionalidad del Arraigo y La PPO En México' 8 <www.cmdpdh.org/publicaciones-pdf/Amicus_Arraigo_PPO_2022.pdf> accessed 16 August 2024; José Antonio Guevara Bermúdez, *La Prohibición de Las Detenciones Arbitrarias y La Organización de Las Naciones Unidas* (UBIJUS 2022) 181–84.

[87] Constitution of 1917, Art 16 para 10, Art 19 para 1, Diario Oficial de la Federación (5 February 1917).

[88] SCJN, 6 September 2005, AI 20/2003, 103–11.

[89] Chávez Vargas and Carrasco Solís (n 86) 25–26.

Obrador submitted a wide-ranging set of constitutional amendment initiatives that, among other things, included yet another expansion of the catalogue of crimes in Article 19.[90]

At this point, the reader might ask: why would the government knowingly insist on doubling down on policies that are widely known to violate human rights? The answer to this question is obviously multifactorial but one answer is particularly relevant when we think of constitutional change as a function of political entrenchment, as explained in Chapter 3. All other things being equal, if a government has the opportunity to shield its preferred policies from the hassle of being potentially reviewed, modified, or struck down, there are not many reasons (if any) one could think of for that government not to choose the means of entrenchment that allow such shielding. For example, by the time *arraigo* detention and *prisión preventiva oficiosa* were adopted in 2008, the government already had an indication of what the position of the Supreme Court was in terms of reviewing the constitutionality of constitutional amendments—ie, the precedent set in the case against the Indigenous Peoples Rights Reform in CC 82/2001. However, the composition of the Supreme Court had changed eversince that decision was handed down: four new justices were appointed between 2003 and 2006.[91] The change of membership was important because the new appointees replaced the justices who voted with the majority in CC 82/2001. Therefore, it meant it could potentially shift the balance in favour of judicial review of constitutional amendments. Yet, as we know, the stance of the Supreme Court on this question did not change in the end.

Incidentally, the adjudication of the challenges against the Electoral Reform of 2007 in AI 168/2007 could not have come at a better time: the claims were dismissed on 26 June 2008, just a few days after the adoption of the Criminal Justice System Reform that made *arraigo* detention and PPO part of the constitution. In practice, with this decision the Supreme Court confirmed that constitutional amendments were not subject to judicial scrutiny (or any kind of scrutiny). The message to the political elite was clear: the amendment power is above the law—those holding the necessary majorities to amend the constitution may exercise said power without any limitation, formal or substantive.[92]

[90] César Jiménez, 'AMLO Incurriría en Desacato de una Sentencia de la Corte IDH con Reforma sobre Prisión Preventiva Oficiosa', *Infobae* (8 February 2024) <www.infobae.com/mexico/2024/02/08/amlo-incurriria-en-desacato-de-una-sentencia-de-la-corte-idh-con-reforma-sobre-prision-preventiva-oficiosa> accessed 16 August 2024.

[91] José Ramón Cossío (2003), Sergio Valls (2004), Margarita Luna Ramos (2004), and Fernando Franco González Salas (2006).

[92] Three months later, after the decision on AI 168/2007 was handed down, there was a remarkable (non-binding) interpretative shift when deciding one of the constitutional challenges against the Electoral Reform of 2007 but in *amparo*. In this case, which came to be known as *Amparo Empresarios*

In other words, the logic behind the non-justiciability doctrine (and later the constitutional restrictions doctrine) was to make the abuse of the amendment power constitutionally permissible .

The abusive move to entrench *arraigo* detention in the Constitution in 2008 was put to the test in the Supreme Court through an *amparo* in 2015. The claimant argued that Article 133 bis *Código Federal de Procedmientos Penales* was unconstitutional for impermissibly expanding the type of crimes subject to *arraigo* detention by including the broad category of *delitos graves* (felonies) instead of only those related to organized crime, as provided in the Constitution.[93] Since *arraigo* detention was not constitutionally allowed for *delitos graves*, the claimant argued, an *arraigo* detention executed in the context of such crimes would unduly violate the right to liberty, due process, and the presumption of innocence. In a 6:4 decision, however, the Supreme Court found that the Federal Congress was competent to expand the types of crimes subject to *arraigo* detention because the sunset clauses of the Criminal Justice System Reform of 2008 allowed

(SCJN, 29 September 2008, AR 186/2008), the Supreme Court reviewed a district court decision dismissing an individual constitutional complaint challenging—both in formal and substantive grounds—the Electoral Reform of 2007. According to the lower court, the Congress and state legislatures could not be considered as state authorities subject to judicial review in *amparo*. The Supreme Court (sitting *en banc*) decided 6:4 to revoke the dismissal on the grounds that as a constituted power the amendment power is necessarily limited and thus subject to judicial review. According to the majority, the power to amend the Constitution could not entail the power to destroy it (SCJN, 29 September 2008, AR 186/2008, 22). The opinion distinguishes between the constituent and the amendment power. The former is unlimited and is inextricably connected to the principle of popular sovereignty, while the latter is limited by both the principle of constitutional supremacy and the principle of popular sovereignty (SCJN, 29 September 2008, AR 186/2008, 21–22). Moreover, echoing the 'basic structure' doctrine of the Indian Supreme Court, the judgment asserts that in the absence of unamendability clauses, the Mexican Constitution establishes implicit limits to the amendment power: formal and substantive. While the formal limit is the amendment process of Article 135, which provides the rules to which those who are part of the process are bound, the substantive limits can only be indirectly determined through constitutional interpretation based on at least two core principles: rights protection and the separation of powers. Any amendment against these two core principles could not be understood as an act amending the Constitution but as an act aiming to destroy it (SCJN, 29 September 2008, AR 186/2008, 22–23). Unlike the disconnection from reality of the non-justiciability and constitutional restriction doctrine, this decision is remarkably aware of the effect of an unlimited amendment power. The emphasis is placed on the importance of not conflating the concept of the constituent power with the constitutional amendment power. The Court makes it clear that constituent power and the amendment power are two separate entities—one outside the constitutional order and the other within it. To make the principle of constitutional supremacy effective, as a constituted power, the amendment power is limited and has to be controlled. Thus, constitutional amendments would necessarily be subject to judicial review. As two different entities, these two powers have different sources of authority; whereas the source of authority of the amendment power is the Constitution, the constituent power's is popular sovereignty (SCJN, 29 September 2008, AR 186/2008, 27). This decision appeared to suggest that the Supreme Court could decide to exercise its jurisdiction with respect to the rest of the *amparos* against the Electoral Reform of 2007 that were already on track to reach the Court. Yet, three years later, when the cases were set for adjudication at the Supreme Court, this interpretative shift changed back to the original position, holding the unlimited nature of the amendment power in *Amparo Intelectuales*.

[93] SCJN, 14 April 2015, Amparo Directo en Revisión [ADR] 1250/2012.

it.[94] Most importantly, for the purposes of our discussion, the Court considered that even though before 2008 it had declared the *arraigo* detention scheme unconstitutional things had changed since then: in 2008 'the permanent Constituent power adopted a far-reaching constitutional amendment' whereby the *arraigo* detention was made part of the master-text Constitution.[95] In so doing, according to the Court, it established the *arraigo* detention as an 'adequate mechanism to provisionally restrict [the right to personal] liberty' which, based on the non-justiciability doctrine, cannot be declared unconstitutional.[96] Additionally, the Court determined that even though the *arraigo* detention is contrary to the right to personal liberty, the presumption of innocence, and due process, according to the constitutional restrictions doctrine (whereby restrictions to human rights should prevail over national and international protection standards) it should be considered as a constitutionally allowed human rights restriction.[97]

In September 2022, the *prisión preventiva oficiosa* came into focus as the Supreme Court was set to decide a set of cases in abstract review (AI 130/2019 and AI 136/2019) and in *amparo* (AR 355/2021) challenging its constitutionality. The abstract review cases, among other things, challenged the constitutionality of several provisions of the *Código Nacional de Procedimientos Penales*, *Ley de Seguridad Nacional*, *Ley Federal Contra la Delincuencia Organizada*, and *Código Fiscal de la Federación* which classified tax-related crimes as organized crime and as crimes against national security, making them subject to automatic pre-trial detention. The Supreme Court draft opinion, penned by Justice Luis María Aguilar Morales, included a proposal to strike down the challenged provisions that implied the overturning of the constitutional restrictions doctrine and, in line with Article 1 of the Constitution, disapplying the section of Article 19 of the Constitution that codifies the *prisión preventiva oficiosa* for violating the right to liberty and the presumption of innocence.[98] The deliberation in the Supreme Court focused almost exclusively on the question of whether it is constitutionally permissible to disapply constitutional provisions. Opposition to the proposal within and outside the Court quickly emerged. During the hearings where the Supreme Court discussed Justice Aguilar proposal in September 2022, it quickly became clear that a majority of justices were against it.[99] The Justices' interventions were filled with

[94] ibid 43–44.
[95] ibid 37.
[96] ibid 38.
[97] ibid 45–47.
[98] SCJN, draft opinion, AI 130/2019 at 52–113; SCJN, draft opinion, AI 136/2019, 52–113.
[99] SCJN, 5 September 2022, Versión Taquigráfica Sesión de Pleno, AI 130/2019; SCJN, 6 September 2022, Versión Taquigráfica Sesión de Pleno, AI 130/2019; SCJN, 8 September 2022, Versión Taquigráfica Sesión de Pleno, AI 130/2019.

references to the 'permanent constituent power' and to the constitutional restrictions doctrine. For instance, in the view of Justice Yasmín Esquivel Mossa,

> the reasons that the Permanent Constituent power had to adopt the *prisión preventiva oficiosa* cannot be questioned by the Supreme Court of the Nation.
>
> [. . .] we can like or dislike the *prisión preventiva oficiosa* [. . .] but it's not us, the Justices of the Supreme Court [. . .] who should review this catalogue of crimes or determine if it should be eliminated from the Constitution [. . .] that authority corresponds exclusively to the Permanent Constituent power as the only one allowed to determine whether changing the constitutional text is necessary.[100]

Similarly, Justice Alberto Pérez Dayán considered that the principle of constitutional supremacy, preserved by the constitutional restrictions doctrine, does not allow the Supreme Court to review the constitutionality of the Constitution or disapply any of its provisions under any circumstances. In his words,

> even in an extraordinary case where a constitutional provision [or amendment] caused such a significant upset in the general order or reversed its tenets, impacting public life and threatening the integrity of the Nation [. . .] even in that extreme scenario, my hesitation to review the constitutionality of the Constitution would remain firm.[101]
>
> as controversial as the *prisión preventiva oficiosa* may be, it's not the judges, not even the Supreme Court [. . .] the one with the duty to amend the vices it creates, [that duty belongs] to that who represents the nation, in the form of the Reforming Power according to Article 135 of the Federal Constitution, nothing more, nothing less.[102]

The opposition and pressure from outside the Court are particularly instructive to exemplify not only how much the government values an arbitrary amendment power but also that the non-justiciability doctrine and the constitutional restrictions doctrine are an important element that maintains the equilibrium of the CPER. When it was made public that the Supreme Court was set to analyse the constitutionality of the *prisión preventiva oficiosa*, sheer pressure from the president, governors, cabinet members, and legislators

[100] SCJN, 5 September 2022, Versión Taquigráfica Sesión de Pleno, AI 130/2019, 24–25, 32 (emphasis added).

[101] ibid 46.

[102] ibid 50.

emerged swiftly. On different occasions, President López Obrador doubled down on fearmongering falsely claiming that the abolition of automatic pre-trial detention would result in thousands of 'criminals' being released from jail and the loss of human lives.[103] Moreover, the governors affiliated with the ruling party, MORENA, did not shy away from openly calling out the Supreme Court. In a joint statement, nineteen out of a total of thirty-two governors questioned the power of the Court to 'remove or amend parts of the constitution' and demanded the justices to strictly observe Article 19 and uphold the automatic pre-trial detention:

> Removing parts of the constitutional text [. . .] or modifying the text is NOT among the Supreme Court's powers. [. . .] the members of the Supreme Court [. . .] DO NOT HAVE THE POWER TO [. . .] AMEND THE CONSTITUTION, even less so when [the constitutionality of] article 19 WAS NOT CHALLENGED [. . .].
>
> [. . .]
>
> [. . .] we respectfully call upon . . . the Supreme Court TO RESPECT THE SEPARATION OF POWERS, STRICTLY OBSERVE THE CONSTITUTIONAL TEXT [. . .]. We ask [the Court] to take into account these considerations so that we can continue to guarantee the peace and tranquility that Mexicans wish for.[104]

After three days of deliberation (and strong political pressure), Justice Aguilar decided to withdraw the draft opinion and craft a new one to capture the view of the majority of the Court.[105] The next day, President López Obrador publicly thanked the Supreme Court for its decision to withdraw the draft opinions because 'removing' the automatic pre-trial detention would have created

[103] '#ConferenciaPresidente: Viernes 2 de Septiembre de 2022' (directed by Gobierno de México, 2022) mins 34:34–1:08:38 <www.youtube.com/watch?v=uNF5SwaSres> accessed 16 August 2024; Emmanuel Carrillo, 'Eliminar Prisión Preventiva Significaría Pérdida de Vidas de Civiles, Soldados, Jueces: AMLO' [2022] *Forbes México* <www.forbes.com.mx/eliminar-prision-preventiva-significaria-perdida-de-vidas-de-civiles-soldados-jueces-amlo> accessed 16 August 2024.

[104] Cuitláhuac García [@CuitlahuacGJ], 'Las gobernadoras, los gobernadores y la jefa de gobierno abajo firmantes exhortamos a la SCJN a respetar la Constitución, no tienen la facultad para modificarla y por lo tanto el artículo 19 de la Carta Magna debe prevalecer en sus términos. https://t.co/GXxz3LhDeD'. The use of capital letters is from the original statement. <https://x.com/CuitlahuacGJ/status/1567478527624101891> accessed 16 August 2024.

[105] Juan Omar Fierro, 'Ministros Retiran Proyectos sobre Prisión Preventiva Oficiosa; Buscan Consensos', *Aristegui Noticias* (8 September 2022) <https://aristeguinoticias.com/0809/mexico/ministro-de-la-scjn-retira-proyecto-para-invalidar-prision-preventiva-oficiosa-busca-repleantearlo> accessed 16 August 2024.

'lots' of problems for the government.[106] Even though the cases were not adjudicated and, therefore, the Supreme Court did not decide on the constitutionality or the conventionality of the Constitution, less than a week after the withdrawal of the draft opinions, a jurisdiction-stripping bill was presented in the Chamber of Deputies by Deputy Reyna Ascencio of MORENA to ban the Court from assessing the constitutionality of the Constitution and impose an obligation to observe constitutional restrictions.[107] Among other things, the preamble explicitly states that the bill is in response to the 'recent judicial discussion on the constitutionality of the *prisión preventiva oficiosa*'.[108] It adds:

> This initiative tries to limit the political power of the Supreme Court [. . .] against the backdrop of the temptation to disapply a constitutional provision or interpret it in a way that undermines its legal force and efficacy. [. . .] Can the Supreme Court [. . .] invalidate a constitutional provision? The categorical answer is no, otherwise [. . .] the Court would illegitimately rise above the constitutional text that is defined by the people.
>
> [. . .]
>
> If we accept that the Supreme Court has the power to 'disapply' or invalidate a constitutional provision, we would be in the face of arbitrariness and we would, de facto, be giving the power to change the Constitution to the eleven members of the Court when [that power] has to entail a process that involves parliamentary discussion under the principle of deliberation with the participation of the representatives of the People.[109]

Months later, in November 2022, the Supreme Court adjudicated the abstract review cases without touching on the question of whether Article 19 of the Constitution should be disapplied for violating human rights.[110] Instead, it left

[106] Animal Político [@Pajaropolitico], '@lopezobrador_ agradeció a la @SCJN por retirar la iniciativa para eliminar la prisión preventiva oficiosa. "Nos iba a generar muchos problemas quitar la medida por la corrupción que todavía existe no solo en el Poder Judicial sino en el Legislativo y Ejecutivo", declaró'. <https://x.com/Pajaropolitico/status/1568244392581791745> accessed 16 August 2024.

[107] Redacción, 'Morena vs. Suprema Corte: Iniciativa Prohibirá Que Pueda Invalidar Normas de La Constitución' *El Financiero* (Mexico, 13 September 2022) <www.elfinanciero.com.mx/nacional/2022/09/13/morena-vs-suprema-corte-iniciativa-prohibira-que-pueda-invalidar-normas-de-la-constitucion> accessed 16 August 2024.

[108] Cámara de Diputados, Gaceta Parlamentaria, núm. 6110-IV, LXV Legislatura, Primer Periodo Ordinario (13 September 2022) <https://gaceta.diputados.gob.mx/PDF/65/2022/sep/20220913-IV.pdf> accessed 16 August 2024.

[109] ibid.

[110] For a discussion on why the government's sheer pressure was partly provoked by the justice in charge of the opinion draft and the chief justice, see Mariana Velasco-Rivera, 'The Enforcement of International Human Rights Standards on Personal Liberty and the Presumption of Innocence in Mexico: When the Supreme Court Became Its Own Worst Enemy' (IACL-IADC Blog 17 November

the constitutional restrictions doctrine untouched and struck down the challenged provisions on the grounds that the tax-related crimes under study could not be considered as threats to national security or organized crime as provided by Article 19. As such, said tax-related crimes would not be subject to *prisión preventiva oficiosa*.[111] The claims made in *amparo* (AR 355/2021) challenged the constitutionality of Article 167 of the *Código Nacional de Procedimientos Penales*, which mirrors the constitutional provisions establishing the *prisión preventiva oficiosa* scheme (ie Article 19). The proposal in the draft opinion was penned by Justice Norma Piña. Like Justice Aguilar's, Justice Piña's suggested overturning the constitutional restrictions doctrine and proposed a new methodology to assess whether a restriction of rights is permissible. Under the proposed reasoning, Article 19 was to be disapplied and the challenged provisions struck down.[112] The case was listed to be adjudicated after the cases in abstract review; however, when Justice Aguilar decided to withdraw his proposal to work on a new one that captured the position of the majority of justices, Justice Piña did the same. The case, however, was soon after reallocated to Justice Jorge Mario Pardo Rebolledo roughly a month later—when Justice Piña was selected by her peers as Chief Justice.[113] Justice Pardo would now be in charge of the new opinion draft. The case was decided in June 2024, over a year later, by the First Chamber (ie a five-judge panel) of the Court, which unanimously decided to dismiss the case for procedural reasons.

Both *arraigo* detention and *prisión preventiva oficiosa* have been under scrutiny at the Inter-American Court of Human Rights (IACoHR), which offers further evidence of how much arbitrary power is valued in the CPER. Mexico was condemned by IACoHR in the case *Tzompaxtle Tecpile y Otros v México* (2022) and *García Rodríguez y Reyes Alpízar v México* (2023), where *arraigo* detention and *prisión preventiva oficiosa* were determined to be against the American Convention of Human Rights for breaching the right to personal liberty and the presumption of innocence. The reparations ordered by the IACoHR included, among other things, an order to eliminate *arraigo* detention as a pre-trial mechanism and to alter the *prisión preventiva oficiosa* scheme to be in line with the Convention (ie it must be exceptional and justified). Eliminating *arraigo* detention would necessarily entail a constitutional

2022) <https://blog-iacl-aidc.org/new-blog-3/2022/11/17/uglnx8vnxfm5kpl6bsdng22pkyjz7p> accessed 16 August 2024.

111 SCJN, 24 November 2022, AI 130/2019; SCJN, 24 November 2022, AI 136/2019.
112 SCJN, opinion draft, AR 355/2021, 37–131.
113 SCJN, 26 June 2024, AR 355/2021.

amendment, while altering the *prisión preventiva oficiosa* to be in line with IACoHR would only entail establishing a scheme that in practice stops automatic pre-trial detentions. Judging only by the official press releases in response to the notification of the rulings, one would think the government was willing to comply with the IACoHR judgments.[114] But the words and actions of the president, governors, and cabinet members in reaction to the IACoHR decisions once again showed that they value the arbitrariness allowed by the amendment power so much that they are seemingly ready not to comply with the IACoHR decisions while ignoring the basic tenets of international public law. When asked about what measures the government would take to comply with the IACoHR rulings, the minister of the interior, Adán Augusto López, said the following:

> [I]t is an absurdity for the Inter-American Court to put itself above the Constitution, and therefore disrespect Mexico, [nothing] can be above Mexico as a State [. . .] our supreme law has to be respected by international tribunals. [. . .] No court, however Inter-American it may be, can oblige Mexico to modify its Constitution.[115]

Interestingly, in his answer, the minister of the interior referred to the Supreme Court decision made months earlier in abstract review where the *prisión preventiva oficiosa* as provided in Article 19 and the constitutional restriction doctrine were left untouched: 'on that occasion the *prisión preventiva oficiosa* was declared constitutionally valid [sic]. If I remember correctly, it was modified [sic] only regarding crimes related to tax fraud'.[116] Even though it is not true that in that case the *prisión preventiva oficiosa* was declared constitutionally valid (the Court, in the end, did not make an official declaration on the constitutionality of Article 19), the practical implication of the absence of such

[114] The press releases relaying the notifications of both cases use very similar wording. The press release of García Rodriguez y otro v México reads: 'Mexico will carefully analyze the remedies [section] of the judgment issued by Inter-American Court [. . .] with the objective of being in a position to comply with [it] and to ensure the greatest respect for the obligations contained in the American Convention of Human Rights in line with [the State's] international commitments and its internal democratic processes.' See Secretaría de Relaciones Exteriores and Secretaría de Gobernación, 'Corte IDH Notifica Sentencia sobre Caso García Rodríguez y otro al Estado Mexicano' (12 April 2023) <www.gob.mx/sre/prensa/corte-idh-notifica-sentencia-sobre-caso-garcia-rodriguez-y-otro-al-estado-mexicano?state=draft> accessed 16 August 2024; Secretaría de Relaciones Exteriores and Secretaría de Gobernación, 'Corte IDH notifica sentencia sobre caso Tzompaxtle Tecpile y Otros al Estado Mexicano' (27 January 2023) <www.gob.mx/sre/prensa/corte-idh-notifica-sentencia-sobre-caso-tzompaxtle-tecpile-y-otros-al-estado-mexicano?idiom=es> accessed 16 August 2024.

[115] *Atención a Medios de Comunicación Desde Tlaxcala* (directed by Secretaría Gobernación, 2023) mins 32:03–35:51 <www.youtube.com/watch?v=59LBtMvOwd0> accessed 16 August 2024.

[116] ibid mins 33:27–33:44.

a declaration (and what matters to the government the most) was that the constitutional restrictions doctrine and, by implication, the non-justiciability doctrine remained untouched. For our purposes, it is telling to see how officials keep coming back to the idea that as long as policy decisions are entrenched in the constitutional text, they should be beyond scrutiny and accountability. Such an understanding is also illustrated by President López Obrador actions and by the joint statement of twenty-three MORENA governors in connection to the IACoHR rulings. In February 2024, in an act that would be in direct conflict with the reparation measures ordered by the IACoHR in *Tzompaxtle Tecpile y Otros v México* (2022) and *García Rodríguez y Reyes Alpízar v México* (2023), President López Obrador submitted a set of amendment proposals that included yet another expansion of the catalogue of crimes in Article 19.[117] Similarly, in a joint statement in connection with an internal proceeding in the Supreme Court to determine how, as a branch of government, the judiciary has to implement the IACoHR rulings, twenty-three MORENA governors' issued a public statement that goes back to the idea that the Constitution, as the expression of the 'permanent constituent power', should be above all kinds of scrutiny:

> giving preference to an international norm over domestic law would translate into affirming that, in practice, an international tribunal has the power to disapply a constitutional provision, which would lead to undermining the Constitution itself, which emanates from the will of the permanent constituent power and not from an agreement between member States from the international community.
>
> [. . .] it is important to mention that [the Constitution] establishes the process to modify or amend it, therefore we ask for the strict observance of Article 135.[118]

By implication, the statement is calling for the Supreme Court to ignore the IACoHR rulings. The reference to Article 135 of the Constitution suggests that they are aware that complying with the rulings would require, among other things, a constitutional amendment. Yet, judging by President López Obrador's

[117] Jiménez (n 90). The proposals relating to Article 19 of the Constitution were passed in November 2024, already under López Obrador's successor, President Claudia Sheinbaum of MORENA, and enacted on 31 December of that year. See Constitution of 1917, article 19, as amended, Diario Oficial de la Federación (31December 2024).

[118] Redacción, 'Gobernadorxs de Morena Piden a la SCJN no Tocar la Prisión Preventiva Oficiosa' *Aristegui Noticias* (22 February 2024) <https://aristeguinoticias.com/2202/mexico/gobernadorxs-de-morena-piden-a-la-scjn-no-tocar-la-prision-preventiva-oficiosa> accessed 16 August 2024.

choice to double down on the commitment to the *prisión preventiva oficiosa* scheme by proposing another amendment to expand the crime catalogue in Article 19, it does not look like there would be political will to comply with the rulings. Referring to the Supreme Court's internal proceedings to implement the IACoHR rulings, President López Obrador mockingly said the following:

> now they want to remove the *prisión preventiva* [*oficiosa*], the justices are suddenly internationalists and say that even though it is in our Constitution, the rulings of the IACoHR [. . .] say it should not exist [. . .]. And because Mexico is part of international treaties, our Constitution should be thrown into the trash.[119]

More generally, this episode illustrates how specific understandings of the scope and limits of the amendment power influence the choices of the relevant political actors among the different means of entrenchment provided in a constitutional order. In the case of Mexico, the president, governors, political parties, and high officers are convinced that the constitutional amendment power should shield their policy choices from any type of scrutiny, even if that means violating the country's international human rights commitments and obligations. The belief is also reflected by the strong reaction of the government against the Supreme Court when the doctrines that make that shield effective were due to be revisited and potentially modified.[120] It is that strong reaction that shows that the non-justiciability and the constitutional restrictions doctrines play a crucial role in contributing to the availability of constitutional amendment in Mexico's economy of constitutional change.

* * *

Ironically, the non-justiciability and constitutional restrictions doctrines can be read as a vestige of what the judiciary was in the PRI era. The first time the judiciary dealt with a question regarding the constitutionality of a constitutional amendment was in 1982, still under the PRI hegemonic rule. The

[119] Pedro Domínguez, 'AMLO Va Contra Ministros por ir Contra Prisión Preventiva' *Milenio* (Mexico, 4 March 2024) <www.milenio.com/politica/amlo-va-contra-ministros-por-ir-contra-prision-preventiva> accessed 16 August 2024 (emphasis added).

[120] As of September 2022, when AI 130/2019 and AR 355/2021 were set to be adjudicated, six out of the eleven justices who had not done so before, were going to express their views on the constitutional restrictions doctrine. Since 2013, the year in which it was set, six new justices had joined the Court: Norma L Piña (2015), Javier Laynez Potisek (2015), Juan L González Alcántara Carrancá (2018), Margarita Ríos Farjat (2019), Yasmín Esquivel Mossa (2019), and Loretta Ortiz (2021).

case was brought against the nationalization of the bank industry discussed in Chapter 5. As a response to the deep economic crisis that pushed the country to the brink of bankruptcy, President López Portillo issued an executive order to nationalize the bank industry in clear violation of Article 28 of the Constitution—which established a general ban on economic monopolies. Immediately after, a constitutional amendment was passed to shield the executive order from being struck down. In response to this, more than a dozen banks filed an *amparo* against the constitutional amendment, arguing that 'it violated a fundamental political decision that could only be modified by the constituent power and not by the amendment power'.[121] In other words, the claimants challenged the attempt to use the amendment power to avoid scrutiny and accountability and, by implication, the idea that such power is unlimited. But the government was convinced of the opposite. A district judge admitted the *amparo* suit—a decision that was thereafter challenged by the government. Perfectly mirroring today's understanding of the scope and limits of the amendment power, the government argued that the case was notoriously inadmissible because the amendment power could not be subject to judicial scrutiny.[122] The Circuit Court in charge of deciding on the government's claim ruled in their favour, arguing that Article 103-I of the Constitution (which establishes the admissibility hypothesis in *amparo*) only referred to 'laws'—a concept that by no means could include a constitutional amendment. Therefore, the Circuit Court concluded that a constitutional amendment was not the kind of act subject to judicial scrutiny in that the Constitution is not a law strictly speaking.[123] Additionally, it considered that attempting to use the *amparo* suit to defend the Constitution against the Constitution itself was absurd and against legal logic.[124]

The claimants filed an appeal that reached the Supreme Court, which in a 15:2 (sitting *en banc*) decision was dismissed on procedural grounds in late 1983.[125] Although in this case the Supreme Court did not study the claim on its merits, the dismissal is important for three main reasons. First, the practical effect of the dismissal was to shield the policy measure from judicial scrutiny. Second, the case resembles much of Mexico's current constitutional reality. Politicians in the past took advantage of the homogenous political landscape

[121] Ramón Sánchez Medal, *El Fraude a La Constitución y El Único Amparo En México Contra Una Reforma Demolitoria de La Constitución* (1st edn, Porrúa 1988) 49.
[122] ibid 93, 98.
[123] ibid 111.
[124] ibid.
[125] ibid 119–37.

to access the amendment mechanism and exercise arbitrary power (ie power shielded from any scrutiny or accountability). Today, even though the political landscape is plural and on paper there is a strong constitutional justice system, the political elite is still able to exercise the constitutional amendment power arbitrarily. Third, despite the transition to democracy, the empowerment of the Supreme Court, and the number of reforms to the constitutional justice system during the last three decades (and what they were supposed to entail for the quality and scope of constitutional justice), the deferential attitude of the Circuit Court to dismiss an individual constitutional complaint against constitutional amendments is still very much alive in today's constitutional doctrine.

Developing an unconstitutional constitutional amendment doctrine would mean allowing citizens to have a say in the development of constitutional law. Yet, by invalidating a constitutional amendment the Supreme Court could be disrupting the CPER. In this context, the absence of an unconstitutional constitutional amendment doctrine is hardly surprising. Judicial scrutiny of the bargains directly entrenched in the Constitution would risk upsetting the political equilibrium reached by the political parties through cross-party agreements. Most importantly, such judicial intervention could result in a challenge to the Court's authority and legitimacy. In this sense, judicial restraint helps the Court to protect its legitimacy. Until recently, no one had challenged the legitimacy of the Supreme Court because it did not pose a challenge to the equilibrium of the CPER.

8
Conclusion

The previous chapters presented an analytical framework that seeks to capture the political dimension of constitutional rigidity. The chapters challenge the dominant approaches to constitutional rigidity found in the literature and were developed through an examination of the history and trends of constitutional change in Mexico, with particular attention to the period between 1988 and 2024. By looking at the case of Mexico in detail, the chapters sought to unveil the non-institutional factors that influence the ease of amendment in that country. The approach to constitutional change offered here can be summarized in the following way:

1. Constitutional change (formal and informal) takes place in an economy of constitutional change.
2. Formal and informal constitutional change is the product of political entrenchment.
3. Understanding the reasons for constitutional rigidity/flexibility requires us to go beyond a constitution's amendment rule. Constitutional rigidity/flexibility can and are most likely determined by factors other than the amendment rule. Those factors include but are not limited to: (a) political parties and party systems (as a general rule, political parties are the actors with the legal power to activate the amendment mechanism); (b) constitutional culture, understood as the understandings, beliefs, assumptions, and attitudes of the relevant group (eg political parties, the relevant legal community, or society at large) regarding the different mechanisms of constitutional change; and (c) choices made by key political actors.
4. The analysis of constitutional change through the lenses of these factors allows us to unveil the unwritten rules that explain how a constitution changes and why certain mechanisms of political entrenchment are available and others are not. In the Mexican case, they help to explain why the amendment mechanism is available in that country's economy of constitutional change even in the context of a divided government.

The Politics of Constitutional Rigidity. Mariana Velasco-Rivera, Oxford University Press.
 DOI: 10.1093/9780191981876.003.0008

5. The study of constitutional culture in Mexico sheds light on the origin of attitudes and understandings that see constitutional amendment as an effective mechanism of political entrenchment, as well as the unwritten rules that allowed access to the amendment mechanism pre-1988 (when the PRI lost the ability to amend the Constitution on its own). Constitutional change trends post-1988 suggest that practices/unwritten rules that developed throughout the twentieth century are still present and are the main drivers of the current cross-party entrenchment regime.
6. Examining the choices made by key political actors in a critical juncture allowed us to unveil the development of a new unwritten rule (ie the rule of cooperation) that enables access to the amendment mechanism. The emergence of the rule of cooperation explains formal constitutional change in Mexico after 1988.
7. Given that the availability of different mechanisms of entrenchment is largely determined by the choices made by key political actors and that those choices and preferences, at the same time, are shaped by understandings, attitudes, and beliefs about their effectiveness as entrenchment mechanisms, it is important to shed light on the factors that might be informing them. In the case of Mexico, two constitutional doctrines developed by the Supreme Court have rendered the constitutional amendment power unlimited. As such, these doctrines help to explain the preference of the political elite for constitutional amendment as a mechanism of entrenchment.

The interplay of the factors that comprise Mexico's economy of constitutional change (ie political parties and party system, constitutional culture, choices made by political actors) explains the relative flexibility of the Mexican Constitution despite its stringent amendment rule. The general applicability of the framework offered in this book is out of the scope of this work. However, there are reasons to think that it has potential to contribute to explaining constitutional rigidity or flexibility in other jurisdictions. The analytical framework offered in Chapter 3 is formulated at a relatively high level of abstraction that is intended to allow the systematic study of constitutional change in general and constitutional rigidity in particular. The idea of an economy of constitutional change comprises elements that are common to all constitutional democracies with written constitutions. First, there is the possibility of direct and indirect political entrenchment. Second, political parties (and therefore party systems) exist as the actors that as a general rule have the legal power to activate the amendment mechanism. Third, parties and key political actors are immersed in a given constitutional culture where their preferences for the different means of political entrenchment would have been formed.

To be sure, this is not to say that the different components of the economy of constitutional change identified in this book are the only possible components. Naturally, there will be jurisdictions where other factors (eg referendums and the politics and culture around them) would be essential to explain constitutional rigidity or flexibility. The analytical framework developed throughout the book should be understood only as a starting point for the systematic study of constitutional change in general and constitutional rigidity in particular.

Index

For the benefit of digital users, indexed terms that span two pages (e.g., 52–53) may, on occasion, appear on only one of those pages.

Tables and figures are indicated by an italic *t* and *f* following the page number.